Edexcel International GCSE History

Edexcel Certificate in History

Student Book – 2nd edition

Robin Bunce, John Child, Laura Gallagher, Jane Shuter, Steve Waugh

Contents

Unit 1: Development of dictatorship: Germany, 1918–45

Overview	4
The German Revolution, 1918	6
The Weimar Republic and the Treaty of Versailles	8
Economic problems, 1918–23	12
Political problems, 1918–23	14
The Stresemann era, 1924–29	18
The birth of the Nazi Party, 1919–23	20
The Munich Putsch, 1923	22
Reorganising the Nazi Party, 1924–28	24
The impact of the Wall Street Crash, 1929	26
Nazi support grows, 1929–32	28
The Nazis win power, 1932–33	30
The removal of opposition, 1933–34	32
The Nazi police state	36
Censorship and propaganda	40
Persecution of the Jews, 1933–39	42
Youth and education in Nazi Germany	45
Women in Nazi Germany, 1933–39	46
Work and employment, 1933–39	48
War and the Final Solution	50
The Home Front and opposition to Hitler	54
Defeat and the death of Hitler	58
Examzone	60

Unit 2: A world divided: superpower relations, 1945–62

Overview	66
Why did the Cold War begin?	68
Fear of war	72
The development of the Cold War: Truman Doctrine and Marshall Aid	74
The development of the Cold War: satellite states	78
The development of the Cold War: first confrontation	80
The Korean War	84
Hungary under Soviet rule: liberation and oppression	86
The Berlin Crisis: a divided city	90
The Berlin Crisis: the Berlin Wall	92
The Cuban Missile Crisis: origins	94
The Cuban Missile Crisis: the 'Thirteen Days'	98
The Cuban Missile Crisis: immediate and long-term consequences	100
Examzone	102

Unit 3: A divided union: Civil Rights in the USA, 1945–74

Overview	108
Reasons for the Red Scare	110
Villains or victims?	112
The role of McCarthy	114
Segregation and discrimination	116
The Montgomery Bus Boycott	118
Integrating schools	120

Martin Luther King 122
Sit-ins and freedom rides 124
Civil rights legislation of the 60s 128
Malcolm X and the Nation of Islam 130
Rising anger 132
The assassination of Martin Luther King 134
Reasons for protest 136
Student protest 138
The position of women in the early 60s 140
Women's liberation movements 142
Opposition to women's liberation 144
Re-electing President Nixon 146
The impact of Watergate 150
Examzone 152

Unit 4: The USA, 1917–29

Overview 158
Impact of the First World War 160
Reactions to the War 162
Immigration 164
Prohibition and crime 168
Why Prohibition failed 170
The US government 171
Mass production 172
Boom! 174
Not all winners 178
The Roaring Twenties 180
Consumerism 181
That's entertainment! 182
New women 184
More open-minded? 186
Racism 188
Examzone 194

Unit 5: The changing role of international organisations: the League and the UN, 1919–2000

Overview 202
The birth of the League of Nations 204
The birth of the United Nations 208
The organisation of League of Nations 212
The organisation of United Nations 216
Successes of the League of Nations 220
Successes of the United Nations 224
Failures and weaknesses of the League of Nations 228
Failures and weaknesses of the United Nations 232
A study in change 236
Examzone 238

Glossary

Glossary 244

The history of Germany from 1918 to 1945 was a real rollercoaster ride. It started with revolution and defeat in war. It ended in defeat in war. In between, a new democracy was created, the Weimar Republic. You will study its early problems and recovery and the later economic crash and political chaos. Finally, a dictator – Adolf Hitler – emerged and transformed Germany, then started the war which destroyed him.

You could picture it all like this:

The Weimar Republic	Economic Depression	Hitler takes power	The Nazi State during peacetime	The Nazi State at war
1918–1929	1929–33	1933–34	1933–39	1939–45
The German Revolution Weimar Republic Treaty of Versailles Political and economic problems Stresemann and recovery Growth of the Nazi Party	The Wall Street Crash Unemployment Political crisis Nazi Party support grows	Hitler becomes Chancellor Hitler removes opposition Hitler takes powers of the President and becomes Führer	Persecution of the Jews Nazi schools and youth policies Nazi policies towards women Nazi policies towards work	The war and the Final Solution The German Home Front Opposition to Hitler grows Defeat The death of Hitler

The exam

This page shows you exactly what your Paper 1 exam paper will look like. This is an option from Group B. You answer the two questions on Paper 1 that relate to the options you have studied.

> There are four questions, parts (a), (b), (c), and (d). **You must answer all four.**

5: Development of dictatorship: Germany, 1918–45

(a) Study these events which occurred in Germany in the years 1918–24.

The Dawes Plan	Hyperinflation	French occupation of the Ruhr	The Treaty of Versailles	The Kapp Putsch

Write these events in the correct chronological sequence.

(3)

(b) Choose **either** | Hyperinflation | **or** | The Treaty of Versailles |

Explain **one** effect on the Weimar Republic of the event you have chosen.

(4)

(c) Why was there increased support for the Nazi Party in the years 1929–32? Explain your answer.

(8)

(d) Study the source below and then answer the question that follows.

Source: from a modern textbook

The Nazis believed that men and women had different roles to play in Germany. Boys and girls were sent to separate schools and studied different subjects. The training continued in the Nazi youth movements. Men were expected to become soldiers and workers. Women were discouraged from doing paid work.

Use the source, and your own knowledge, to explain the changes in the position of women in Nazi Germany in the years 1933–39.

(10)

(Total for Question 5: 25 marks)

> Pay special attention to part (b). You have to choose **one** of the two events which are in boxes, and then write about the effects of that event.

> Notice the marks for each question. Part (a) is worth 3 marks, but part (c) is worth 8 and (d) 10. You need to spend the most time on (c) and (d) questions.

> The pattern of questions will be the same:
> (a) chronology
> (b) the effects of an event
> (c) causation
> (d) an essay where you need to write more.

> In part (d) you get a source which will help you answer the question. However, it says use the source **and your own knowledge**, so in order to get a good mark you have to use information not in the source.

The German Revolution, 1918

> **Learning objectives**
>
> In this chapter you will learn about:
> - the causes of the German Revolution
> - the events of the German Revolution.

In late 1918, there was unrest across the whole of Germany. The emperor fled for his life and a new government took control. These events are called the German Revolution.

What caused the German Revolution?

One reason was failure in the First World War. Germany went to war in September 1914, confident of victory. But, by 1918, Germany's enemies, known as the Allies, remained undefeated and now had the combined might of Britain, France, Russia and the USA. In March 1918, Germany made a spring offensive – a last, desperate, attack upon Paris. But in July, the Allies counter-attacked and drove the Germans back. Two million German troops had died since 1914, yet defeat seemed near. Morale amongst troops was very low.

Another reason for the German Revolution was the hardship that the war had caused. Allied navies were blockading the German coast, preventing imports of basic supplies. Food shortages led to great suffering and military failure caused a sense of hopelessness. Public hardship was made worse by a deadly influenza infection which spread through Europe from August 1918.

We have no meat, and potatoes cannot be delivered because we lack the 4000 trucks a day we need. The shortage is so great, it is a mystery to me what the people of Berlin live on. They say 'Better a horrible end than unending horror'.

Source A: *A member of the German government, writing in October 1918.*

Source B: *Berlin in 1918. Women searching through garbage for food.*

The Russian Revolution also helped to cause discontent in Germany. In November 1917, Russians had overthrown their emperor, the Tsar, and replaced him by a government of the people. By November 1918, many Germans were demanding similar changes in Germany. They wanted to replace the undemocratic rule of their emperor, the Kaiser, by councils of workers and soldiers.

The events of the Revolution

On 29 October, German sailors at the naval base of Wilhelmshaven refused to follow orders to set sail. The mutiny spread to the base at Kiel. On 4 November, 40,000 sailors there joined dockers, set up a workers' and soldiers' council and took over the dockyard. This sparked similar revolts all across Germany in towns like Hamburg, Bremen and Lübeck. In Hanover, soldiers refused to control the rioters. Government was breaking down. It soon got worse.

On 7 November, in the German state of Bavaria, thousands of workers, led by Kurt Eisner, marched on the state capital of Munich. The local ruler, King Ludwig III, feared for his life, so he left the country. Next day, Eisner set up a workers' and peasants' council and declared Bavaria a people's state. In other parts of Germany, four kings, five dukes and twelve princes feared similar revolts and fled.

In Berlin, even the Kaiser's own ministers deserted him. As defeat in the war came closer, the Allies said they would only negotiate with 'representatives of the people'. Ministers therefore told the Kaiser he had to go. On 9 November, Kaiser Wilhelm agreed to abdicate and, the next day, fled to Holland. Germany's biggest political party, the Social Democrat Party [SPD] formed a new government. An SPD leader, Friedrich Ebert, became the new Chancellor.

The Effects of the German Revolution

The first effect of the German Revolution was that the new government was able to agree an **armistice**, on 11 November. Germany had to withdraw from all land won in the war, pull its troops back 48 kilometres (30 miles) inside its border with France, surrender its munitions and put its navy under Allied control. A second effect, a new government, took longer to achieve. The terms of the armistice were not popular and economic suffering continued. So the winter of 1918–19 was one of political turmoil. (See pages 12–13). But gradually Ebert's government gained control. By mid-1919, in the town of Weimar, new rules for governing the country were agreed and the new German state became known as the Weimar Republic.

Watch out!

The way Germany was governed can be confusing. The German emperor (or Kaiser) was the ruler of Germany. He appointed a government for Germany; this was based in the capital, Berlin, and it was led by the Kaiser's chief minister, the chancellor.

But Germany was made up of many states: some large, like Saxony, and some very small. Each of these states had their own local rulers who controlled local affairs.

Many revolts in the German Revolution were against the local rulers. Some were replaced by groups who didn't agree with the new government in Berlin. Ebert had to struggle all through the winter of 1918–19 to get control of the whole country.

Activities

1 Create a timeline to show, in chronological order, the events described in this chapter.

2 The events on your timeline help to explain why the German Revolution took place.

   Here are three causes of the German Revolution:

   ● failure in war
   ● public hardship
   ● events in Russia.

   List the events under the causes which they help to explain.

3 Here are two effects of the German Revolution:

   ● the armistice
   ● the Weimar Republic.

   Write a detailed sentence explaining why each one was an effect.

The Weimar Republic and the Treaty of Versailles

Learning objectives

In this chapter you will learn about:

- how a new constitution was agreed
- the terms, strengths and weaknesses of the new constitution
- the terms of the Treaty of Versailles
- its effects upon the Weimar Republic.

After the Kaiser's departure, there was unrest all around Germany. Armed groups with extreme political views clashed with the army and even claimed control in some towns. But Ebert began to take control by introducing slow, careful changes. Civil servants kept their jobs. Six moderate social democrats formed a Council of People's Representatives, a temporary government. They organised elections for a National Assembly. This met in February 1919 to create a new **constitution**. With so much unrest in Berlin, the Assembly met in Weimar. The new republic was called the Weimar Republic, even after the government moved back to Berlin. By August 1919 the Assembly had drawn up the new constitution.

The constitution had a number of strengths. Firstly, it made Germany more democratic than it had been under the Kaiser. More people voted, and there was a general election every four years. Secondly, it had a system of checks and balances. For example, there were two houses in the new parliament and the power of one, the Reichstag, was checked (limited) by the power of the other, the Reichsrat. There were also two key offices, the president and the chancellor. Power was shared – or balanced – between the two. So no single group or person had all the power.

The terms of the constitution

Local government was run by the 18 regions of Germany (e.g. Bavaria, Prussia); they kept local parliaments.

Central government was given more power than before.

The **Reichstag** was the dominant house of the new German parliament; it controlled taxation.

- Members of the Reichstag were elected every four years.
- All men and women over 20 years could vote, using a secret ballot (rather than all men over 25, as had been the case before).
- **Proportional representation** was used. This meant that the number of Reichstag seats which political parties were given depended on the percentage of votes they gained.

The **Reichsrat**: the other house of the German parliament.

- A number of members were sent by each local region, according to its size.
- The Reichsrat could delay new laws unless overruled by a two-thirds majority of the Reichstag.

The **chancellor** was the head of the government.

- The chancellor chose ministers and ran the country.
- But to pass laws, he needed majority support in the Reichstag.

The **president** was the head of state; the president was directly elected by the people every seven years.

- The president took no part in day-to-day government.
- But the president was a powerful figure.
  - He chose the chancellor (usually the leader of the largest party).
  - He could dismiss the Reichstag, call new elections and assume control of the army.
  - Also, under Article 48, the president could suspend the constitution, and pass laws by decree.

Friedrich Ebert was elected by the Assembly as the first president. He carefully gained the support of powerful groups in society.

- He promised General Gröner, the head of the German Army, that there would be no reform of the armed forces.
- He reassured the industrialists' leader, Hugo Stinnes, that there would be no nationalisation of private businesses.
- He ensured the support of trade unions by promising their leader, Karl Legien, a maximum eight-hour working day.

With this support, the new government overcame the opposition of the protesters and gradually gained control of the country. The new republic was successfully launched but it had its weaknesses.

Weaknesses of the constitution

Firstly, proportional representation meant that even a party with a small number of votes gained seats in the Reichstag. During the 1920s, 28 parties were represented in the Reichstag. To get majority support, chancellors needed **coalitions** of several parties – usually the Social Democrats, the People's Party, the Democratic Party and the Centre Party.

But these all wanted different things, making stable government difficult.

Secondly, the careful balancing of powers made strong, decisive government by the chancellor very difficult in times of crisis.

This second weakness meant that, whenever compromise broke down, the chancellor had to ask the president to suspend the constitution, under Article 48, and rule by decree. This gave the impression that the new constitution didn't really work.

The Weimar Republic was built on shaky foundations. Extremist parties didn't support it; moderate Germans feared it was too weak.

Build Better Answers

Explain one **effect of the new constitution on Germany.** **(4 marks)**

Paper 1 part (b) questions will ask about the effect of one event on another.

■ **A basic answer (level 1)** will give a consequence, or effect, but no supporting detail. For example, *Germany became more democratic.*

● **A good answer (level 2)** will make a statement giving a consequence and then develop this statement by giving extra detail or explanation. For example, *Germany became more democratic, because women could now vote and there was a general election, to elect a new government, every four years.*

Did you know?

Because the National Assembly could not meet in Berlin, its meetings were held in Weimar's National Theatre, complete with stage, circle and box seats.

Source A: *A 1950s painting of Ebert addressing the National Assembly in the National Theatre, Weimar, 1919.*

The terms of the Treaty of Versailles

Germany had to pay reparations to the Allies

- Reparations were eventually fixed, in 1921, at 136,000 million marks (£6600 million).

Germany lost all its colonies

- The 11 German colonies in Africa and the Far East were given to victorious countries as 'mandates' – territories to look after.

German military forces were cut

- The army was limited to 100,000; to be used internally only.
- The navy was limited to 6 battleships, 6 cruisers, 12 destroyers and 12 torpedo boats. No submarines were allowed. The rest of the fleet was destroyed.
- No air force was allowed. The existing air force was destroyed.
- The Rhineland was demilitarised – the German army was not allowed in the Rhineland, which bordered France.

Germany lost land

- Alsace and Lorraine were lost to France.
- Eupen and Malmédy were lost to Belgium.
- Posen and West Prussia were lost to Poland
  - the loss of Posen and West Prussia divided Germany in two, cutting off East Prussia from the rest of the country.
- Plebiscites (public votes) had to take place in other areas, to decide whether they should leave Germany.
  - Upper Silesia voted to become part of Poland.
  - Northern Schleswig decided to become part of Denmark.
- The German port of Danzig was made an international city – not governed by Germany.
- Altogether, Germany lost:
  - about 13% of its European territory
  - almost 50% of its iron and 15% of its coal reserves.

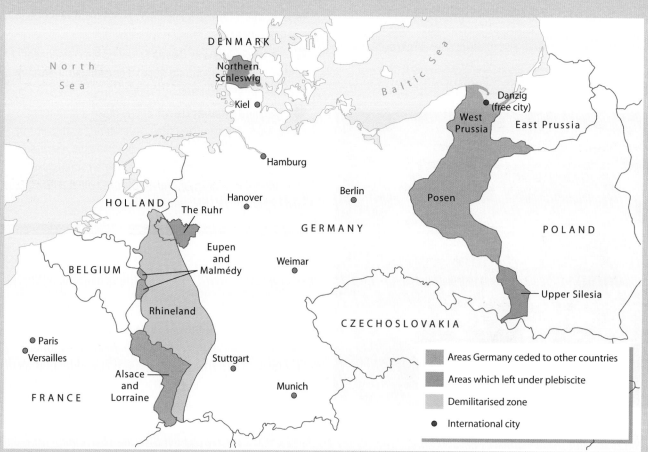

Germany and the Treaty of Versailles.

The Diktat

Making peace with the Allies was one of the first jobs for the new German government. But it wasn't given much influence over peace terms.

On 11 November 1918, just two days after the Kaiser had abdicated, Matthias Erzberger, representing the new government, signed the armistice – an agreement to stop fighting. The Allied leaders – David Lloyd George (Britain), Georges Clemenceau (France) and Woodrow Wilson (United States) – then spent several months drawing up the peace treaty.

The Germans were given 15 days to respond to the treaty. It said Germany had to accept the blame for starting the war, pay **reparations** (compensation) to the Allies and agree to reductions in Germany's armed forces and territory. The Germans were bitterly opposed and asked for several changes; all were refused. They called the treaty a 'diktat' – they were not invited to the negotiations, just told what the terms were. Because of Germany's military collapse, they had to accept. On 28 June 1919, the German delegation signed the Treaty of Versailles.

The terms of the treaty were very unpopular with the people of Germany. They did not believe they deserved such harsh treatment. But that was not the only reason why the treaty was unpopular.

Dolchstoss – the stab in the back

The treaty was particularly difficult to take for the German people because they believed that their army had never been defeated in the war. It had failed to win but it had not been defeated. Critics of the treaty claimed that the army had been ready to fight on. They said that the army had been betrayed by politicians in Berlin – in effect, that they had been 'stabbed in the back' (the *Dolchstoss* in German).

So, the politicians who signed the Treaty were blamed for undermining the army, for being weak and for accepting its harsh terms. These politicians became known as the 'November Criminals' and resentment about the Treaty of Versailles followed the new republic all the way to its collapse in 1933.

The treaty therefore had lasting effects on Germany.

- It weakened the popularity of the Weimar Republic.
- It stirred up political protest
- It harmed Germany's economy.

Build Better Answers

Why was the Treaty of Versailles unpopular with the German people? (8 marks)

Paper 1 part (c) questions expect you to explain why something happened.

■ **A basic answer (level 1)** will give a generalised reason why the treaty was unpopular. For example, *The treaty was unpopular with the people because it took away land from Germany.*

● **A good answer (level 2)** will support the statement with detail. For example, *The treaty was unpopular because Germany lost land. For example, it lost Alsace and Lorraine to France, Eupen and Malmedy to Belgium and also Posen and West Prussia to Poland.*

▲ **A better answer (level 3)** will give more than one reason and will explain each of them. The very best answers will also show how causes combined to lead to the outcome. For example, *The treaty was unpopular because it said Germany was to blame for starting the war. ...This was linked to another reason why it was unpopular. Because it was blamed for the war, the treaty made Germany pay reparations. These totalled £6,600m and crippled government funds. So the cost of these reparations was another reason the treaty was hated by the German people.*

Economic problems, 1918–23

> **Learning objectives**
>
> In this chapter you will learn about:
> - the bankruptcy of the new Weimar government
> - the occupation of the Ruhr
> - the causes and effects of hyperinflation.

Bankruptcy

At first, Germany's biggest problem was that its government was bankrupt; its reserves of gold had all been spent in the war. The Treaty of Versailles made things worse. It deprived Germany of wealth-earning areas, such as coalfields in Silesia. It also made the German government pay reparations. Germany asked for reductions, but the victors, especially France, needed money to pay war debts to the USA. With no gold reserves and falling income by 1923, Germany could no longer pay.

Occupation of the Ruhr

In retaliation, the French sent troops into the German industrial area of the Ruhr (see the map on page 10). They confiscated raw materials, manufactured goods and industrial machinery. The German government urged passive resistance; workers went on strike; there was even some **sabotage**. The French replied by arresting those who obstructed them and bringing in their own workers.

The Germans bitterly resented what the French had done. However, many Germans also resented the failure of the Weimar Republic to resist, even though, realistically, they had no choice. Germany's reduced troop numbers of 100,000 were no match for the 750,000 in the French Army.

The occupation of the Ruhr did the French little good, but it crippled Germany. Many factories and 80% of German coal and iron were based there. The disruption increased Germany's debts, unemployment and the shortage of goods.

Inflation

These shortages meant that the price of things went up – this is called **inflation**. People had to pay more money to get what they needed.

The government needed money to pay their debts, but unemployment and failing factories meant they received less money from taxes. During 1919–23, government income was only a quarter of what was required, so the government just printed more money. In 1923, the government had 300 paper mills and 2000 printing shops just to print more money.

Source A: *This 1923 poster shows German bitterness. France is seen ravaging German industry. The caption reads 'Hands off the Ruhr area!'*

Hände weg vom Ruhrgebiet

Source B: *German cartoon from 1922 – Gutenberg, the German inventor of the printing press, says 'This I did not want!'*

This made it easier for the government to pay reparations, but it made inflation even worse. It was a vicious circle: the more prices rose, the more money was printed and this made prices rise again. By 1923, prices reached spectacular heights. A loaf of bread cost 1 mark in 1919; by 1922 it cost 200 marks; by 1923 it cost 100,000 million marks. This extreme inflation is called hyperinflation.

The results of hyperinflation were complex. There were benefits for some people:

- **Farmers** profited from rising food prices – although they still had to pay higher prices for other goods.
- **Some businesses** were able to pay off loans, as the loans lost value. Others were able to buy up smaller, failing, businesses very cheaply.

However, most people suffered in some way.

- **Everyone suffered from shortages**. This was because German marks became worthless in comparison with foreign currency. In 1918, £1 cost 20 marks; by 1923, £1 cost 20 billion marks. Foreign suppliers refused to accept marks for goods, so imports dried up and shortages of food and other goods got worse – for everyone.
- **Everyone found it difficult to buy what they needed** – even if their wages went up. People had to carry bundles of money in baskets and even wheelbarrows. Many workers were paid twice a day – so they could rush out and buy goods before prices rose even further. Some suppliers refused to take money at all, asking for payment in kind (swapping goods).
- **People with savings** were hit hardest – those with money in bank accounts, insurance policies or pensions; their savings became worthless. Those affected were mainly from the middle classes.

Eventually, things improved. In September 1923 a new chancellor was appointed – Gustav Stresemann. In November 1923, he cancelled the old mark and issued a new currency – the Rentenmark. This led to a period of stability. However, most Germans had suffered and many blamed the Weimar Republic. The middle classes had suffered most; they had been the Weimar Republic's greatest supporters.

Examination question

Explain why there was so much social hardship in Germany between 1918 and 1923. **(8 marks)**

Activities

1 Write the following on small cards: fall in value of pensions; shortage of industrial goods; government bankruptcy; fall in value of savings; inflation; reparations; occupation of the Ruhr; printing more money; loss of land after Versailles.

2 Organise the cards into causes and effects. Draw lines to link causes and their effects. (Note: some cards may be both a cause of one thing and an effect of another.)

3 What does the resulting diagram tell you about:
- the causes of the bankruptcy of the German government
- the causes of the social and economic problems of the German people?

Political problems, 1918–23

The start of the Weimar Republic was marked by political unrest all over Germany. This unrest came from right-wing and left-wing groups.

Right-wing and left-wing

Generally those on the right 'wing' of politics:

● want to keep society very stable

● want a strong government dominated by powerful leaders

● support capitalism – the private ownership of land and business

● stress the importance of the family unit, law and order and traditional values

● are nationalist – placing the interests of the nation over the individual.

Fascism and Nazism are extreme right-wing movements.

Generally, those on the left 'wing' of politics:

● want to change society rapidly

● aim to treat all people as equals and give political power to workers

● oppose capitalism; they want to abolish private ownership of land or business and put these in the hands of workers

● are internationalist; they stress co-operation of nations.

Socialists are left-wing. Communism is an extreme left-wing movement.

Did you know?

The terms 'left' and 'right' to describe political views date back to the French Revolution. In the new 1789 parliament, members who wanted to limit change and keep power in the hands of the king and a small elite sat on the king's right. Those who wanted to change the political system and give the people more power sat on the king's left.

Source A: *This right-wing cartoon shows Karl Liebknecht, leader of Germany's communists, attacking German property, industry, money and families.*

At this time, the right wing in German politics included many small nationalist parties.

● They resented that the Weimar Republic's Social Democrat politicians had abandoned the army in 1918.

● Even more, they hated the communists who had undermined the Kaiser with riots and mutinies in 1918.

● They feared the damage communists would do to their property and German traditions.

● They wanted to reverse Versailles, reinstate the Kaiser, boost the army and return Germany to her former strength.

● They gained support from the military, the **judiciary** and the civil service, who were opposed to giving power to ordinary people in the new, democratic Weimar Republic.

The left wing in Germany was dominated by the KPD, the Communist Party of Germany.

- They wanted a revolution in Germany like the one in Russia in 1917.
- They thought that the Weimar Republic gave too little power to the workers.
- They wanted government by councils of workers or soldiers.
- They wanted to abolish the power in Germany of the land-owning classes and the army.

From 1918–23, the German people were unhappy about:

- the Weimar leaders' decision to admit defeat in 1918
- the 1919 Versailles Treaty, which Germans regarded as punitive and vindictive
- the hardships caused by unemployment and inflation.

All this persuaded many people in Germany to support extreme left-wing or right-wing political groups between 1918 and 1923. If they did support extremist groups, German workers tended to support the socialists and communists, while the German Army, business classes and landowners tended to support the right-wing groups.

Source B: *A left-wing political poster produced by the KPD – Communist Party of Germany. They portray themselves as the slayers of German capitalism, militarism and the German landed nobility – the Junker. The Spartacists were part of the Communist Party.*

The main political parties in the Weimar Republic

KPD	SPD	DDP	ZP	DVP	DNVP	NSDAP
Communist Party	Social Democrats	Democratic Party	Centre Party	People's Party	National Party	Nazi Party
Extreme left-wing	Moderate left-wing	Left-wing Liberal	Moderate	Right-wing Liberal	Right-wing	Extreme right-wing
Opposed Weimar Republic	Supported Weimar Republic	Supported Weimar Republic	Supported Weimar Republic	Supported Weimar Republic in 1920s	Opposed Weimar Republic	Opposed Weimar Republic
Supported by workers and some middle classes	Supported by workers and middle classes	Backed by business	Originally the party of the Catholic Church	Backed by upper middle classes	Landowners, wealthy middle class and big business	

Violent political unrest

One thing which made politics in the Weimar Republic so violent was that political parties had their own private armies. They recruited mainly ex-soldiers, who were often unemployed and bitter that their government had accepted peace. The left wing had its Rotfrontkämpfer (Red Front Fighters). The Stahlhelm (Steel Helmets – a veterans' group) were a conservative organisation on the right wing. Even the moderate SPD had its Sozi force.

At first, private armies were for protection, but they quickly caused political activity to become violent.

- Hugo Hasse, one of Ebert's Council of People's Representatives, was murdered in 1919.
- Matthias Erzberger, a moderate politician who signed the surrender of Germany in 1918, was shot and killed walking in the Black Forest in August 1921.
- Walther Rathenau, the Weimar foreign minister, was machine-gunned to death in the street in Berlin in June 1922.

Between 1919 and 1922 there were 376 political murders, mostly of left-wing or moderate politicians. However, not a single right-wing murderer was convicted and executed; ten left-wing ones were. The judiciary was filled with right-wing supporters.

The Spartacist League (a left-wing movement)

Sometimes, extreme political groups tried to overthrow the government by force. For example, during the winter of 1918–19 there were left-wing uprisings throughout Germany, which set up workers' and soldiers' soviets – local councils – in towns across Germany. A central Council of Commissars was created, claiming to be the true government, as a direct threat to the new moderate government of Ebert in Berlin.

The most influential communist leaders were Rosa Luxemburg and Karl Liebknecht, organisers of the Spartacist League – named after Spartacus, the head of a slaves' revolt in Ancient Rome. On 6 January 1919, inspired by the Spartacists, 100,000 communists demonstrated in Berlin and took over key buildings, such as newspaper offices.

Chancellor Ebert, and his defence minister, Gustav Noske, realised the regular army (the Reichswehr, many of whom were still loyal to the Kaiser, not the republic) would not be able to put down the revolt alone. They had been considering disbanding the Reichswehr and now persuaded it to work with the Freikorps in return for not being disbanded. The Freikorps were **demobilised** soldiers who had refused to give back their arms. By March 1919 there were about 250,000 of them. They were anti-communist.

The Social Democratic politicians into whose lap the German government fell in 1918 didn't have widespread support. Instead, they faced a bitter, suffering population, filled with unrealistic ideas about what peace could bring and divided about…the road ahead.

Source C: *From a modern textbook.*

Source D: *A recruitment poster for the Freikorps, 1919.*

With the help of the Freikorps, the Weimar government was able to put down the Spartacist uprisings in early 1919. Several thousand communist supporters were arrested or killed, mostly in Berlin. Both Rosa Luxemburg and Karl Liebknecht were arrested on 15 January and both were murdered by the Freikorps. Leibknecht was shot; Luxemburg was shot in the head and her body dumped in a canal.

The Kapp Putsch (a right-wing revolt)

But the unrest continued. In 1920, 5000 right-wing supporters of Dr Wolfgang Kapp marched on Berlin to overthrow the Weimar Republic and bring back the Kaiser. For a while, the rebels controlled the city. The government fled to Dresden; they urged people not to co-operate and instead go on strike.

Many workers obliged – they had socialist leanings and no desire to see the Kaiser return. Essential services – gas, electricity, water, transport – stopped and the capital ground to a halt. Kapp realised he could not govern and fled. He was caught and put in prison, where he later died.

Still the unrest continued. In 1923, there was another right-wing uprising – the Munich Putsch – led by Adolf Hitler (see pages 22–23).

Unrest subsides

It wasn't until the end of 1923 that the political unrest calmed down. A new chancellor, Gustav Stresemann, came to power; inflation was brought under control; suffering was reduced and politics became more moderate.

However, by this time, the Weimar Republic was permanently weakened by the political unrest.

- It had not been able to govern on its own authority. It relied upon workers' strikes and the violence of the Freikorps. Government forces had killed thousands of Germans to keep themselves in power.
- Extremist parties had gathered strength during the turbulent years of 1918–23. They still had their private armies and events had taught the worrying lesson that those with most military power could eventually win.

Build Better Answers

Use Source C and your own knowledge to explain why there was widespread political unrest in Germany 1919–23. **(10 marks)**

Paper 1 part (d) questions expect you to use a source and your own knowledge to explain something.

■ **A basic answer (level 1)** will make simple generalisations from the source, with little support from own knowledge. For example, *Germany had a bitter, suffering population which protested.*

● **A good answer (level 2)** will give reasons supported by detail from their own knowledge and the source (more than one would get a higher mark). For example, *Germany had a bitter population. They were bitter about Versailles. During the Spartacist revolt in 1919, many people joined in.*

▲ **An excellent answer (level 4)** will be the 'good' answer from above with more than one factor showing how they combined to produce the outcome. **At least two factors must be used**. For example, *Germany had a bitter, suffering population. Germans blamed the Weimar politicians for Versailles, so they supported unrest against the government. …This unrest was made worse by hyperinflation – it made it hard to buy daily supplies and ruined middle class savings. All kinds of people were hit, so unrest was widespread.*

Activity

How well had the new Weimar Republic done by 1923? Set out your conclusions in a table like this:

	Successes	Failures
the new constitution		
the Treaty of Versailles		
economic problems		
political problems		
overall conclusion		

The Stresemann era, 1924–29

Learning objectives

In this chapter you will learn about:

- Gustav Stresemann's economic and foreign successes
- the Rentenmark, Dawes Plan and Young Plan
- League of Nations, Locarno and Kellogg–Briand Pacts.

In August 1923, during the occupation of the Ruhr, President Ebert appointed Gustav Stresemann as his chancellor and foreign secretary. Stresemann resigned as chancellor in November 1923, but remained foreign secretary until 1929. He led a number of policies which brought recovery to the Weimar Republic between 1924 and 1929.

The Rentenmark

Germany's biggest problem in 1923 was hyperinflation. Stresemann tackled this by abolishing the existing German currency and setting up a new, temporary one, the Rentenmark. The new notes were trusted because, if the currency failed, the government promised to exchange them for shares in German land or industry. Confidence in German money was restored. By August 1924, Stresemann was able to replace the Rentenmark with a new, permanent currency. This was called the Reichsmark and it was controlled by a newly independent national bank, the Reichsbank. The effect was that confidence rose in the currency and banking system. Deposits in German banks rose from 900m marks at the start of 1924 to 4,900m marks at the end of 1926.

The Dawes Plan, 1924

Next, Stresemann tackled reparations. These were so high that Germany had been unable to pay. In April 1924, Stresemann and the Allies agreed the Dawes Plan.

- Annual payments were reduced to an affordable level.
- American banks agreed to invest 800,000,000 marks in German industry.

The effects of the Dawes Plan were that:

- Germany resumed reparations payments
- the French left the Ruhr
- the German economy recovered.

Coal output rose from 275,000,000 tons in 1924 to 350,000,000 tons in 1929. Manufactured goods sales doubled 1923-29. Unemployment fell in 1928 to its lowest for 10 years.

Most Germans were reassured by this economic progress. But the extreme political parties hated Versailles and were furious that Germany had, again, agreed to pay reparations. Furthermore, this fragile economic recovery depended on American loans.

Activities

1 As you read this chapter, look carefully at the *effects* of Stresemann's economic and foreign policies. Decide how successful they were. Set out your answer in a table, like the one on page 17, with Success and Failure columns for each of the following issues:

- the German currency
- the reparations issue
- the Locarno Pact
- the League of Nations
- the Kellogg-Briand Pact.

2 Add a conclusion to your table, just like the one in the table on page 17.

3 Compare your table with the one you did on page 17. What does the comparison tell you?

In foreign policy, Stresemann tried to co-operate with other nations so they would trust Germany and treat Germany as an equal. He hoped they would reduce reparations and make other changes to the terms of the Treaty of Versailles.

The Locarno Pact, 1925

In October 1925 Stresemann signed the Locarno Pact with Britain, France, Italy and Belgium. Germany agreed to keep to its new 1919 border with France and Belgium. In return, the Allies agreed to remove their troops from the Rhineland and discuss German entry to the League of Nations. One effect of this was that Germany was being treated as an equal, not dictated to, at Versailles in 1919.

The League of Nations, 1926

In 1919, the Allies had founded the League of Nations to work for world peace. Germany was excluded. In 1926, Stresemann persuaded the League to accept Germany as a member. Again, an effect was that Germany was trusted and treated as an equal. Germany even got a place on the League's Council.

Kellogg–Briand Pact, 1928

In August 1928, Germany became one of 65 countries to sign the Kellogg-Briand Pact – an international agreement by which states promised not to use war to achieve their foreign policy aims. The effect of this was to show Germany as a respectable member of the international community.

The Young Plan, 1929

Success in foreign policy linked to success in economic policy. In August 1929, the Young Plan cut reparation payments from £6.6 billion to £2 billion, with 59 more years to pay. This had the effect of strengthening the Weimar Republic. Linked with the other successes in economic and foreign policy, it made the new republic look trusted and stronger. However this didn't last.

- There was criticism of the Young Plan. Repayments were still £50 million per year – to be paid until 1988. The leader of the Nazi Party, Adolf Hitler, said that this was 'passing on the penalty to the unborn'
- On 3 October, Stresemann died of a heart attack.
- Then, in late October 1929, a world economic crisis began. Germany was plunged back into turmoil.

Source A: *A German peace rally in 1926; the banner reads 'Thou shalt not kill.' Stresemann restoring healthy diplomatic relations abroad was warmly welcomed by many, though not all, Germans.*

Build Better Answers

Write these events in the correct chronological order:
   French occupation of the Ruhr ends
   The Young Plan agreed
   Germany enters League of Nations
   The Dawes Plan agreed
   The Locarno Pact   **(3 marks)**

Section A part (a) questions ask you to list events in chronological order.

Any 2 in correct sequence:	**1 mark**
3 in correct sequence:	**2 marks**
4 or 5 in correct sequence:	**3 marks**

The birth of the Nazi Party, 1919–23

Adolf Hitler had been a corporal in the German army during the First World War; he had been a brave soldier and was awarded the Iron Cross (First Class). After the war, Hitler was sent by the army to check up on political groups. One was the German Workers' Party (DAP), a small group, founded on 9 January 1919 by Anton Drexler. At Hitler's first meeting, in September 1919, there were only 23 people present; at his third, the treasurer announced its entire funds – 7 marks and 50 pfenning.

The DAP members were bitter and angry about:

● communists and socialists, whom they blamed for bringing down the Kaiser
● Weimar politicians who had agreed to the Treaty of Versailles
● the weakness of democracy as a means of government
● the Jews, who they blamed for weakening the economy.

Although sent to spy on the group, Hitler found that he actually agreed with their views. In late September 1919, he joined the party.

The 25-Point Programme

By 1920, Hitler was working as Drexler's right-hand man. In February 1920, the two men revealed the new 25-Point Programme of the DAP. This included:

● scrapping the Versailles Treaty
● expanding Germany's borders to give its people lebensraum – more land to live in
● depriving the Jews of German citizenship.

The programme also made clear that the DAP were willing to use force to achieve all this.

Hitler was an energetic, passionate speaker and his public speaking started to attract larger numbers to meetings. Many people were dissatisfied with the Weimar Republic in the period up to 1923, and Hitler's group attracted supporters from the army, the police and small businesses. Membership grew rapidly, to about 1100 in June 1920.

In 1921 Hitler became party leader and in the same year founded the *Sturm Abteilung* ('Stormtroopers' or 'Brownshirts'). The SA was a paramilitary organisation that paraded in full uniform, wearing the Nazi 'swastika'. Its main task was to protect Nazi meetings and 'disrupt' those of its opponents.

Source A: *From a modern textbook.*

Hitler's role grows

On 7 August 1920, at Hitler's suggestion, the DAP changed its name to the National Socialist German Workers' Party (NSDAP, or Nazi Party for short). The party then adopted the swastika as its emblem, and its members began to use the raised arm salute. Membership increased to 3000 during 1920. Increased membership boosted funds and the party was able to buy a newspaper – the *Völkischer Beobachter* – for 180,000 marks, enabling it to spread its views even further.

In mid-1921, Hitler pushed Drexler aside and became the party Führer, or leader. He gathered around him loyal party leaders:

- Ernst Röhm, a scar-faced, bull-necked soldier
- Hermann Goering, a wealthy hero of the German Air Force
- Rudolf Hess, a wealthy academic who became Hitler's deputy
- Julius Streicher, founder of another Nazi paper, *Der Stürmer*.

Hitler also cultivated powerful friends, such as General Ludendorff, leader of the German Army during the First World War.

In 1921, Hitler created the Sturmabteilung (SA), or storm troopers. These were the party's private army. They were recruited from demobilised soldiers, the unemployed and students. These 'Brownshirts' provided security at meetings and bodyguards for Nazi leaders; they also broke up meetings of opposition groups. Hitler put Röhm in charge of the SA. Many of the SA were thugs and difficult to control, so in 1923 Hitler selected trusted members of the SA and formed his own bodyguard, the *Stosstrupp* or Shock Troop.

In 1923, Hitler was an unlikely future ruler of Germany. His control of the NSDAP was shaky. Furthermore, it was only one of many right-wing groups in Germany. It had no seats in the Reichstag and was mainly confined to Bavaria, in southern Germany. But with his loyal lieutenants and SA thugs, Hitler had the nucleus of the party that would later take him to power.

Source B: *Social Democrats noticed the threat of the NSDAP. This SPD poster from 1922 says 'Your enemy is on the Right' and shows an SA trooper, complete with brown uniform and swastika.*

Build Better Answers

Use Source A and your own knowledge to explain the part played by Hitler in the early development of the Nazi Party 1919–23. **(10 marks)**

Paper 1 part (d) questions expect you to use a source and your own knowledge to explain something.

■ **A basic answer (level 1)** will make simple generalisations from the source, with little support from own knowledge. For example, *Hitler became leader of the party and controlled the changes.*

● **A good answer (level 2)** will give examples, with detail from their own knowledge and the source (more than one will get a higher mark). For example, *In mid-1921, Hitler became party leader. He created the SA, nicknamed the Brownshirts. They were the party's private army. They were used to protect Nazi meetings. They made the Nazis appear strong and well organised.*

▲ **An excellent answer (level 4)** will be the 'good' answer from above with more than one factor showing how they combined to produce the outcome.

At least two factors must be used. For example, *The SA gives us a link to another way Hitler shaped the Nazi Party. Hitler turned the Nazis onto the attack. He used the SA to disrupt the meetings of his opponents, like the Communists. ... This weakened the opposition, so people heard less about other policies.*

The Munich Putsch, 1923

> **Learning objectives**
>
> In this chapter you will learn about:
> - the causes, events and results of the Munich Putsch.

Causes

In November 1923, Hitler launched the Munich Putsch – an uprising against the German government. He had three reasons for doing so.

- Firstly, hyperinflation was making the lives of Germans miserable. The French occupation of the Ruhr had also angered them. Hitler wanted to exploit this discontent. Membership of the NSDAP had grown to about 55,000, mainly people from around Munich, the capital of Bavaria, in the south of Germany. This was Hitler's chance to make an impact nationally.
- Secondly, Hitler sensed that the new government of Gustav Stresemann would soon get on top of Germany's economic and international problems. He needed to act before unrest died down.
- Thirdly, Stresemann's government was starting to crack down on extremist groups. The army had recently put down a left-wing revolt in Saxony. Hitler could see a crackdown on right-wing groups coming next.

Events

On the evening of 8 November 1923, there was a meeting of 3000 officials of the Bavarian government in a beer hall, called the Burgerbrau Keller, in Munich. The three main speakers were von Kahr, the leader of the Bavarian government, von Seisser, the head of the Bavarian police, and von Lossow, the head of the army in Bavaria.

Hitler burst in, with 600 SA storm troopers, brandishing a gun. He released a shot into the ceiling and announced that he was taking over the government of Bavaria. He claimed that, after taking control in Munich, he would then march against the German government itself. He was supported by the famous German general, Erich von Ludendorff. Kahr, Seisser and Lossow were taken off into a side room. Confronted with Hitler, his troops and their weapons, they agreed to support the uprising.

However, the next morning, Hitler heard that Kahr, Seisser and Lossow had changed their minds and opposed him. This was a blow. The SA had only 2000 rifles, far fewer than the local police and army forces, but Hitler pressed on. He sent 3000 supporters to key buildings around the town, each group supported by the SA.

Causes

Hitler's new policy

When he was released from prison, Hitler realised he needed a new approach to gaining power because:

- his imprisonment had given him time to think through his beliefs and ideas (expressed in *Mein Kampf*)
- the failure of the Munich Putsch, in the area of Germany where the NSDAP were strongest, showed taking power by force was unlikely to work
- partly because of the publicity of the Putsch and Hitler's trial, the NSDAP began to win seats, under the name of the National Socialist Freedom Movement, in the Reichstag even before the ban on the party was lifted in 1925.

Activity

You are a newspaper reporter. On the evening of the Munich Putsch, you are asked to write a 400–word article for the next day's paper.

Write the article. Your editor has particularly asked you to explain:

- why the revolt took place
- the events of the revolt.

Hitler, his key supporters and his Shock Troop marched on the town centre to declare him the president of Germany. But, in the Residenzstrasse, they were met by state police, who opened fire. A bodyguard, Graf, threw himself in front of Hitler and was hit by several bullets. Goering fell, shot in the thigh. Hitler was dragged to the ground by his bodyguards with such force that his left arm was dislocated. In all, 14 of Hitler's supporters and four police were killed.

Ludendorff was arrested. Other rebels fled; one group entered a nearby ladies' academy and hid under the beds. Hitler fled the scene in a car. He hid at the house of a friend, ten miles south of Munich, but was later found and arrested.

Source A: *A group of Hitler's Stosstrupp (Shock Troop), in Munich on the morning of the Putsch.*

Results

Hitler and three other leaders of the Putsch were put on trial, found guilty of treason and sentenced to five years in gaol at Landsberg Castle. The NSDAP was banned. In the short term, the Munich Putsch was therefore a defeat and a humiliation for Hitler.

However, it could have been worse. The judge was quite lenient – five years was the minimum sentence allowed for treason. Ludendorff, incredibly, was even found not guilty. Furthermore, in the longer term, the results were not all bad.

- Hitler used his trial to get national publicity for his views.
- The ban on the NSDAP was weakly enforced and then lifted in 1925. As a result of the publicity, the NSDAP won its first seats in the Reichstag – 32 seats in the 1924 election.
- Hitler was released after only nine months.
- Hitler used his time in gaol to write his autobiography – *Mein Kampf (My Struggle)*. It contained his political ideas and became the guiding light of the Nazi Party.
- Finally, Hitler realised he needed a new approach to gain power in Germany.

Examination question

Explain **one** effect on Hitler of the Munich Putsch. **(4 marks)**

 Top Tip

Your examination paper will always have a question like the one above, which asks you to describe an *effect* of something.

To get good marks in these questions, you need to support the effect you give with detailed information. For example, if you say one effect on Hitler was that he was leniently treated, you should support this by saying he was given the minimum sentence of 5 years and then released after only nine months.

Instead of an armed coup, we shall have to hold our noses and enter the Reichstag…If outvoting them takes longer than outshooting them, at least the result will be guaranteed…Sooner or later we shall have a majority and, after that – Germany!

Source B: *From a letter written by Hitler from gaol. The strategy he describes did later get him into power.*

Did you know?

Hitler spent two days hiding in the attic at his friend's house after the failure of the Munich Putsch. The family gardener informed police and Hitler was arrested after he was found hiding in a wardrobe.

Reorganising the Nazi Party, 1924–28

Learning objectives

In this chapter you will learn about:

- the organisation and funding of the NSDAP
- the growth of the SA and founding of the SS
- Joseph Goebbels and Nazi propaganda
- Nazi Party election results in 1928.

Activity

Copy the diagram below. Add to each box detailed notes to show how Hitler strengthened the Nazi Party 1924–28.

```
  administration          funding

       NAZI PARTY ORGANIZATION

      the SS              the SA

            propaganda
```

Hitler left prison in 1924 and he re-launched the Nazi Party in February 1925 – ironically at the Burgerbrau Keller, scene of the Munich Putsch. He still had personal appeal: 4,000 people heard him speak; a further 1,000 were turned away.

New organisation and funding

As the party grew, it needed better organisation. Hitler appointed two efficient administrators to run Nazi headquarters: Philipp Bouhler as secretary and Franz Schwarz as treasurer. He also divided the party into regions; he appointed a network of *gauleiters* answerable only to him, who ran the NSDAP in each *gaue*, or region.

To fund all this, Hitler improved party finances. He befriended Germany's most wealthy businessmen. They shared his hatred of communism and hoped Hitler would limit the power of trade unions. By the early 1930s, the Nazis were receiving donations from giants of German industry, such as Thyssen, Krupp and Bosch.

The SA and SS

This extra income also helped Hitler to strengthen the SA. As well as protecting Nazi meetings and intimidating opponents, the uniformed men gave the Nazis the appearance of strength and order. He expanded the SA to 400,000 members by 1930.

But the Munich Putsch had taught Hitler the importance of a loyal bodyguard – and Hitler didn't trust the SA. Many Storm Troopers were violent thugs, difficult to control; and, while Hitler was in prison, the SA had developed a dangerous loyalty to Ernst Röhm, its commander. So, in 1925, Hitler set up a new party security group. He called them the Schutzstaffel (Protection Squad), or SS.

At first, the SS was run by Hitler's personal chauffeur and bodyguard, Julius Schreck, and soon after by Heinrich Himmler, one of his most loyal supporters. The SS, in their black uniforms, were soon widely feared for their ruthlessness.

Source A: *Adolf Hitler, in 1929, in SA uniform and surrounded by storm troopers.*

Goebbels and Nazi Propaganda

Dr Joseph Goebbels was the Nazi Party *gauleiter* for Berlin. He and Hitler worked together to improve Nazi party propaganda. Propaganda is the information or the ideas that you spread to help your own cause or harm other people's.

Hitler and Goebbels had a simple message, but they created many ways to get it across.

They created scapegoats whom they blamed for Germany's problems: the Jews, the communists and the moderate leaders of the Weimar Republic – especially the Social Democrats, who had signed the armistice and the Treaty of Versailles.

They promoted Hitler as the voice of the Nazi Party. By the 1930s, his speeches were reported in 120 daily or weekly Nazi newspapers, read by hundreds of thousands of Germans across the whole country.

They used the most up-to-date technology, including radio, films and gramophone records, to keep Hitler in the public eye. Hitler used aeroplanes to fly from venue to venue, so that he could speak in up to five cities a day.

They created a clear image for the party – an image of strength. The image was set by:

- Hitler's passion
- the spectacle of mass Nazi rallies
- the impressive power of the SA and the SS.

Nazi Party progress by 1928

By 1928, the Nazi Party was well organised. It had 100,000 members and Hitler was a national figure. However, in some ways, these were lean years.

- Since 1923, inflation had eased, employment had increased and the public were better off.
- Stresemann seemed to be regaining status for Germany on the world stage.
- In 1925, Paul von Hindenburg, the 78-year-old ex-field marshal of the German Army, had become president; his reputation was a boost to the Weimar Republic.

As a result, voters supported moderate parties, such as the SPD, and all the extreme parties lost ground. In the general elections of May 1928:

- the Nazis won only 12 seats
- were only the ninth biggest Reichstag party
- polled only 810,000 votes – just 2.6% of votes.

> A numerically insignificant…radical-revolutionary splinter group incapable of exerting any noticeable influence on the great mass of the people and the course of political events.

Source B: *A confidential report on the Nazis by the Interior Ministry, July 1927.*

> Propaganda must confine itself to very few points and repeat them endlessly. Here, persistence is the first and foremost condition of success.

Source C: *Hitler, writing in* Mein Kampf, *1925.*

Build Better Answers

Why was the Nazi Party so unsuccessful in elections in 1928? Explain your answer. **(8 marks)**

Paper 1 part (c) questions expect you to explain why something happened.

■ **A basic answer (level 1)** will just make a simple statement giving a reason why Nazis were unsuccessful. For example, *They got few votes because the economy had improved.*

● **A good answer (level 2)** will give reasons supported by detail (more than one would get a higher mark). For example, *They got very few votes, only 2.6% of votes cast in the 1928 general election. This was because the economy improved.*

▲ **An excellent answer (level 3)** will be the 'good' answer from above with more than one factor showing how they combined to produce the outcome. For example, *The Nazis only got 2.6% of the votes cast in the 1928 general election. One reason was that the economy had improved; inflation had eased and employment had increased. This was linked to another reason. Because the economy had recovered, Germany was making reparations payments again. …So it was accepted by other countries. This was another reason for Nazi failure. Stresemann was regaining German status on the world stage. People supported the moderate parties in government, not parties like the Nazis who wanted to remove them.*

The impact of the Wall Street Crash, 1929

> **Learning objectives**
>
> In this chapter you will learn about:
> - the causes of the Great Depression in Germany
> - the effects of the Great Depression in Germany.

The Wall Street Crash

In October 1929, share prices began to fall on the Wall Street **stock exchange** in New York. Falling shares meant people's investments fell in value. Worried about losing money, people rushed to sell shares before they fell further. On 'Black Thursday', 24 October 1919, 13 million shares were sold. But this panic selling sent prices even lower. Shares worth $20,000 in the morning were worth $1000 by the end of the day's trading. Within a week, investors lost $4000 million. This is called the Wall Street Crash.

Economic effects

Banks were major investors in shares and suffered huge losses. German banks lost so much money that people feared they couldn't pay out the money in bank accounts. People rushed to get their money back – causing some banks to run out of cash.

All this spelt disaster for the German economy. German and American banks urgently needed the return of money they had lent to businesses. But German companies were dependent upon these loans. They either had to reduce operations or close. German industrial output fell and unemployment rose.

It was equally bad for companies that sold at home or abroad. The worldwide **depression** was a disaster for export industries but high unemployment meant that domestic demand for goods fell too. Unemployment rose further.

Social and political effects

The economic collapse caused suffering.

- The middle classes lost savings, their companies or their homes.
- Workers became unemployed.

People demanded political action, but the Weimar government failed them. From 1930 to 1932, the chancellor was Heinrich Brüning. He proposed:

- raising taxes to pay the cost of unemployment benefit
- reducing unemployment benefit to make payments more affordable.

Activities

1 As you read this chapter, make a list of the effects of the Great Depression.

Your list will include things like: banks made huge losses people rushed to withdraw saving some banks ran out of cash.

Aim for a list of at least 12 effects.

2 Some of your effects will be linked, for example: *workers became unemployed* would be linked to *the unemployed roamed the streets; some joined the private armies of political parties.*

List and explain as many links as you can find.

Source A: *Some effects of the Crash on German industry.*

Years	Fall in industrial production (per cent)
1929–30	10%
1929–31	30%
1929–32	40%

Source B: *Some effects of the Crash on German employment.*

Date	Unemployment
September 1929	1.3 million
September 1931	4.3 million
September 1932	5.1 million
January 1933	6.0 million

This pleased no one. Right-wing parties, the middle classes and the wealthy opposed higher taxes. Left-wing parties and workers opposed lower benefits. The coalition of parties which Brüning's government depended upon collapsed in 1930. Brüning could only govern by decree. There had only been five presidential decrees in 1930. As the crisis deepened, Brüning's government had to rely on 44 decrees in 1931 and 66 in 1932.

But even this was in vain – the causes of suffering were beyond government control and the crisis continued. Useless decrees merely undermined confidence in the Weimar Republic still further.

The unemployed roamed the streets; some joined the private armies of political parties. Violent clashes became common. Brüning had lost control of the Reichstag, the economy and the streets.

Effects

The Depression

The depression created a situation where:

- a drop in spending
- factory closures
- unemployment

led to:

- a further drop in spending
- more factory closures
- more unemployment.

These things became both causes and effects as they spiralled out of control, linked together and setting each other off.

Source C: *A 1950s painting showing the unemployed and beggars outside a closed German factory in the Great Depression.*

Nazi support grows, 1929–32

As Germany's problems grew during the Great Depression, Chancellor Brüning's supporters in the Reichstag deserted him. He had to resort to governing by presidential decree. He tried raising taxes to pay benefits to the poor. He tried banning demonstrations to calm unrest. All failed. When elections took place, voters increasingly turned to extreme right-wing and left-wing parties to solve their problems.

Nazi support rose during this time, partly because the Nazis had very effective campaigning techniques and partly because they appealed to many different types of Germans.

Hitler's appeal

Part of Hitler's success was that he didn't appeal to just one group or class. His appeal was universal. Hitler played a central role in Nazi election campaigning. He was the party's figurehead and a key part of their propaganda material. He appeared everywhere. He used aeroplanes in a whirlwind campaign for the 1930 and 1932 elections. Germans saw him as man who could:

● unite the country under a strong leader

● restore order from social unrest

● scrap the Treaty of Versailles

● persuade other nations to treat Germany fairly.

The strength of the SA

The SA was also vital to Nazi election campaigns. By 1930, the SA had 400,000 Storm Troopers. These were used in rallies to make the Nazi Party seem strong, organised, disciplined and reliable.

But they were also used to against opposition parties. The elections of 1930 and 1932 were violent. Armed, uniformed men tore down opposition posters, intimidated their candidates, broke into their offices and disrupted their rallies.

	May 1928	**Sept 1930**	**July 1932**
National Socialists	12	107	230
Communists	54	77	89
Nazi	1 million	6 million	13 million

General Elections 1928–32: seats in the Reichstag and votes for the Nazis.

Source A: *A painting showing a lorry full of SA storm troopers driving through a communist rally outside KDP headquarters.*

Activity

Many different groups of people supported the Nazis. Copy and complete the table below.

Who supported the Nazis	Why they supported the Nazis

Working-class support

Many working people were attracted by Nazi support for traditional German values and a strong Germany. There was an economic appeal too – Nazis promised 'Work and Bread' on posters. But part of the appeal was just propaganda. The Nazis used posters which gave the impression that many workers already supported them. And, of course, they called themselves the National Socialist German *Workers* Party. But the Nazis never really dominated the working-class vote. When times were hard, most workers supported the communists, so Nazi working-class support was important; but it wasn't enough.

Middle-class support

The middle class contained professional people, like teachers and lawyers, business people and small farmers. They often owned land or businesses and had savings. Between 1929 and 1932, they deserted more moderate parties, like the Social Democrats, and supported the Nazis. There were several reasons for this.

The Great Depression hurt the middle classes. Many lost their companies, their savings or their pensions. They saw Hitler as a strong leader who could help the country recover. Secondly, the middle classes were afraid of the growing German Communist party (the KPD), which wanted to abolish private ownership of land and businesses. The middle classes saw the Nazis as a strong party which could protect them from this. Finally, there was a view that there had been a moral decline under the Weimar Republic, including more drinking and sexual openness. The Nazis represented a return to traditional German values. This went down well with the middle classes.

…he was offering unity. He welcomed all. There was no class distinction; the only demand was to follow Hitler in his fight against Jews and Reds, in his struggle for Lebensraum and the glory and good of Germany.

Source B: *From a modern textbook.*

Farmers

The Nazis targeted farmers' votes. The Nazi policy of confiscating all private land (in the 25 Points of 1920) was changed in 1928. The new policy said that private land would only be confiscated if owned by Jews. This way, Hitler could promise to protect the farmers from the Communist Party, which would have confiscated their land.

Big business

The business classes usually supported the National Party. But this party's Reichstag seats halved from 1929–32. Big business saw Hitler as protection from the KPD. Their support brought a boost to Nazi funds and help from powerful newspaper owners, like Alfred Hugenberg.

Young people and women

The young were attracted by Hitler's passionate speeches, his ambitions for the future and the atmosphere of Nazi rallies. At first, women did not support Hitler; his policies limited their roles to the home. But, Nazi propaganda made special appeals to women, saying voting for the NSDAP was best for their country and best for their families.

Top tip

Someone once asked a US president, Bill Clinton, what was the most important thing in an election. His reply was "The economy, stupid."
If an examiner asks why Nazi support grew in elections, don't call him or her stupid. But do stress the economy. As economic problems and unemployment grew in Germany 1929–32, Nazi votes grew too.

The Nazis win power, 1932–33

By July 1932, the NSDAP had become the biggest party in the Reichstag. In addition to this, in March 1932, Hitler stood for election as president.

The presidential elections of 1932

Germany was in turmoil at this time. The Wall Street Crash had caused the collapse of German industry and banking. Unemployment and the loss of savings caused hardship and unrest. As in the general elections, people protested by voting for extreme candidates. Hindenburg, president since 1925, hung on with 18 million votes. The Communist leader, Ernst Thällmann, polled 5 million. Hitler polled 11 million votes.

Because no candidate had achieved 50 per cent of the vote, the election was repeated in April. This time, Hindenburg polled 19 million and was re-elected president. However, while the Communist vote fell to 4 million, Hitler's vote grew to 13 million. Hitler was now a major political figure in Germany.

The fall of Chancellor Brüning

In April 1932, the moderate socialist chancellor, Brüning, used a presidential decree to ban the SA and SS. He wanted to calm unrest and control the Nazis. But right-wing parties were angered. An ambitious general, Kurt von Schleicher, decided to remove Brüning. He organised a coalition of right-wing groups, consisting of landowners, industrialists and army officers. Then he persuaded Hindenburg that they had a majority in the Reichstag, and Brüning was sacked.

Von Papen becomes chancellor

Von Schleicher controlled the new government from behind the scenes. He chose a wealthy gentleman politician, ex-General Franz von Papen, as the figurehead for this new coalition. Hindenburg made von Papen chancellor in May 1932.

Von Schleicher offered the NSDAP a place in the coalition. He thought he could control the Nazis, seeing them as 'merely children who had to be led by the hand'. Hitler agreed to the offer. From May 1932, therefore, Hitler and the Nazi Party were, for the first time, part of the government of Germany.

Date	Elections and government	Chancellor
1932		
March & April	Hitler stood for president and lost.	Brüning
May	Nazis asked to join government coalition.	von Papen
July	Reichstag election: Nazis now biggest party (230 seats).	von Papen
Nov	Reichstag election: Nazis still biggest party (190 seats).	von Papen
Dec	New chancellor	von Schleicher
1933		
Jan	New chancellor	Hitler

The key events of 1932–33.

Activity

1 a Copy the key events diagram above, adding two columns: 'Causes' and 'Significance'.

b Complete one or both of these new columns for each event using the information in the text.

Von Papen's coalition was weak from the start. In the general elections of July 1932, the NSDAP won 230 seats in the Reichstag. It was now the largest party. Hitler demanded that Hindenburg should sack von Papen and appoint him chancellor. Hindenburg, who had been field marshal of German forces during the First World War, detested Hitler – in his eyes he was a vulgar, jumped-up corporal. He refused.

Instead, von Papen hung on to office and called a new election for November 1932. He was gambling that the Nazi support would fall. Nazi seats in the Reichstag did fall to 196, but they were still the largest party. Without Hitler's support, von Papen could no longer command a majority in the Reichstag, nor the confidence of Hindenburg. Von Papen resigned.

Von Schleicher becomes chancellor

Thirty-nine business tycoons like Krupp, Siemens, Thyssen and Bosch signed a letter asking Hindenburg to appoint Hitler as chancellor. They thought that, with their donations to his party, they could control him. But Hindenburg was still opposed. On 2 December, he appointed von Schleicher as chancellor.

Von Schleicher was confident that support for the Nazis was fading. He told a visiting Austrian minister that 'Herr Hitler is no longer a problem; his movement is a thing of the past'. But he consistently failed to get a majority in the Reichstag. He informed Hindenburg that von Papen and Hitler were conspiring against him – as in fact they were – and that he needed Hindenburg to suspend the constitution and declare von Schleicher head of a military dictatorship. Hindenburg refused, but news of von Schleicher's plan leaked out and he lost any remaining support in the Reichstag. His time was up.

Hitler becomes chancellor

Throughout all this, von Papen had continued to plot against von Schleicher with Hindenburg and right-wing parties in the Reichstag. He told them that, if they supported Hitler as chancellor, with von Papen as vice-chancellor, they could make all the decisions themselves and use Hitler as a figurehead. He said he had Hitler 'in his pocket'.

So, reluctantly, Hindenburg agreed that there was no alternative. 'It is my unpleasant duty then to appoint this fellow Hitler as Chancellor,' he grumbled. And on 30 January 1933, Adolf Hitler was legally and democratically appointed chancellor of Germany.

> The men of the German Right thought that the clever von Papen could outwit the hysterical ex-corporal, who lacked experience of high office. They became the gravediggers of the Republic.

Source A: From a modern textbook.

Activities

1 Make a table showing how Hitler was helped by:
   - economic conditions
   - elections
   - disagreements between other politicians
   - other politicians underestimating him.

   Re-read this chapter and, each time something happens to help Hitler, explain it in the appropriate place in the table.

2 Now look at what you've written. How could you use this to answer an examination question like:

   Why was Hitler able to become chancellor in 1933?

Source B: *This 1933 British cartoon shows Hindenburg and von Papen lifting Hitler to power, while cursing him under their breath.*

THE TEMPORARY TRIANGLE.
VON HINDENBURG AND VON PAPEN (*together*)—
"FOR HE'S A JOLLY GOOD FELLOW,
FOR HE'S A JOLLY GOOD FELLOW,
FOR HE'S A JOLLY GOOD FE-EL-LOW,
(*Aside:* "Confound him!")
AND SO SAY BOTH OF US!"

The removal of opposition, 1933–34

Learning objectives

In this chapter you will learn about:
- the Reichstag fire and election of March 1933
- the Enabling Act and banning of political parties and trade unions
- the Night of the Long Knives
- the death of President Hindenburg.

From 30 January 1933, Hitler was chancellor of Germany but his power was limited.

- The Weimar constitution controlled chancellor's powers.
- Hindenburg retained all the powers of the president.
- Hitler's cabinet of 11 had only two Nazi Party members.
- Only a third of the Reichstag were Nazi Party members.

But, almost immediately he became chancellor, Hitler began to remove restrictions on his power.

The Reichstag fire

On 27 February 1933, the Reichstag building was destroyed by fire. A young Dutchman, a communist supporter named Marinus van der Lubbe, was caught on the site. He confessed, was put on trial, found guilty and executed.

But Van der Lubbe's execution was not enough for Hitler. He said that the fire was part of a communist conspiracy and persuaded Hindenburg to declare a state of emergency. He could now legally use decrees to govern Germany.

The 1933 elections

Hitler also asked Hindenburg to call an election for 5 March 1933. He hoped for more Nazi seats in the Reichstag. To help his election campaign, Hitler:

- raised millions of marks from rich businessmen
- used a decree to imprison political opponents
- used the SA to attack political rivals.

It was a bloody election campaign; violent clashes led to 70 deaths. But it worked for Hitler. The Nazis increased their Reichstag members to 288.

Source A: *A 1933 cartoon showing Joseph Goebbels, head of Nazi propaganda, pulling a communist plotter out of a box. Some historians have suggested that the Nazis made up the plot to turn people against the communists.*

Furthermore, Hitler used his emergency powers to ban the Communists from taking up their 81 seats. With the support of the other nationalist parties, this gave Hitler a two-thirds majority in the Reichstag. This was crucial. He now had enough votes to change the constitution of the republic.

The Enabling Act

The Enabling Act was passed on 23 March 1933. It changed the constitution of the Weimar Republic and gave Hitler the right to make laws for four years without the consent of the Reichstag. The Enabling Act was passed by 444 votes to 94. Communist members of the Reichstag could not attend the session, having been banned. Hitler also posted members of the SA and the SS all around and inside the Kroll Opera House where the Reichstag had met since the fire. Members from other parties who might have considered opposing the act were intimidated by their menacing presence. The act marked the end of democracy and the end of Weimar because:

- Hitler, not the elected Reichstag, made the laws
- the laws he passed laws that turned Germany into a **totalitarian state**, not a democracy.

Trade unions

Trade unions were potential sources of opposition to Hitler. If communists among working men were able to control their trade unions, they could use strikes to attack the government. So, in May 1933, Hitler used his new powers to ban trade unions and make strikes illegal.

Political parties

In July 1933, Hitler issued another decree. It was called the Law Against the Establishment of Parties. Article 1 of this new law removed all opposition to the NSDAP (Nazis). It said 'The National Socialist German Workers' Party constitutes the only political party in Germany.'

Local government

The next step was for Hitler to strengthen the central government in Berlin – which he controlled – and to weaken local government. Under the Weimar constitution, all regions (*Länder*) of Germany had their own parliament, which ran local government in the area. But in January 1934, Hitler abolished the Länder parliaments and declared that governors, appointed by him, would run every region.

> The Enabling Law gave Hitler the power to pass any law he liked. At once the Nazis set about bringing the whole of Germany under their control and, in July 1933, Germany became a one party state.

Source B: *From a modern text book.*

Activities

1. To understand properly how Hitler became a dictator in Germany, it is important to analyse his actions carefully.

   Make a table, like the one below.

Legal changes	Illegal changes

2. As you work through this chapter, take notes on the ways in which Hitler increased his power, putting each of them in the appropriate column of your table. Continue your table for the events on pp. 74–75.

Build Better Answers

Choose either **the Reichstag Fire** or **the Enabling Act.**

Explain one **effect on the democracy in the Weimar Republic of the event you have chosen.** **(4 marks)**

Paper 1 part (b) questions will ask about the effect of one event on another.

■ **A basic answer (level 1)** will give a generalised effect. For example, *The Enabling Act increased Hitler's power.*

● **A good answer (level 2)** will give more detail, relevant to the question. For example, *The Enabling Act meant the end of democracy in the Weimar Republic. It gave Hitler the power to make laws himself, and he banned other political parties. He was a dictator.*

The Night of the Long Knives

By the start of 1934, Hitler had made Germany a one-party state. He now made sure that he was the unrivalled leader of that one party – the Nazi Party.

Hitler feared Ernst Röhm, the leader of the SA.

- Röhm had merged an army veterans' group, the *Stahlhelm*, with the SA. This brought SA numbers to three million. With so many SA members loyal to him, Röhm was in an ideal position to challenge Hitler.

- Röhm also opposed Hitler's policies. He criticised Hitler's links with rich industrialists and army generals. He wanted more socialist policies, to tax the rich and help the working classes.

The German Army also worried about the power of Röhm. After the Versailles Treaty the army had only 100,000 men; it was dwarfed by the SA. Röhm wanted the SA to replace the German Army.

Leaders of the SS, like Himmler and Heydrich, resented Röhm too. They wanted to reduce the power of the SA, so that they could increase their own power and the status of the SS.

In 1934, leaders of the SS and the army warned Hitler that Röhm was planning to seize power. So, on 30 June 1934, Hitler arranged for Röhm and several other senior officers of the SA, to be arrested, imprisoned and shot. This is known as the Night of the Long Knives.

> Adolf is a swine. His old friends are not good enough for him. Adolf is turning into a gentleman. He wants to sit on a hilltop and pretend he is God.

Source D: *Röhm, drunk in 1934, quoted by H. Rauschning, in his book* Hitler Speaks *(1940).*

> With an SS escort, the Führer knocked gently on Röhm's door: 'A message from Munich', he said in a disguised voice. 'Come in' Röhm shouted, 'the door is open'. Hitler tore open the door, fell on Röhm as he lay in bed, grabbed him by the throat and screamed, 'You are under arrest, you pig!' Then he turned him over to the SS.

Source C: *extracts from the diary of Alfred Rosenberg, a leading Nazi politician, for 30 June 1934.*

Röhm was taken to Stadelheim jail, where, on 1 July, an SS brigade leader arrived. He left a loaded pistol, with one bullet, in Röhm's cell, thereby inviting Röhm to commit suicide. After 15 minutes, hearing no sound, he entered the cell with his deputy, where they both shot him. In addition to Röhm, six other SA leaders were shot, on Hitler's orders, at Stadelheim.

In the middle of all this, von Papen, still vice-chancellor, protested to Goering. He was told that the SS had things under control and he should return home for his own safety. SS squads were rounding up suspects; one group reached von Papen's office before he did, shot his press secretary and arrested his staff.

Von Papen's home was surrounded and his telephone cut off – so much for having 'Hitler in his pocket'.

Activity

Read back through pages 32–35.

Copy and complete the list below, so that you have a list of all the changes which increased Hitler's power. Where possible, give dates.

a Hitler able to rule by decree (February 1933)

b He is able to imprison rivals

c He is able to ban KPD papers

d He controls two-thirds of Reichstag (March 1933)

Over a period of about four days, about 400 people, including 150 senior members of the SA, were shot without trial. These included:

- General von Schleicher – the ex-chancellor – who was gunned down along with his wife. Goering announced they had been shot resisting arrest.
- Gregor Strasser, a Nazi member with socialist views similar to Röhm, who was locked in a Gestapo cell before gunmen sprayed bullets through a window. A lone gunman entered to finish him off.

Hitler was now clearly acting illegally by murdering his rivals for power. He claimed to be doing this in the interests of Germany. Some Germans objected to the violence, but few knew how terrible it had been. Most were grateful that the SA, hated for their brutality, had been restrained.

The SA continued after 1934 but it was limited to giving muscle to the Nazi party and no longer rivalled the army. It was also now firmly under Hitler's control.

> I ordered the leaders of the guilty to be shot. If anyone asks why I did not use the courts of justice, I say this: in this hour, I was responsible for the fate of the German people and I became the supreme judge of the German people.

Source E: *Hitler, in a speech to the Reichstag on 13 July 1934.*

The death of President Hindenburg

Finally, on 2 August 1934, President Hindenburg died, aged 87, and Hitler moved in to take over supreme power.

- He declared himself Germany's Führer.
- He decreed that, as Führer, he would add all of the president's powers to those he already held as chancellor.
- He forced an oath of loyalty to him from every soldier in the Army.

A plebiscite (public vote) was organised to confirm Hitler as the Führer. Bombarded by pro-Nazi propaganda, 90% of voters decided in favour. The Weimar Republic had ended; Hitler's Third Reich had begun.

THEY SALUTE WITH BOTH HANDS NOW.

Source F: *A British cartoon from July 1934. The ranks of the SA are shown desperately saluting with both hands, as Hitler looks on with his gun still smoking.*

Examination question

Study Source B on page 33. Use the source and your own knowledge to explain the changes in Hitler's powers 1933–34. **(10 marks)**

Top tip

The best answers to questions like the one above do three important things.

1. Consider at least two changes.
2. Use the source to give *details* of at least one of the changes.
3. Explain each of the changes in detail.
4. Try to *link* the changes, and show how they combined to produce the outcome – for example explaining how one change (such as extra powers under the Enabling Act) was linked to another change (such as being able to ban rival political parties).

The Nazi police state

> ## Learning objectives
>
> In this chapter you will learn about:
> - Himmler, the SS and the Gestapo
> - Nazi concentration camps and the law courts
> - repression of the Church in Nazi Germany.

Nazi Germany was a police state. This is a state in which the government uses the police – sometimes secret police – to control people's lives. Views opposed to the Nazis were suppressed. The main organisations used by Hitler to exert this control over Germany were the SS and the Gestapo.

> Right from the start, I have taken the view that it does not matter in the least if our actions are against some clause in the law; in my work for the Führer and the nation, I do what my conscience and common sense tells me is right.

Source A: *Himmler addressing the Committee for Police Law in 1936.*

The SS (Schutzstaffel)

The SS was a military group, set up in 1925 as a personal bodyguard for Hitler. From 1929 it was run by Heinrich Himmler. The main role of the SS was to be the Nazi Party's own private police force. They were totally loyal to Hitler. It was the SS who warned him about Röhm in 1934 and Hitler used SS officers to murder SA leaders during the Night of the Long Knives. Gradually, during the 1930s, the SS was expanded to 50,000 men and put in charge of all the other state security services.

Another role of the SS was to carry out the Nazi policy of racial purification. One part of the SS was the Totenkopf (Death's Head Units), who ran concentration camps. Himmler was careful about recruitment to the SS. He ensured that members were Aryan in appearance; they were expected to marry 'racially pure' wives.

Source B: *Nazi SA. Their banner reads 'We don't like sabotage of the work of the Führer'. Their poster shows what the Nazis would not accept – whispered criticisms and a Jew being baptised as a Christian.*

The Gestapo

The Gestapo (*Geheime Staatspolizei*) was Hitler's non-uniformed secret police force. They were set up in 1933 by Hermann Goering and placed under the control of the SS in 1936. The Gestapo was led by Reinhard Heydrich. Germans particularly feared the Gestapo because they could not tell them apart from other members of the public. The Gestapo arrested people who acted against or spoke out in any way against Nazi ideas. Offenders could be imprisoned without trial.

All states have police forces. But in most states the police have to act within the law and can be held to account in the courts. However, the SS and Gestapo could arrest people without being responsible to anyone but their commanders and Hitler.

> To discover the enemies of the state, watch them and render them harmless at the right moment…In order to fulfil this duty, the political police must be free to use every means suited to achieve the desired end.

Source C: *Werner Best, Heydrich's deputy.*

By 1939, 150,000 people were 'under protective arrest' in prisons. This means that they had not committed criminal acts, like stealing. They were just locked up for doing things that the Nazis disapproved of, such as voicing opposition to Hitler and the Nazis. Once in the prisons, they were at the mercy of their guards.

Concentration camps

The first Nazi concentration camp was opened at Dachau in 1933. Later that year, the first camp for women was opened at Moringen. Camps were normally located in isolated areas outside cities and away from the public gaze. They were secretive places, not controlled by normal prison rules.

Inmates were mainly political prisoners or 'undesirables' – like prostitutes and minority groups, such as Jews or gypsies – of whom the Nazis disapproved. From 1938 onwards, the SS used camp inmates as forced labour for business enterprises, for example producing army uniforms.

There were six concentration camps by 1939, holding about 20,000 people in total. After 1939, concentration camps grew in number and size and some were used for the mass murder of minority groups, such as the Jews.

The law courts

Finally, Hitler also took control of what happened in the courts. Firstly, he set up the National Socialist League for the Maintenance of the Law. He insisted that all judges must be members. If any judges displeased the Nazis, they were denied membership. Certain that judges would support Nazi ideas, Hitler gave them freedom to punish people even when they had not broken the law. He also set up a new People's Court, to hear all treason cases – offences against the state. Judges for this court were hand picked. Even then, if Hitler thought sentences too lenient, he increased them himself.

The Führer has seen the press cutting about the sentencing of the Jew, Markus Luftgas, to two-and-a-half years in prison. He desires that Lufgas should be executed. Please make the arrangements.

Source D: *A letter from Hitler's private office, quoted in* World Conflict in the Twentieth Century, *by S.M. Harrison (1987).*

The SS was supported by the Gestapo (or secret police). The Gestapo used any method they could to find opponents of the regime, including phone tapping and spying on people. Informers were everywhere, in every street, every workplace and even in every classroom.

Source E: *From a modern textbook.*

Top tip

Paper 1 part (d) questions expect you to use a source and your own knowledge to explain something.

Use the following question as an example.

Use Source E and your own knowledge to explain the changes involved in creating the Nazi police state. (10 marks)

These are the five most important things to remember.

1 You must give explain at least two changes (for example two or more from, *Gestapo, SS, concentration camps, control of law courts, control of churches*).
2 You must use information from the source **and** your own knowledge (not just one of these) to support your answer.
3 Don't just state the changes; explain *how* they were made and what *impact* they had.
4 Show *links* between the changes and how they combined to produce the outcome (for example, ... *the Gestapo made arrests; it was no use arresting people if the courts freed them, so the Nazis also needed to control the law courts ...*).
5 Plan your answer. The examiner wants a piece of writing that discusses the changes, makes links between them and reaches a conclusion. Plan your answer before writing it.

Activity

It's easy to confuse the SS and the Gestapo. To help you to remember the difference, make a table with one column for the SS and one for the Gestapo and list their main features. Include things like when each was set up, what their main task was, who their leaders were, key events in their history.

The Nazis and Christianity

The Christian religion was one aspect of life in Germany repressed by Hitler's police state. The likelihood of friction was obvious. Whereas the Nazis glorified strength and violence and taught racial superiority, Christianity preached tolerance and peace and respect for all people. At first, Hitler tried to control the Christian churches by reassuring them and encouraging them to work with the Nazi government.

However, this approach didn't work for long. Soon, Hitler turned the full force of the police state against Christians.

The Catholic Church

One-third of Germany's Christians were Catholic. Again, there were obvious sources of friction here.

- On social issues, Catholics owed their first allegiance, not to Hitler, but to the Pope.
- Catholics also had their own schools, which taught values different from Nazi state schools.

Hitler tried, at first, to reach agreement with the Catholic Church. In July 1933, he reached a concordat (agreement) with the Pope. Hitler agreed:

- to confirm freedom of worship for Catholics
- not to interfere with Catholic schools in Germany.

The Roman Catholic Church:

- agreed that its priests would not interfere in politics
- ordered German bishops to swear loyalty to the National Socialist regime.

But Hitler didn't keep his promise to the Catholic Church. As the 1930s went on:

- Catholic priests were harassed and arrested; many ended up in concentration camps
- Catholic schools were brought in line with state schools or closed
- Catholic youth activities, like the Catholic Youth League, were banned.

By 1937, Pope Pius XI realised that the Concordat was worthless. He issued a stinging criticism of the Nazi regime in a statement known as 'Mit Brennender Sorge' ('With Burning Anxiety').

Source F: *This NSDAP poster from 1933 shows the swastika knocking out the Catholics and the communists. This suggests that Hitler was always half-hearted about working with the Catholic Church.*

Christianity is the unshakeable foundation of the moral and ethical life of our people. The National Government's concern will be for co-operation of the Church with the State. It expects, however, that [this] will meet with similar appreciation from their side.

Source G: *Extract from a speech by Hitler in the Reichstag on the Enabling Law (March 1933).*

In my spiritual office, for the welfare and interest of the German Reich, I will endeavour to avoid all detrimental acts which might endanger it.

Source H: *Extract from the oath of allegiance to the Nazi regime, sworn by German Catholic bishops in 1933.*

The Protestant Church

Hitler also fell out with Christians in the Protestant churches. At first, some Protestants were so grateful that Hitler had protected them from anti-Christian communists that they worked with the Nazis. They even allowed Nazi flags to be displayed inside their churches. These Protestants formed the German Christian Movement. Its leader was Ludwig Müller. Hitler made Müller the Reich bishop of Germany in September 1933. Protestant pastors who supported Hitler were allowed to carry on with their church services as normal.

However, many Protestant Christians opposed Hitler's policies; some even spoke out against him. The most famous of these was Pastor Martin Niemöller. In 1933, he was one of the Protestant pastors who set up the Pastors' Emergency League (PEL), to campaign against Nazi actions. These Protestants became increasingly troublesome to Hitler. In 1937, Niemöller was sent to a concentration camp and the PEL was banned.

By this time, Hitler controlled the Reichstag, the NSDAP, the army, the police and the legal system. He treated the Christian Church with contempt. This was truly a totalitarian state, in which the central government controlled every aspect of the country.

We all know that, if the Third Reich were to collapse, communism would come in its place. Therefore, we must show loyalty to the Führer, who has saved us from communism and given us a better chance.

Source I: *A leader of the German Christian Church, 1937.*

Activity

Prepare for an exam question asking you to explain the changes which made Germany a police state, using pages 36–39.

a List all the changes Hitler made to create his police state.

b Alongside each change, record some facts, to use as supporting detail in an essay.

Source J: *A British cartoon from 1934 commenting on Hitler's police state. He controlled most aspects of the lives of German people; now he wanted control of their religious beliefs too.*

OATH OF LOYALTY TO HITLER

SIGN HERE

It is rumored that Fürer-President-Chancellor Hitler, unable to settle Germany's religious "mutiny" in any other way, contemplates taking over yet another High Office.

LOW

SIGN! OR—— !

Censorship and propaganda

Learning objectives

In this chapter you will learn:

- how the Nazis used censorship to ban information and ideas they disliked
- how the Nazis used propaganda to publicise information and ideas which they wanted to promote.

Nazi Germany was a totalitarian state. This means a state in which the government seeks to control all individuals and every aspect of society. **Censorship** and **propaganda** were two of the ways the Nazis exerted control in their totalitarian state.

When Hitler became chancellor in 1933, Joseph Goebbels was made the Minister of People's Enlightenment and Propaganda. He used censorship and propaganda to campaign for the Nazi Party. But he also used them to control the political, cultural and artistic life of Germany.

Nazi Party campaigning

Goebbels could now use government resources to publicise Hitler and his views. Some propaganda just continued methods used by the Nazis since the 1920s. For example:

- government posters advertised Nazi views
- Goebbels expanded his use of rallies and parades
- a mass rally was held each year at Nuremberg to create a sense of German unity and advertise Nazi strength.

But some methods were new, such as radio and cinema.

Radio

Goebbels quickly saw the value of radio. He placed all radio stations under Nazi control and Hitler made frequent broadcasts. Cheap mass-produced radios were sold or placed in cafes, factories and schools; speakers were even placed in the street. By the 1930s there were more radios per person in Germany than anywhere else in Europe.

Cinema

With audiences of over 250 million in 1933, cinemas had excellent potential for getting Nazi views across.

- Films were shown alongside a 45-minute official newsreel, publicising Germany's achievements.
- From 1934, film-makers had to send the plot of every new film to Goebbels for approval.
- Some films had overtly political messages, like *Hitlerjunge Quex* (1933), in which a young member of the Nazi Party was killed by communists.

Watch out!

Sometimes students think that one set of things (for example, the press, books and universities) was linked to Nazi censorship and a different set of things (for example, radio, posters and rallies) was linked to Nazi propaganda.

Don't fall into this trap. Most of these things were part of Nazi censorship and Nazi propaganda. For example, papers were censored <u>and</u> used for propaganda, as were films.

Attention! On Wednesday 21st March, the Führer is speaking on all German (radio) stations from 11am to 11.50 am... All factory owners, stores, offices, shops, pubs and flats must put up speakers an hour before, so that the whole workforce can hear.

Source A: *Part of a Ministry of Propaganda order, March 1934.*

The Press

Newspapers had to print views which the Ministry agreed with or face the consequences. Journalists were given briefings with information the government wanted to publicise. And it wasn't only papers that were controlled.

Universities

University researchers and lecturers were directed by the Ministry to support Nazi views or face dismissal. Between 1933 and 1938, 3000 academics were dismissed.

The arts

Goebbels also controlled the arts. He set up the Reich Chamber of Culture. All writers, musicians, artists and actors had to be members. Those of whom the Nazis disapproved were barred from working.

- The Nazis decided what books would be available. Books with views they didn't like were banned. Millions of books were taken from university and public libraries and burned on huge public bonfires.
- Music was also censored. Jazz music was banned; it was seen as black music and therefore inferior. The work of Mendelssohn was banned because he was part Jewish.
- Art was heavily censored. The Ministry disapproved, for example, of almost all modern art. The Nazis preferred art that showed heroic German folk tales.
- In the theatre, plays about German history were favoured as long as they gave Nazi views. Cheap theatre tickets were made available to get Nazi views across.

Sport

Hitler and Goebbels also used the 1936 Berlin Olympics to show Nazi Germany in a good light.

- The Nazis built an Olympic stadium seating 110,000 people to reflect the power of Germany.
- All the events were faultlessly organised, to show off German efficiency.
- Germany won 33 gold medals, more than any other country – and more silver and bronze too. The Nazis claimed this was proof of Aryan superiority.

There was only one embarrassment for the Nazis: the black American athlete Jesse Owens won four gold medals.

Hitler the figurehead

A key feature of Nazi propaganda was Hitler himself. His image was used to personify the Nazi Party and unify the nation. He was shown as strong and decisive figure – but also frequently pictured with children to show that he was a caring father-figure for the nation.

Activities

Make two lists.

1 A list of ways information in Nazi Germany was censored.

2 A list of ways Nazi propaganda was spread.

Where possible, add a piece of detailed information to support your answer. For example: books with anti-Nazi views were banned – thousands of books were burned on huge public bonfires.

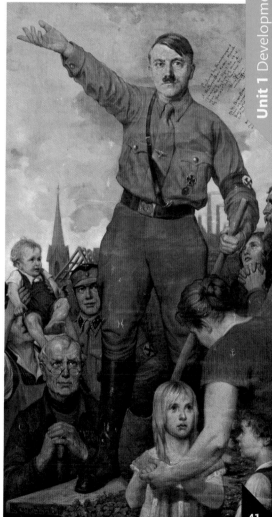

Source B: *A portrait of Hitler. Note his uniform, his pose, the spade in his left hand and the men, women and children around him. What impressions do you think the painting intended to give?*

Persecution of the Jews, 1933–39

Learning objectives

In this chapter you will learn about:

● beliefs which led to persecution of Jews
● the first stages of persecution 1933–38
● Kristallnacht and persecution 1938–39.

Anti-Semitism: the background

Anti-Jewish views, sometimes called anti-Semitism, had been common in Europe for centuries. There were several reasons:

● their religion, customs and looks made Jews stand out as 'different'
● some Christians hated Jews, blaming them for the execution of Christ.

When times were hard, some people looked for scapegoats and blamed the Jews. This had several effects in Germany.

● Some Germans wrongly blamed the Jews for defeat in the First World War.
● Jews were criticised for being communist rebels – like Kurt Eisner, the Jewish leader of the communist rising in Munich in 1918.
● Other Jews were criticised for being selfish capitalists, since many Jews were wealthy business people.

Hitler was one of those who blamed Germany's problems on the Jews.

Hitler's views

In 1925, Hitler set out his racial views in *Mein Kampf*. He claimed that there was a hierarchy of races.

● The Aryan race was the superior race – the *Herrenvolk* or master race. They were portrayed as tall, blond, blue-eyed and athletic.
● Other races, such as the Slavs of Eastern Europe, were lesser races.
● Then there were the *Untermenschen*, or sub-humans; this included Africans.
● Worst of the *Untermenschen*, according to Hitler, were gypsies and Jews. Later, Hitler deemed these *Lebensunwertes* – unworthy of life.

Persecution starts

As soon as they came to power, the Nazis could officially persecute Jews, including passing laws against them. Step by step, in 1933,

● there were Nazi boycotts of Jewish businesses
● Jews were banned from government jobs
● Jews were banned from inheriting land.

In 1935,

● Jews were banned from the army
● Jews were banned from restaurants.

The Nuremberg Laws and after

When the Nazis became the only political party, persecution increased. On 15 September 1935, the Nuremberg Laws were passed. Jews:

● could not be German citizens
● lost the right to vote, hold government office or have German passports
● could not marry German citizens

In 1938, restrictions were increased.

● Jewish doctors, dentists and lawyers were forbidden to work for white Aryan Germans.
● Jewish identity cards had to carry a large letter 'J' for 'Jew'.
● Jews had to register all possessions – making it easier for the government to confiscate them.

Activity

Design a diagram called *The Road to Persecution*.

Use the events from 1925 to 1939 on pages 42–43 to annotate your diagram. The aims are:

a to show how persecution grew AND

b to record enough information to describe the persecution of the Jews in the examination.

Kristallnacht

On 7 November 1938, a young Polish Jew, Hershel Grynszpan, went into the German embassy in Paris and shot Ernst von Rath, a German. Grynszpan hated the Germans for the way they treated Jews. A wave of anger swept Germany. On 9 November, von Rath died. Goebbels told Hitler. He then announced that the Führer said that, if Germans took revenge on the Jews for this, the government would do nothing to prevent it. This was printed in *Der Stürmer*, the Nazi paper.

The result was a storm of attacks on Jews. Some Nazis stood back from the events; others, especially the SA, took it as an order to attack the Jews. Local SS groups were ordered to 'organise demonstrations' and arrest 'as many Jews as we can fit into prisons'.

So, on 9 and 10 November, gangs smashed up Jewish property and attacked Jews. Some Germans were horrified; others watched with pleasure. The official figures underestimate the violence. Even they say 814 shops, 171 homes and 191 synagogues were destroyed. At least 100 Jews were killed. The damage was so bad, that these events were called Kristallnacht ('Crystal Night', or 'the Night of Broken Glass').

Longer term effects of Kristallnacht

Goebbels blamed the Jews for Kristallnacht. As a result, he said, Jews would be:

- fined 1 billion marks to pay for the damage
- banned from running shops or businesses
- banned from German schools or universities.

The SA and SS also started to round up Jews as punishment. By 12 November 1938, 20,000 Jews had been sent to concentration camps.

Persecution increased in 1939.

- In January, the Reich Office for Jewish Emigration was set up to rid Germany of its Jews altogether – by enforced emigration. However, progress was slow.
- So in April, orders went out that all Jews were to be evicted from their homes. They were forced to move into particular areas of some cities (often walled or fenced off) called ghettos. Here they had to wait to be deported (forcibly taken out of the country).

When war broke out, in September 1939, persecution escalated (see pages 50–53).

Source A: *Jews arriving at the Sachsenhausen concentration camp on 19 December 1938.*

Youth and education in Nazi Germany

Nazis had very clear ideas about young people that affected their policies. They believed that:

- young people should be trained to be good Germans and good Nazis
- education should prepare young people to serve the state
- boys should be educated to go out to work and serve the army; girls should be educated to become good wives and mothers.

Schools

All children attended school until they were 14 years old. After that, school was voluntary. Boys and girls went to separate schools. Nazi ideas had several effects on the timetable.

- New subjects, such as Race Studies, taught pupils that Aryans were superior and that they should not marry Jews.
- *Mein Kampf* became a compulsory school text.
- History lessons criticised communism and the Treaty of Versailles.
- Even subjects like maths were used for Nazi propaganda (see Source A).
- Girls had different lessons from boys. Domestic science, including cookery and needlework, was compulsory for girls.
- PE took up about one-sixth of school time, to emphasise good health for girls (to be a good mother) and boys (to be a good soldier).

Teachers had to swear an oath of loyalty to Hitler and join the Nazi Teachers' League. They were expected to pass on Nazi political views. Teachers taught the Nazi salute and started each lesson with the children saying '*Heil Hitler*'. Classrooms were decorated with Nazi posters and flags.

The Jews are aliens in Germany. In 1933 there were 66,060,000 people in Germany of whom 499,862 were Jews. What is the percentage of aliens in Germany?

Source A: *A question from a German maths textbook, 1933.*

Source B: *A German primary school in 1935.*

Youth movements

Outside school, the Nazi government closed down activities for young people run by other groups, such as the churches, and set up their own youth movements. Like schools, these reflected Nazi ideas about young people. Boys and girls had separate groups, as they did at school.

Boys:
- started, aged 6, in the *Pimpf* (Little Fellows)
- moved on to the *Jungvolk* (Young Germans) when they were 10
- moved on the Hitler *Jugend* (Hitler Youth) between 10 and 14.

Girls:
- had *Yung Mädel* (Young Maidens) aged 10–14
- and the *Bund Deutscher Mädel* (League of German Maidens) from 14–18.

Similarities and differences

All the groups had uniforms and all members had to swear loyalty to the Nazi Party. The activities all encouraged good health, good citizenship and support for the Nazis. There was some overlap in the activities. Boys and girls both went camping and hiking, for fitness. They did group activities which encouraged co-operation and comradeship. They went to rallies and camps attended by groups from all over the country. After 1939, the Hitler Youth was also used to help the war effort on the Home Front, helping air raid wardens and fire brigades during bombing.

However, boys and girls had different activities that reflected Nazi expectations of them as adults (just as they did in school). Boys did marching drills, map-reading, signalling and rifle shooting – all useful for fitness and military service. Girls did more activities which prepared them for motherhood, cooking and setting up camps.

Opposition

Not everyone supported Nazi youth movements.
- Some parents disliked their children being taught to be loyal to the Nazis above all else.
- Some young people disliked the rules, the uniforms, the regimented activities and marching. Some even started opposition youth groups, like the Edelweiss Pirates (see page 56).

The Nazis also wanted to control the young in their spare time. This was achieved through the Hitler Youth. All other youth organisations were banned. From 1936, membership was compulsory. By 1939, there were seven million members.

Source C: *From a modern textbook.*

Build Better Answers

Use Source C and your own knowledge to explain the changes in the lives of young people in the years 1933–39. **(10 marks)**

Paper 1 part (d) questions expect you to use a source and your own knowledge to explain something.

■ **A basic answer (level 1)** will make simple generalisations. For example, *They had to study different things at school and join youth groups.*

● **A good answer (level 2)** will give examples, with detail from their own knowledge and the source (more than one will get a higher mark). For example, *They had less time to themselves. Source C says the Nazis wanted to control young people in their spare time. The Nazis worked to provide groups and special camps and mass rallies, which would take up a lot of time.*

▲ **An excellent answer (level 4)** will be the 'good' answer as above, with more than one factor, showing how they combined to produce the outcome. For example, *If you think about how much time all the activities provided would take up, and how the Nazis also got rid of other youth groups like the church ones, it all strongly supports a big change – the Nazis were taking up a lot of the young people's time so that they could control them and feed them Nazi ideas.*

Women in Nazi Germany, 1933–39

> ## Learning objectives
>
> In this chapter you will learn about:
> - Nazi views on the role of women
> - Nazi policies to increase marriage
> - Nazi policies to increase childbirth.

During the 1920s, women's lives changed in most European countries. For example, in Weimar Germany:

- women over 20 years were given the vote and there were about 20 female members of the Reichstag
- women were also more likely to go out to work and more likely to work in the professions, where they were often paid on an equal basis to men. For example, there were about 100,000 female teachers in Germany by 1933.
- women also started to enjoy more social activities outside the family and express their freedom in the way they dressed.

But the Nazis had a very different view of how women should fit into society. They believed that, like Germany's youth, women should serve their society, and the best way that they could do this was to be good mothers.

To be good mothers, German women should:

- stay healthy
- learn housecraft – cookery and needlework
- marry and enable their husbands to be useful workers
- have children and bring them up to be good Germans
- stay at home and concentrate on domestic matters, not work or politics.

Furthermore, 'good' German women were not expected to wear make-up or trousers, or to dye or perm their hair.

When the Nazis came to power, their policies towards women were driven by these ideas.

- The German Women's Enterprise was formed, to arrange classes and radio broadcasts, teaching good motherhood.
- Women were encouraged to leave work and concentrate on the 3Ks – *kinder, küche, kirche* (children, kitchen and church).
- Some professional women were forced to leave their jobs as doctors, lawyers or teachers.

Nazi policies towards women had the extra benefit of freeing up jobs for men – and thus reducing unemployment.

Source A: *A 1939 painting called 'A Farming Family from Kalinberg'. The painting reflects Nazi ideas of the dominant male figure and women concerned with children and housework.*

Source B: *Girls in the League of German Maidens practising their housecraft in preparation for motherhood. Nazi policies towards girls were driven by their views on women.*

Marriage and childbirth

The birth rate was falling in Nazi Germany, and the Nazis wanted to reverse this. So, as well as their general views on the role of women listed above, they had several policies specifically intended to increase marriage and childbirth.

- In 1933, the Law for the Encouragement of Marriage was introduced. Loans of 1000 marks, worth about nine months' wages, were provided for young couples to marry, as long as the wife left work. For each one of their first four children, the couple could keep a quarter of the loan. There were other payments to encourage large families too.

- The Mother's Cross also encouraged large families. It was an award given to women for the number of children they had: bronze for four or five children, silver for six or seven children, and gold for eight or more children. Each year, on 12 April (Hitler's mother's birthday), medals were distributed to women with large families.

- The *Lebensborn* (meaning 'fountain of life') programme was another policy to encourage childbirth. This was started in 1935 by the SS leader, Heinrich Himmler. At first, the policy just provided nurseries and financial aid for women who had children with SS men. Later, it even made 'single women available for fertilisation by SS men'. This was to create 'genetically pure' children for adoption by worthy German families. In one home alone, over 540 mothers gave birth from 1938 to 1941.

By the end of the 1930s, German industry was expanding so fast that the Nazis needed women to do some work, so some of their earlier policies were reversed. Nevertheless, fewer women were working in Germany in the late 1930s than had been working during the early 1920s.

Hitler believed that these policies were fair to women. In a speech in 1935, he said: 'Both sexes have their rights, their tasks. These tasks are equal in dignity and value.' But some women remained strongly opposed to this view of women. Some even said that the Nazi view of women encouraged men to see women as inferior.

> I was proud. When I got the gold, there was a big celebration in a school, where the mothers were all invited for coffee and cake.

Source C: *Wilhelmine Haferkamp eventually had ten children.*

> A son, even the youngest, laughs in his mother's face. He regards her as his servant and women in general are merely willing tools of his aims.

Source D: *An extract from a letter to a Leipzig newspaper in 1934.*

> I got 30 marks per child from the Hitler government and 20 marks from the city. That was a lot of money. I sometimes got more 'child money' than my husband earned.

Source E: *Wilhelmine Haferkamp, who was 22 years old in 1933.*

Activity

As you read through this chapter, draw a spider diagram.

On the body of your 'spider' write the words

Nazi policies towards women 1933–39.

At the end of your 'spider's legs' give examples of:

- *a way women were treated in Germany before 1933*
- *a Nazi belief about the role of women*
- *a Nazi policy to encourage good motherhood*
- *a Nazi policy to encourage marriage*
- *two Nazi policies to increase childbirth.*

Examination question

Use Source C and your own knowledge to explain the changes in the position of women in Nazi Germany in the years 1933–39. **(10 marks)**

Work and employment, 1933–39

Learning objectives

In this chapter you will learn about:
- the German Labour Front (DAF)
- reducing unemployment using the National Labour Service (RAD) and rearmament.

The Nazis intended to make the economy, just like youth and women, serve the needs of the state.

Nazi policy towards workers

Hitler believed that powerful trade unions could disrupt the economy, so the government banned these in 1933. In their place, Hitler set up the DAF (German Labour Front). The DAF's key role was to ensure that workers served the best interests of the Nazi regime. However, to ensure that the economy worked for the best interests of the state, the DAF also controlled the power of the employers. It set out new employment rights of all workers in factories, mines, munitions plants and shipyards. It regulated working hours (which increased on average by six hours per week) and rates of pay. The DAF also had powers to punish workers.

Although German workers lost their freedom to act collectively against employers, at least the DAF established what the minimum working standards should be, which prevented serious exploitation of labour by employers.

Nazi policy towards the unemployed

Solving unemployment was important to Hitler for many reasons. Unemployed workers were potential supporters of the communists, Hitler's rivals. Nazis also believed that unemployed workers sapped the strength of a nation. Men needed to be put to useful work, in the service of their country.

So, in 1933 the Nazis set up the RAD (National Labour Service). This provided manual work for the unemployed. At first it was a voluntary scheme, but from 1935 it was made compulsory for all young men to serve for six months in the RAD.

Men in the RAD were organised along the lines of an army. Workers wore uniforms, lived in camps and did military drill and parades as well as work. Rates of pay were very low and some complained of very poor food. Those in the RAD were used to work in the fields and build public buildings and autobahns (motorways). Apart from giving men work, these projects were also good for Germany. By 1939, Germany had 7000 miles of autobahns.

It was a system in which owners of property and workers were all subjects of the state. The great industrial magnates, like Krupp and Thyssen, remained – but they were forced to serve the needs of Germany. Trade unions were abolished… labour was put at the disposal of the Reich, in the form of the new Labour Front.

Source A: *From a modern textbook.*

Source B: *Hitler starts the first autobahn project, 1933.*

Rearmament

As you have seen, the Nazi view was that the health of a nation depended upon constant struggle against other nations and that the German race needed *lebensraum* (living space outside its existing borders). These views required military power. Therefore, Nazi policy towards the economy – like its policy towards youth – was organised to make Germany strong as a military nation.

In 1936, Hitler issued a secret memo declaring that the economy must be reorganised to make Germany able to wage war within four years. Hitler's 'Four Year Plan' had several effects on the economy.

- Government spending on **rearmament** increased:
  - in 1933, spending on arms was 3.5 billion marks
  - by 1939, it was 26 billion marks.
- The army's need for iron and steel increased:
  - German production of these trebled from 1933 to 1939.
- The government wanted to reduce the damage any naval blockade might do so they boosted German production of products like plastic, oil and rubber:
  - German production of plastic increased by 460% in the 1930s.
- The German army grew; it numbered:
  - about 100,000 in 1933
  - about 500,000 in 1936
  - about 900,000 in 1939.

As the army increased in size so demand for uniforms and equipment also grew. In economic terms, rearmament was a huge boost for Germany. Unemployment went down, while production and profits went up.

Effects of these policies

There were political benefits for some of Hitler's actions. Banning unions and reducing unemployment reduced political opposition to the Nazis. There were social benefits too. Protecting workers' rights and reducing unemployment helped all ordinary Germans – workers and their families. Unemployment fell from 4.8 million in 1933 to 1.6 million in 1936 and 0.5 million in 1938. There were also military reasons for Hitler's actions: by 1939, Germany was ready for war.

However, funding public works and rearmament was expensive. In addition, some of the employment had only been achieved by moving women and Jews out of jobs and by expanding organisations like the SS and Gestapo.

Did you know?

In 1933 the DAF set up Strength Through Joy, an organisation that organised activities for workers in their leisure time. Some activities were free, others partly paid for. It set up libraries, ran courses and organised walks and tours. It also organised holidays.

Build Better Answers

Choose either **The National Labour Service** or **rearmament**.

Explain one **effect on unemployment of the Nazi policy you have chosen. (4 marks)**

Paper 1 part (b) questions will ask about the effect of one event on another.

■ **A basic answer (level 1)** will give a generalised answer, or give an effect with no supporting detail.

● **A good answer (level 2)** will give one valid effect and will support the answer with detailed information.

Activity

You are the employment spokesman for the Nazi Party. You are going to be interviewed, in 1939, for a radio broadcast.

Outline your answers to the following possible questions.

a Why is reducing unemployment so important?

b Have you succeeded in reducing unemployment?

c How has the RAD lowered unemployment?

d How has rearmament lowered unemployment?

War and the Final Solution

Learning objectives

In this chapter you will learn about:

● how war changed policies towards the Jews

● ghettos, camps and *Einsatzgruppen*

● Wannsee, the Final Solution and death camps.

On 1 September 1939, German troops invaded Poland. By the end of 1941, Germany controlled most of Europe, and a large area of the USSR. As Britain and the Allies fought back, the Second World War went on for almost six years.

The war made treatment of the Jews much worse.

● The Nazis no longer worried about the need to have policies acceptable to world opinion.

● Invasions brought many more Jews under Nazi control. There were 3 million in Poland and a million in the southern Soviet Union.

At first, the Nazis merely expanded the existing ways in which they persecuted the Jews.

Ghettos

When the Nazis invaded Poland in 1939, they built ghettos there. Ghettos were walled-off, guarded, parts of cities where Jews were forced to live. Jews from Germany and occupied countries were sent there. In the Polish capital of Warsaw, the Nazis crushed 380,000 Jews, 30% of the population of the city, into less than 3% of its area. By 1942, 50,000 Jews had died of hunger, cold and disease in the Warsaw ghetto.

Concentration camps

The Nazis had built prison camps as early as 1933. They housed a variety of prisoners, including many Jews. But after 1939 the number and size of the camps grew. For example, in 1937 a camp for 1,000 prisoners was set up at Buchenwald, in Germany. It had 10,000 prisoners by the end of 1939 and 80,000 by the end of the war.

Prisoners in concentration camps were used as slave labour. From the outset, many prisoners died of overwork, starvation or mistreatment. During the war, this became worse. Germany set a deliberate policy to exterminate prisoners by working them to death. From 1937 to 1945, 56,000 Jews died at Buchenwald.

Activities

Persecution of the Jews by the Nazis can be seen in three stages: 1933–39, 1939–42 and 1942–45.

1 Look back at pages 42–43.

  List four examples of persecution of the Jews in Nazi Germany 1933–39.

2 Now look at what happened 1939–42.

  a How were the Jews treated?

  b In what ways was this treatment different?

  c What was the reason for this change of treatment?

3 Finally, look at what happened 1942–45.

  a How were the Jews treated?

  b In what ways was this treatment different?

  c What was the reason for this change of treatment?

Causes and effects

Ghettos

The Nazis set up ghettos because they wanted to:

● isolate Jews from the rest of the community

● free valuable Jewish property in the rest of the cities for Nazi use

● control the movements of the Jewish population.

Ghettos had the following effects. They:

● had a high death rate due to overcrowding and poor facilities

● re-enforced Nazi propaganda about Jews being dirty and so on: their living conditions made it so

● enabled many people outside the ghettos to see Jews as 'sub-human' and ignore the way that they were treated.

Einsatzgruppen

Unlike the ghettos and camps, the *Einsatzgruppen* were new. They were SS death squads. In 1939 and 1941, they followed the German army into Poland and the Soviet Union, systematically murdering any civilians whom the Nazis regarded as undesirable. In the village of Ponary in Lithuania, for example, a small committee of Jews was asked to summon local Jews from all the towns in the province, for 'relocation'. As they came, the Jews were marched to open pits and shot. Over two weeks, 50,000 were shot. In all, by 1945, the *Einsatzgruppen* had killed 1.5 million Jews, gypsies and communist leaders.

Source A: *An* Einsatzgruppen *death squad in the Ukraine in 1942.*

Wannsee meeting and Final Solution

By 1941, the treatment of Jews was a fiercely debated issue among Nazi leaders. But, incredibly, this was not a moral debate. Their key concern was cost.

After the invasion of the Soviet Union in June 1941, the question became urgent. In all, there were four million Jews in the western Soviet Union. Some Nazi leaders, such as Hitler's deputy Göring, argued against killing the Jews. For him, they provided cheap labour vital to the war effort. But others, such as Himmler, head of the SS, said that ghettos, camps and death squads were too expensive to run and used men who were needed in the army.

Some time during the summer of 1941, Himmler's view prevailed. It was decided that all Jews under German control would be exterminated in death camps. This policy has been called the Final Solution. In January 1942, leading Nazis met at Wannsee House, in Berlin, to work out the details.

Reinhard Heydrich, the head of the Gestapo, was in charge of the plans. All Jews were to be transported to areas of Eastern Europe under Nazi control. There, some of the fit were to be housed in labour camps and worked to death on building projects; any survivors were to be killed. Others were to be sent to death camps. There, they were to be gassed to death.

Work started in the camps. First, gas chambers were built to do the killing, then crematoria to burn the bodies. In March 1942, the first death camp started operating at Belzac, in Poland.

> In the summer of 1941, Himmler received me and said in effect "The Fuhrer has ordered that the Jewish question be solved once and for all. The Jews are the sworn enemies of the German people and must be eradicated. Every Jew that we can lay our hands on is to be destroyed now, during the war, without exception."

Source B: *Rudolf Höss, commandant of Auschwitz concentration camp, in his memoirs written while he was waiting for execution for war crimes in 1947.*

The death camps

There were six death camps at first. Auschwitz, Chelmno and Majdanek were converted from concentration or labour camps. New death camps were built at Belzec, Sobibor and Treblinka. The camps were run by SS officers. But they were built well away from Germany. Local troops, not the German army, were used as guards.

Prisoners arrived by train. Some were sent to labour camps. Fit prisoners were kept back to help run the camp, for example disposing of the bodies.

But the majority were killed as soon as possible. Children, the aged and sick were killed first. Their belongings were taken. They were usually told they were to have a shower and, perhaps, given soap and a towel. They were then herded, naked, into the gas chambers. Despite the attempts at deception, sometimes the victims guessed what was about to happen. The smell from the crematoria was a clue.

At first, there were two gas chambers at Auschwitz. One held 1,200 people and one held 800. In 1943, a new chamber was built to hold 2,000. After people had been marched in, the doors were screwed shut. People nearest to the poison gas vents died immediately. Others took up to 20 minutes to die.

When the victims had died, the gas was then pumped out from the chambers and the bodies were removed. Fit prisoners were ordered to cut off the women's hair, remove any jewellery and use pliers to extract gold fillings from teeth.

At first, bodies were just buried in deep pits, then covered with lime. But, as the camps developed, crematoria were built to burn the bodies.

The prisoners who were used to help run the camps, were deliberately mistreated. They were given very little to eat and disease was rife. One prisoner, Franciszek Piper, told how teeth extracted from the dead were examined: if the gold had not been properly separated, the prisoner blamed could be thrown, alive, into the crematorium ovens. Some prisoners were used for medical experiments, without anaesthetic, by Nazi doctors. The extermination of Jews was at its height from 1942 to 1944. In 1944, at Auschwitz, 400,000 Hungarian Jews were gassed in just three months.

Deaths in the extermination camps began to slow down during 1944. Germany was being pushed back by the Allies. But, by 1944, about 90% of all Jews in Germany, Austria and Poland, and other areas close to the camps, were already dead.

As the Soviet Army pushed the Germans back in Eastern Europe, the imprisoned Jews were forced to travel west to camps closer to Germany. They were marched through the winter of 1944–45. Another 250,000 Jews are thought to have died on these 'death marches'.

The SS quickly separated the men from the women. They took the old and sick into a special line… (My arm) was tattooed with the number 182699. My entire body was shaved. Then I was given a shower and issued with clothes which had huge red painted marks on them. This was so I could be easily spotted if I tried to escape.

Source C: *Erricos Sevillias describing his arrival at Auschwitz.*

I was ordered to establish extermination facilities at Auschwitz in June 1942. I used Cyclon B, a crystallised prussic acid, dropped into the death chamber from a small opening. It took from three to fifteen minutes to kill. We knew people were dead because the screaming stopped.

Source D: *Rudolf Höss, commandant at Auschwitz, giving evidence to the Nuremberg War Crimes Tribunal.*

We could see the chimneys from where we were. We could smell, first the gas when it was let out from the gas chambers, and then we could smell the burning of the bodies, the human flesh burning. And then they cleaned the bones from the grates and we could hear the grates being cleaned.

Source E: *Ruth Meyerowitz was a German Jew sent to Auschwitz. She did forced labour building roads and also sorted the possessions of gassed prisoners. She survived and left this record of her memories in an interview in 1990.*

The overall outcome

The persecution of Jews in Nazi Germany is a scar on the history of Germany, Jews and the world. The suffering cannot be quantified. We do not know how many Jews were killed.

The most likely estimate to the nearest million is that 6 million Jews died under Nazi rule 1933–45. This is the equivalent of one in every ten people living in Britain today. Or the entire population of London. This mass slaughter of the Jews has become known as the Holocaust.

In addition, we should not forget that other minority groups were also persecuted in Nazi Germany: for example homosexuals, prostitutes, alcoholics and Jehovah's Witnesses. The disabled and mentally ill were often killed. About half a million European gypsies were also worked to death, shot or gassed.

Why?

We have already seen why the Nazi leadership decided on a policy of persecuting the Jews. But we also need to ask ourselves why this policy was allowed to take place by the majority of the German people. It was partly because the worst of the information was kept from them. It was partly because they had been whipped up into hatred of the Jews by Nazi propaganda. It was partly because speaking out against Nazi policy was dangerous; people felt that they could not stop the persecution – or they told themselves so. It was partly because some saw the treatment of the Jews as the price of other benefits which the Nazis brought to Germany.

Source F: *A body pit at a camp at Belsen, 1945.*

> I believed the propaganda that all Jews were criminals and sub-humans and that they were the cause of Germany's decline after the First World War. The thought that one should disobey or evade the order to participate in the extermination of the Jews did not therefore enter my mind at all.

Source G: *A German policeman testifying in a war crimes trial, 1961.*

Effects

Death camps

The setting up of death camps had several effects:

- millions of Jews died
- hundreds of thousands of people in minority groups that were persecuted by the Nazis also died in these camps (e.g. gypsies)
- many Nazis were tried after the war as war criminals.

The Home Front and opposition to Hitler

Learning objectives

In this chapter you will learn about:
- how German people's lives changed during the war
- how opposition to Hitler increased during the war.

Activity

Make a table and record details about life on the German Home Front in the war.

Use two columns, headed 1939–42 and 1942–45.

Give your table three rows of information:
- living conditions
- the impact of fighting
- overall morale.

The Home Front

From 1939–42, life in Germany was relatively undisturbed by the War.

- Overall morale remained good. Germany had a series of victories and there was no fighting on German soil.
- The standard of living remained high. Public suffering had undermined the Kaiser in 1918. So Hitler limited rationing by taking food from occupied countries. And working conditions changed little. More women worked in German war industries, but only gradually, since this clashed with Nazi ideology. Most German factories still worked day shifts only.

However, all this changed from 1942.

- Morale fell as the German attack on the Soviet Union stalled in 1942. By 1943, the Germans were in retreat in Africa and Italy.
- The standard of living fell. In May 1942, food shortages reduced the weekly bread and meat ration to half a loaf and 300 grams of meat a week. But a ration book didn't guarantee food. Some food disappeared into the 'black market' and was too expensive for many people to buy. Families kept rabbits for their meat.
- Another source of suffering was massed bomber attacks on German cities. May 1942 saw the first 1,000-bomber attack, on Cologne. In one series of raids on Hamburg, in July 1943, 50,000 German civilians died in the space of a week.

Children were torn away from their parents' hands by the force of the hurricane and whirled into the fire. People…fell down, overcome by the devouring heat, and died in an instant. People trying to flee had to make their way over the dead and dying.

Source B: *Major-General Kehrl, describing the effects of bombing in Hamburg in 1943.*

Source A: *Devastation caused to the lives of German citizens by Allied bombing of the German city of Hamburg in 1943.*

'Total war'

On 2 February 1943, the 94,000 German soldiers still fighting for Stalingrad (over 200,000 had already been killed) surrendered to the Soviet Army. It was a terrible defeat. Goebbels' reaction was to call for a policy of 'total war'. On 18 February he made his longest ever radio speech calling on all Germans to show the Allies that they were not defeated, or worn out; that they could carry on fighting and make more sacrifices for Germany than ever. Everything was to give way to war production. These sacrifices included:

- longer working hours
- all women aged 17–45 to register for work
- the closure of bars, night clubs, 'luxury' shops (including many clothing shops) and many restaurants
- more rationing
- travel restriction
- the ending of any exemptions for serving in the armed forces.

Goebbels' speech spent some time on the subject of women working. Previous Nazi policy had been for women not to work, and then for some women to do essential war work when there were no men available. Now Goebbels wanted all women at work. He urged them to volunteer at once, not even wait to be called up.

Opposition to Hitler

Opposition to the Nazis grew during the war. As the war began to go badly, new forms of opposition emerged. The Nazis arrested and executed anyone they found passing information out of the country or, once the war had started, helping the Allies.

Political opposition

In 1933 the Nazis had banned all political parties but the Nazi party, so normal political opposition was impossible. But from the moment they came to power, people worked secretly to oppose them. Opposition grew as Nazi policies about freedom of speech, religion and Jews and other 'undesirables' became more extreme. However, it was very dangerous to oppose the Nazis. They had a widespread system of informers. Opposition groups were always in danger of an informer joining the group and betraying it.

Activity

1 As you read pages 55–57 create a spider diagram. Make the 'body' of your spider *Opposition to Hitler.*

At the ends of the 'legs' of your spider make lists to record:

a 3 reasons why people opposed Hitler

b 3 people who opposed Hitler

c 3 organisations that opposed Hitler

d 3 things which opponents did to oppose Hitler

e 3 reasons why there was so little opposition

f 3 reasons why opposition to Hitler grew after 1942.

Among well-informed people in Berlin, I noticed a good deal of despair. The main reasons are that the war cannot be won; realisation of the highly dangerous economic situation; of being led by criminal adventurers; and the disgrace…of the war in Poland, namely the brutal use of airpower and the shocking bestialities of the SS, especially towards the Jews.

Source C: *Ulrich von Hassell describing the feelings of some Germans during the war.*

The White Rose Group

The White Rose Group was a slightly more open form of resistance. It was started at the University of Munich in 1941 by students, including Hans and Sophie Scholl, and their philosophy teacher Kurt Huber. The war triggered this group. Most of the students had been loyal Germans before. But several of them served in the German Army during the war and hated the atrocities it brought. Hans Scholl, for example, had seen Jews murdered in Poland.

The White Rose Group believed in opposing the Nazi regime by peaceful means. They began by mailing leaflets, anonymously, to people all over Germany. They concentrated on lecturers and the owners of bars and restaurants. The leaflets called for democracy and social justice. They also painted messages on walls.

By 1943, wartime suffering made them more confident. They began to leave leaflets in public places. On 18 February, Hans and Sophie Scholl were seen and reported to the Gestapo. Within two days, they were tried and executed. Within weeks, 80 others were arrested and many executed.

The Edelweiss Pirates

An even more open form of resistance was youth groups like the Edelweiss Pirates. Many young people in 1930s Germany accepted Hitler's youth groups. But some rebelled. They formed their own groups. They found simple ways to rebel. Girls mixed with the boys. They listened to modern 'swing' music. The boys grew their hair long. They daubed anti-Nazi slogans on walls; they beat up members of Hitler Youth. The most well-known of these groups was the Edelweiss Pirates. There were about 2,000 of them by 1939.

After the war broke out, members of these rebel youth groups became more political. They supported the Allies; some helped army deserters or distributed Allied leaflets dropped from aeroplanes. At first, the Nazi response was muted; they seemed no real danger to the regime. Youngsters were frequently arrested, their hair shaved off and released. But after 1942, rationing and working conditions became worse.

Then bombing intensified. Popular morale fell. This made some youngsters more daring. They smashed factory equipment to disrupt war production and started to steal guns and explosives. In 1944 Himmler ordered a crackdown. Hundreds of Pirates were arrested. In Cologne 13 young activists, some of them Edelweiss Pirates, were blamed for the death of a local Gestapo chief, arrested and publicly hanged.

Did you know?

Mildred and Arvid Harnack formed a resistance group in the 1930s that included many of the students Mildred taught at university. From 1935, they sent information they gathered to the US and Soviet governments. From 1938, Arvid (who worked for the government) passed on valuable information about Nazi war preparations. In 1942, the Harnacks and another leader of the group, Harro Schulze-Boysen, were caught and executed. A further 32 members of this group, later known as the 'Red Orchestra', were executed in August 1943.

We've got fists and we can fight,
We've got knives and we'll get them out
We want freedom, don't we boys?
We're the fighting Navajos!

Listen, we're talking to you.
Our land isn't free, we're telling you true.
Get out your cudgels and come to town
And smash in the skulls of the bosses in brown.

Source D: *Extracts from a song spread by the Navajos, a branch of the Edelweiss Pirates from Cologne.*

Religious opposition

In the 1930s some members of the Protestant and Roman Catholic churches criticised the Nazi regime. During the war, some individual clergy tried to do more. For example, Dietrich Bonhoeffer was a Protestant pastor who joined German military intelligence and tried to use his position there to undermine the Nazis. He passed messages to the Allies and helped Jews escape into Switzerland. He was caught in 1943, imprisoned and then hanged in 1945.

Military opposition

The officer class in German society had never been natural supporters of the Nazis. Many of them despised 'Corporal' Hitler and the thugs in his paramilitary SA and SS. While Hitler expanded the army in the 1930s and while the war was successful 1939–42, its opposition to Hitler was subdued. But there were several plots on his life after 1942. The most famous of these was the July Bomb Plot of 1944.

Colonel Claus von Stauffenberg was one of many senior officers at the War Office in Berlin who, by 1944, believed that Hitler was leading Germany to inevitable defeat. They decided to kill him. On 20 July, Stauffenberg took a bomb inside a briefcase into a meeting with Hitler. He placed it under the map-table Hitler was using and, soon after, left to take a phone call. The bomb blew up 12 minutes later. But, the briefcase had been moved by another officer. Hitler had only singed clothes, temporary deafness and a cut hand.

Over 5,000 people were arrested for their suspected part in the plot; 19 generals and 27 colonels, including Stauffenberg, were executed. Military opposition, like all other German opposition to Hitler, had failed.

Build Better Answers

Why was there increased opposition to Hitler after 1939?
(8 marks)

Paper 1 part (c) questions expect you to explain why something happened.

The best answers will:

- include at least two reasons
- explain how they caused more opposition
- use detailed information to support the explanation
- if possible, show how the reasons combined to produce the outcome. (For example, *one reason for popular opposition was the bombing.* The bombing was linked to another reason – *it made Germany more likely to lose the war. The idea that Germany was losing the war caused even more opposition*).

Unit 1 Development of dictatorship: Germany, 1918–45

Source G: *Thirteen youths, some of them members of the Edelweiss Pirates, publicly hanged in Cologne in 1944 for opposing the Nazi regime.*

Defeat and the death of Hitler

> **Learning objectives**
>
> In this chapter you will learn about:
> - the defeat of Germany in the Second World War and the death of Hitler
> - the reasons for Germany's defeat and Hitler's death.

Germany's defeat

Between 1939 and 1941, the Second World War went well for Hitler. In 1939 Germany overran western Poland. In 1940 it defeated Denmark, Norway, Holland, Belgium and France. In June 1941, Germany invaded Yugoslavia, Greece and the Soviet Union.

However, 1941–42 was a turning point. The United States joined the Allies in December 1941. During 1942, Hitler's attack on the Soviet Union stalled and the Allies won important victories in North Africa.

1943–44 saw the tide turn. Germany lost the Battle of Stalingrad in February 1943. In September the Allies invaded Italy from North Africa. Then they invaded France in June 1944. The Germans were in retreat on the southern and western fronts.

Meanwhile, the Soviet Army was advancing towards Germany from the east. By April 1945, they reached Berlin itself.

Why was the Nazi regime defeated?

Germany would have won the Second World War if it had stopped in 1941. The two key reasons why this didn't happen were that

- Germany failed to defeat Britain in an air and sea war
- Hitler decided to invade the Soviet Union.

But the invasion of the USSR turned out to be a mistake. The war went into a long drawn-out struggle, which Germany lost.

- Another reason why Germany lost this second phase was the USA. Once the United States joined the Allies, the men, machines and munitions available to the Allies far outweighed Germany's. It became a war of attrition; Germany was worn down by a stronger enemy.

By 1944 Germany was losing the war of production. Compared to the German side, the Allies were producing

- twice as much steel
- 4 times as many planes and tanks
- 7 times as many rifles and machine guns.

When the Allies invaded France on D-Day (6 June 1944), they had air superiority of 70:1.

Activity

Read the summary of the war 1939–45 on this page. Draw a timeline to record the key events Germany's defeat.

Instead of a straight line for your timeline, you could use a curved line, showing Germany's early successes as an up-slope and gradual defeat as a down-slope, like the rollercoaster on page 4.

Use a colour code to distinguish between events on the western, eastern and southern fronts.

Use your diagram to make sure you know the chronological order of these key events of the war.

Examination question

Why did Nazi Germany lose the Second World War? Explain your answer. **(8 marks)**

Hitler must take some of the blame. It was his decision to invade the USSR. The Soviet economy was weak and its army poorly equipped. But:

- it was a huge country to conquer;
- it had a population of almost 200 million from which to draw its army;
- and its climate made fighting very difficult.

Hitler interfered in military decisions, overruling his generals in key decisions. For example:

- He refused to agree to their pleas for a strategic withdrawal from Stalingrad.
- He did not see the importance of the war in North Africa until it was too late.

He also backed the wrong scientific projects. The Allies developed radar, cipher machines and the **atomic bomb**, and their war effort benefitted. Hitler invested in V1 and V2 rockets. These caused a public stir, but eventually had little effect on the war.

Finally, Hitler's Nazi philosophies slowed down the German war effort.

- He allowed the SS and the German Army much too much control of the economy.
- He was slow to use women in the labour force.

Worried about his political support at home, he tried to protect the German people from rationing and harder working conditions.

In April 1945, Soviet troops entered Berlin. Hitler committed suicide. Admiral Doenitz briefly took control, but, on 7 May 1945, Germany surrendered and the Nazi regime came to an end.

The death of Hitler

In April 1945, Soviet troops surrounded Berlin. Some senior Nazis, such as Himmler, were trying to negotiate peace with the Allies. But Hitler refused to accept defeat or surrender. He also refused to flee from Berlin to regroup elsewhere.

Instead, Hitler moved, with his mistress and his key advisors, to an underground bunker in Berlin.

Hitler prepared for the end. On 28 April, he married his long-term mistress, Eva Braun. Then, on 29 April, he dictated his will. At mid-day on 30 April, he went into his private apartment, along with his wife. Mid-afternoon, his aides discovered them there, dead.

Hitler is thought to have taken cyanide capsules and shot himself in the head. Hitler's aides later said that they took the two bodies to the surface and tried to cremate them. Soviet authorities report that their troops discovered the half-burnt bodies on 4 May and took them away. Dental records were used to confirm their identity.

Russian sources later said that Hitler's remains were secretly buried in Magdeburg, near Berlin, where they remained for many years. However, there were fears that they could be discovered and become a Nazi shrine. So, in 1970, the remains were secretly dug up, thoroughly burned and the ashes flushed into a river.

Source A: *A Soviet poster from 1942. Notice the flags on the cuffs of the people throttling Hitler. The poster suggests Hitler's Nazi regime was doomed once the 'Big Three' combined against him.*

In the Paper 1 final examination you will have to answer questions on the two different options you have studied. Germany 1918–45 is one of them. You will have to answer four questions. Question (a) is on chronology, (b) asks you to explain effects, (c) asks about causation and (d) is an essay using a source and own knowledge.

You have 45 minutes to answer the four sub-questions on each theme (the exam is one hour 30 minutes in total), so the examiners are not expecting you to write huge amounts. The number of marks helps you to judge how much to write. For Question (a) allow 5 minutes, Question (b) 8 minutes, Question (c) 12 minutes and Question (d) 15 minutes, with 5 minutes to read over your answers.

Build Better Answers

Question (a)

Examiner's tip: Part (a) questions will ask you to place a series of events in the correct chronological order. This is only worth 3 marks, so allow about 5 minutes for this question.

Let's look at an example.

Study these events which occurred in the years 1919–29.
Write these events in the correct chronological sequence. **(3 marks)**

Germany joins the League of Nations	Munich Putsch	The Young Plan	The Spartacist Revolt	The Kaiser abdicates

- As part of your revision, ensure you make a timeline of your own showing the key events in Germany in the years 1918–45. This will help you not only with Question (a) but also with the other three questions in this section. It will ensure that you put events in the correct sequence or order.

- Cut out the events and dates separately and test yourself by matching the dates to the events and putting them in chronological order. Here is an example:

1918	Kaiser abdicates	1919	Spartacist Revolt
	New Republic set up		New Weimar Constitution
	Germany agrees to armistice		Germany signs Treaty of Versailles

Student answer	**Examiner comments**
The Kaiser abdicates The Spartacist Revolt The Young Plan Germany joins the League The Munich Putsch	This would be awarded 1 mark as the candidate has the first two in the correct sequence.

Let's rewrite the answer with all the events in the right sequence

The Kaiser abdicates The Spartacist Revolt The Munich Putsch Germany joins the League The Young Plan	The candidate has all five events in the right chronological order and would be awarded full (3) marks.

Build Better Answers

Question (b)

Examiner tip: Question (b) will pick out two of the five events from Question (a). It will ask you to choose one of the two of the events and use your knowledge to explain its effects. This is only worth 4 marks, so allow about 8 minutes for this question. An effect means the results or the consequences of an event – in other words, what the event led to. For example, one effect of the Spartacist Revolt was to force the Weimar Republic to seek the help of the army leaders who, in return, ensured that the army would not be changed. One effect of the Young Plan was to encourage opposition from nationalist groups such as the Nazis and to give Hitler much-needed publicity.

Let's look at an example.

Choose **either** | The Spartacist Revolt | **or** | The Young Plan

Explain one effect on the Weimar Republic of the event you have chosen. **(4 marks)**

- Choose **one** of the events and stick with your choice. Some candidates, half way through writing their answer on the first event, decide to write about the other event. This wastes valuable time.

- Focus on the question. It is about one effect so begin your answer with *One effect was...* Do not just tell the story.

- Give the effect and explain it. Using the word *because* helps you to give a developed description.

- One paragraph is enough because it is only worth 4 marks.

Student answer	**Examiner comments**
The Spartacists were communists who tried to take over the German government. They were led by Rosa Luxemburg and Karl Liebneckt. They wanted a Germany ruled by workers' councils and soviets.	This student tells the story rather than focusing on one effect and describing it. This would be marked in Level 1.

Let's rewrite the answer and focus on one effect.

One effect of the Spartacist Revolt was **to weaken the Weimar Republic**. This was because the Weimar Republic was not strong enough to defeat the Spartacists and made an agreement with the army commanders and the Freikorps to put down the rebellion. In return the Republic promised not to change the army. **As a result** the old army, which supported the Kaiser and opposed the new Republic, remained in existence.	The student immediately focuses on the question by giving the effect. There is a developed explanation of the effect using link words and phrases such as 'because' and 'as a result'. This would be marked in Level 2.

Question (c)

Examiner tip: Part (c) questions will ask you to use your knowledge to explain why something happened. In other words, this is a question about causation. Causation means explaining the reasons why an event happened. In the example given below, you are being asked to explain reasons why Germany was able to recover under the leadership of Stresemann. You will always need to explain at least two reasons, and these reasons should be linked. It is worth 8 marks, so allow about 12 minutes for this question.

Let's look at an example.

Why was Germany able to recover under the leadership of Stresemann in the years 1924–29? Explain your answer. **(8 marks)**

There are several reasons that you could write about for this question. These include:

- the Dawes Plan and how this helped German economic recovery as well as reparations payments
- the Rentenmark, which stabilised the German currency after the hyperinflation of 1923
- Stresemann's policies abroad, such as entry to the League of Nations and the Locarno Treaties
- the political stability of the period, with much less support for extremist parties such as the Nazis and Communists.

Remember to:

- Focus on the question. It is about causation, so ensure you write about the reasons why something happened. Do not just tell the story.
- Write a separate paragraph for each reason. At the beginning of each paragraph, give the reason and then fully explain it. Using the word *because* helps you to give a developed explanation.
- Two paragraphs or explained reasons are enough to achieve the top level.
- For the highest marks you also have to make links between each reason. This means explaining how one reason led to the next. For example, a paragraph on the Dawes Plan and economic recovery could be linked to the stability provided by the introduction of a new currency, the Rentenmark. For example, *The economic recovery brought about by the Dawes Plan was a result of the stability created by the introduction of a new currency, the Rentenmark.*

You would then write a paragraph giving an explanation about the Rentenmark.

Link words or phrases often help to achieve this. Here are some examples: *this led to, as a result, moreover, furthermore, as a consequence, in addition.*

- Write a conclusion confirming how the two factors combined to produce the outcome.

Here is a grid to help you plan your answer to this question.

First reason	Give the reason.
	Fully explain it.
Link	Make a link with the second reason.
Second reason	Give the reason.
	Fully explain it.
Conclusion	Sum up the two reasons stressing the links between them.

Build Better Answers

Student answer

Stresemann negotiated the Dawes Plan with America to help the recovery of Germany. The Americans lent money to Germany to help them recover from the hyperinflation of 1923. Britain and France agreed that reparation payments should be reduced until Germany could afford bigger payments. Stresemann also got Germany into the League of Nations and signed the Locarno Treaties.

Examiner comments

The candidate knows the reasons. For example, mentions the Dawes Plan and gives good supporting detail about loans and reduced payments. The answer also mentions the League of Nations and the Locarno Treaties but does not explain these with supporting detail. In addition, there is no attempt to show links between the two reasons. This would be marked in Level 2.

Let's rewrite the answer with the details added and links shown between the reasons.

The first reason for German recovery was the Dawes Plan. Stresemann negotiated the Dawes Plan with America to help the recovery of Germany. It helped **because** the USA agreed to lend Germany 800 million marks to invest in industry and commerce. In addition, reparation payments were adjusted to match Germany's capacity to pay. Germany was now able to make reparations payments to the Allies, Britain and France, while the loans boosted the growth of German industry and reduced unemployment.

Moreover, the Dawes Plan and reparations payments brought improved relations between Germany and the other major powers, and this encouraged a second reason for German recovery: Stresemann's policies abroad. **As foreign secretary in the years after 1924,** he successfully restored and improved relations with other countries, especially France and Britain. Germany signed the Locarno Treaties of 1925, guaranteeing her frontiers with neighbouring countries. In the following year Germany was allowed to join the League of Nations and seemed, once again, to be fully accepted by the rest of Europe.

The period of recovery was due to the Dawes Plan, which stabilised the German economy and enabled Stresemann to improve relations abroad with Britain and France.

Now we have two clearly explained reasons. Notice how the candidate immediately focuses on the question at the start of the first paragraph. Furthermore, the answer makes links between the first factor, the Dawes Plan, and the second factor, Stresemann's policies abroad. This link is reinforced by the conclusion which explains how the factors combined to produce Germany's recovery. In addition, the answer gives supporting details for the second reason, the League and Locarno.

Build Better Answers

Question (d)

Examiner tip: Part (d) questions will ask you to use a source and your knowledge to describe or explain cause, effect or change. It is worth 10 marks so allow about 15 minutes for this question. If the question is about change you must show change either by comparing the situation before and after the development or you must show how it developed during the period. Let's look at an example.

Study the source and then answer the question that follows.

Source A: *From a modern textbook.*

> Hitler was determined to <u>control</u> the young in Nazi Germany. They were the future supporters of the Nazi Party. The Nazis reorganised every aspect of the <u>school curriculum</u> to make children loyal to them. They also controlled their leisure time through the <u>Hitler Youth</u> and the League of German Maidens.

Use the source, and your own knowledge, to describe the changes in the position of the young in Nazi Germany in the years 1933–39. **(10 marks)**

- The question is asking to use the source as well as your own knowledge. Ensure that you directly refer to the source in your answer.

- It is also asking you to use your own knowledge. Use the source to stimulate your own knowledge by underlining key names, events or dates in the source. This is shown in Source A, where the candidate has underlined <u>control</u>, <u>school curriculum</u> and <u>Hitler Youth</u> and would be able to develop these. Once you explain these in more detail, you are using your own knowledge.

- Focus on the question. It is about change, so ensure you write about changes. Do not just tell the story.

- At the beginning of each paragraph, give the change and then fully describe it. Using the word *because* helps you to give a developed description.

- Two paragraphs or developed descriptions are enough to achieve the top level.

- For the highest marks you also have to make links between each factor. This means explaining how one change led to the next. Link words or phrases help to achieve this. Here are some examples: *this led to, as a result, moreover, furthermore, as a consequence, in addition.*

- Write a conclusion confirming how the two factors combined to produce the outcome.

Here is a grid to help you plan your answer to this question.

The source	Underline or highlight key words, events, people in the source that you can write more about.
First factor	Give the first factor mentioned in the source. Fully describe it.
Link	Make a link with a second factor mentioned in the source.
Second factor	Fully describe the second factor.
Conclusion	Sum up the two factors stressing the links between them.

Student answer

Hitler wanted to control the young because they would be the future supporters of the Nazi Party. He controlled the young by changing their education, especially the school curriculum, and by making them join the Hitler Youth or the League of German Maidens.

Examiner comments

This answer summarise or paraphrases the source. There is little own knowledge except a hint of the young being forced to join the Hitler Youth. It would be awarded Level 1 and needs to bring in a lot more own knowledge.

Let's look at an answer where the student has used some of his or her own knowledge.

The Nazis controlled the schooling of the young. Teachers had to swear an oath of loyalty to Hitler and join the Nazi Teachers' League. They had to promote Nazi ideals in the classroom. In lessons for boys, the emphasis was on preparation for the military. Girls took needlework and home crafts, especially cookery, to become good homemakers and mothers. Subjects such as race studies were taught to put across Nazi ideas on race and population control. Children were taught that Aryans were superior and should not marry inferior races such as Jews.

This time the student has used own knowledge but made no direct reference to the source or to the idea of change. In addition, the answer only describes one factor, schooling and cannot show links to a second factor. This would be awarded a Level 2 mark.

Let's re-write the answer to include the sources and own knowledge and two linked factors focused on change.

Life for the young **changed** a great deal under the Nazis. They exerted much greater control over the education and leisure time of young people than the Weimar Republic. **Moreover**, this control increased during the years 1933-39. The first change, as suggested in **Source A**, was in the school curriculum. Unlike the Weimar Republic, the curriculum was strictly controlled by the Nazis to put across their ideas about the different roles of boys and girls. With the boys the emphasis was on preparation for the military. Girls took needlework and home crafts, to become good homemakers and mothers. There was also a **change** in the subjects taught, and new subjects such put across Nazi ideas on race and population control.

Moreover, this control of the young at school was extended to their leisure time, as is suggested by **Source A**, with the introduction of the Hitler Youth as the Nazis banned the different youth groups, such as the Catholic Youth Organisation, that had existed under the Weimar Republic. The Hitler Youth changed the life of the young because, as with schooling, it was used to pass on Nazi ideas. Boys took part in athletics, hiking and camping. As they got older they practised marching, map reading and military skills. Girls learnt domestic skills as preparation for motherhood and marriage, and there was much less emphasis on military training.

Therefore there was much change for the young in Nazi Germany, with boys and girls prepared for different roles through schooling as well as the Hitler youth movements.

This candidate has used the source and own knowledge to describe two changes and has ensured that the answer focuses on change. Furthermore, the answer links the first change to the second, as well as showing how they combined to produce the outcome in the conclusion.

How many world wars have there been? This seems like an easy question. There were two: the First World War (1914–1918) and the Second World War (1939–1945). However, some American writers have recently suggested that there was a Third World War: a war that started in 1945 between the East and the West; a war that in the early 1960s could have ended the world. This war is better known as the Cold War.

American and Russian troops never faced each other in battle, but in spite of this the Cold War had many of the features of a real war. For example, both sides were involved in an **arms race**, both sides spied on each other and both formed powerful military **alliances** to ensure that if the cold peace turned into an actual war, they were in the best position to come out on top.

In this section you will study:

- the causes of the Cold War
- the early development of the Cold War, 1945–49
- the development of the Cold War in the 1950s
- the Berlin Crisis of 1961
- the Cuban Missile Crisis of 1962.

The exam

This page shows you exactly what your Paper 1 exam paper will look like. This is an option from Group C. You answer the two questions on Paper 1 that relate to the options you have studied.

> There are four questions, parts (a), (b), (c), and (d). **You must answer all four.**

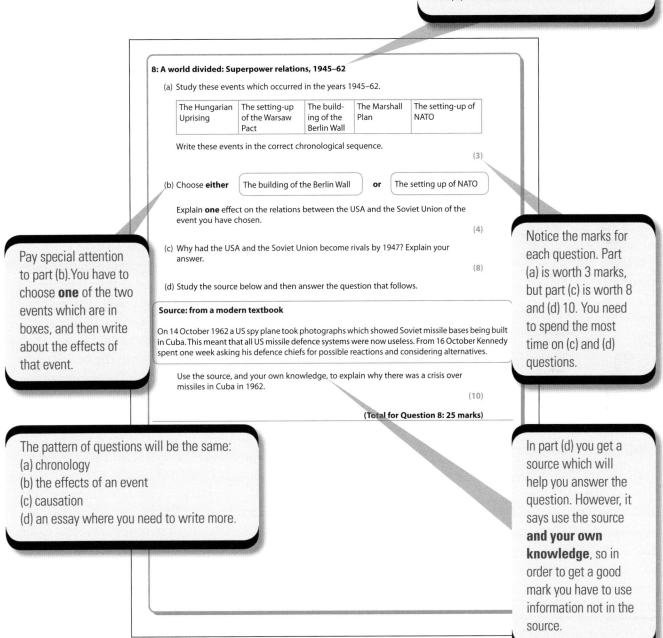

8: A world divided: Superpower relations, 1945–62

(a) Study these events which occurred in the years 1945–62.

The Hungarian Uprising	The setting-up of the Warsaw Pact	The build-ing of the Berlin Wall	The Marshall Plan	The setting-up of NATO

Write these events in the correct chronological sequence.

(3)

(b) Choose **either** [The building of the Berlin Wall] **or** [The setting up of NATO]

Explain **one** effect on the relations between the USA and the Soviet Union of the event you have chosen.

(4)

(c) Why had the USA and the Soviet Union become rivals by 1947? Explain your answer.

(8)

(d) Study the source below and then answer the question that follows.

Source: from a modern textbook

On 14 October 1962 a US spy plane took photographs which showed Soviet missile bases being built in Cuba. This meant that all US missile defence systems were now useless. From 16 October Kennedy spent one week asking his defence chiefs for possible reactions and considering alternatives.

Use the source, and your own knowledge, to explain why there was a crisis over missiles in Cuba in 1962.

(10)

(Total for Question 8: 25 marks)

> Pay special attention to part (b). You have to choose **one** of the two events which are in boxes, and then write about the effects of that event.

> Notice the marks for each question. Part (a) is worth 3 marks, but part (c) is worth 8 and (d) 10. You need to spend the most time on (c) and (d) questions.

> The pattern of questions will be the same:
> (a) chronology
> (b) the effects of an event
> (c) causation
> (d) an essay where you need to write more.

> In part (d) you get a source which will help you answer the question. However, it says use the source **and your own knowledge**, so in order to get a good mark you have to use information not in the source.

Why did the Cold War begin?
The breakdown of the Grand Alliance

Learning objectives

In this chapter you will learn about:

● the difference between communism and capitalism

● the three key meetings of the Grand Alliance

● the difficult relationship between Russia and America.

The Grand Alliance (1941)

Prior to the Cold War, America and the USSR worked together as members of the **Grand Alliance**: an alliance created in 1941 to defeat the **Nazis**. However, the Grand Alliance was a marriage of convenience between communists and capitalists united only in their opposition to Hitler. Once Hitler had been defeated, the Alliance became increasingly uneasy. Between 1943 and 1945, the leaders of the Grand Alliance met at three international conferences: Tehran, Yalta and Potsdam.

	Capitalism	**Communism**
Focus	Individual rights	The rights of the working class
Values	Individual freedom	Equality
Economy	Free trade	Government planned
Politics	Democratic elections	Communist Party controls government

The leaders each wanted the others to recognise that there were countries that fell within their 'sphere of influence' and countries that did not. None of the official documents that were signed laid out these spheres. Nevertheless, by the end of the three conferences, it was clear that there was broad agreement over what these were.

● The USSR would 'influence' Poland, Czechoslovakia, the Baltic States, Hungary and Romania. This would build a line of 'buffer states' between the USSR and the West. Stalin agreed this could be 'influence' only, with these states having free elections and a level of democracy (this was built into the signed document at Yalta).

● The USSR also wanted its influence in Yugoslavia (which had its own communist government) accepted. Yugoslavia was officially accepted as a communist country at Yalta.

● Britain and the USA were keen to get the USSR to accept their influence in Western Europe, Greece and Italy.

The Tehran Conference (1943)

When Churchill, Stalin and Roosevelt met at Tehran (28 November–1 December 1943), they reached some definite agreements and some agreements in principle (without outlining the detail). Stalin was annoyed that Britain and the USA had delayed opening a second front in the war. He was convinced they were waiting for the communist USSR to damage itself fatally in the battle against Nazi Germany before they would intervene.

● The USA and Britain would open a second front to split the German defences and take some of the pressure off the USSR. Stalin had been urging them to do this for some time, while Britain and the USA had wanted to focus on a single front. However, Roosevelt supported the second front idea and it was agreed to start in June 1944.

● The USSR would declare war on Japan once Germany was defeated.

● Poland should be given more land from Germany, but lose some to the USSR.

But there were points of disagreement, over which Roosevelt often sided with Stalin, not Churchill. For example, Churchill wanted to begin an invasion of the Balkans. While this would help the war effort, he mainly wanted it to stop the Soviet advance in Eastern Europe (and via this the spread of communism).

Not surprisingly, Stalin opposed this and Roosevelt supported Stalin. He favoured the second front in the west proposed by Stalin and an invasion of the Balkans as well would have weakened the Allied forces by splitting them up too much.

The Yalta Conference (1945)

When Churchill, Stalin and Roosevelt met at Yalta (4–11 February 1945), they agreed on some of the same things they had agreed at Tehran, but with some changes.

- Germany, when defeated, would be reduced in size, would be demilitarised and would have to pay reparations (these would be taken in materials, goods and labour).
- Plans were begun for how Germany would be divided after the war. The rebuilding of Europe was to be done along the lines of the Atlantic Charter agreed between the USA and Britain in 1941, the most important policy of which was the right of countries to choose their own governments.
- The Nazi Party would be banned and war criminals tried in front of an international court.
- A United Nations Organisation (UN) would be set up to replace the League of Nations. It would meet for the first time on 25 April 1945. It was decided who would be members: all the Allies and those who had agreed to join the UN on 8 February 1945. The Soviet Republics of Ukraine and Belorussia were to be seen as separate countries from the USSR and to have their own voting rights. The USA would draw up the Charter.
- The USSR would declare war on Japan three months after the defeat of Germany. There was an outline of how lands held by Japan would be divided after the war (the USSR would have land Japan had captured returned).
- Poland (at present communist, under Soviet control) should be in the Soviet 'sphere of influence' but be run on 'a broader democratic basis'.

The conference was a success largely because of the understanding between Stalin and Roosevelt, established at Tehran in 1943. Roosevelt also worked well with Churchill. However, splits were growing. Britain and the USA had been reluctant to agree to Poland becoming communist. Britain had entered the Second World War to defend Poland, while America wished to avoid communism spreading further west and antagonising the many Americans who had Polish roots. Stalin, on the other hand, desperately wanted Poland as a buffer between the USSR and the West. The USSR had been invaded from the West no less than three times already that century.

Signs of tension

In spite of the apparent unity, there were important issues that divided the 'Big Three' – Stalin, Roosevelt and Churchill. For example, although they all agreed to work for democracy, there were significant disagreements over what democracy meant.

Stalin believed that a democratic government had to be a communist government because only the communists truly represented the working people. Roosevelt, on the other hand, believed that democracy involved a number of different political parties competing to win the people's support in free elections.

The success of the conference was based largely on Stalin's relationship with Roosevelt. However, within two months Roosevelt had died and the new American President, Harry S. Truman, was less willing to compromise with Stalin. This led to further tensions at the Alliance's final conference.

Source A: *The 'Big Three' at the Yalta Conference, February 1945. From left to right: Churchill, Roosevelt, Stalin.*

The Potsdam Conference (1945)

When Churchill, Stalin and Truman met at Potsdam (July and August 1945), there was far more tension. President Truman had been briefed about the earlier conferences. But he had no relationship with Stalin. To add to the disruption, the result of the British election came during the conference, and the new Labour Prime Minster, Attlee, replaced Churchill.

So the personal trust and understanding built up in earlier conferences was lost. Truman had delayed the first meeting of the conference until after the new **atomic bomb** had been tested. The fact that Stalin had been told nothing of the bomb until this point increased his suspicion of his allies. Also, Germany was defeated, so the Big Three were no longer united by a common enemy.

Despite this, they reached agreement on many points concerning the reconstruction of Europe. It went into great detail about the terms as they applied to Germany – from how reparations were to be paid to how the military equipment was to be broken up. They agreed to:

- set up a Council of Foreign Ministers to organise the re-building of Europe
- ban the Nazi Party and prosecute surviving Nazis as war criminals in a special court run by the Allies at Nuremberg
- reduce the size of Germany
- divide Germany into four zones, to be administered by the USA, the USSR, Britain and France, with the aim of re-uniting it under one government as soon as possible
- divide Berlin, Germany's capital, into four as well, despite it being deep in the USSR's zone
- the USSR could have a quarter of the industrial equipment from the other three zones, because its zone was the least developed industrially, but had to provide the other zones with raw materials such as coal.

Once again, however, there was disagreement on bigger issues.

Examination question

Why was there tension at the Potsdam Conference (1945)? Explain your answer. **(8 marks)**

Reparations

The USSR wanted to impose heavy reparations on Germany, whereas America wanted Germany to be rebuilt. The Conference agreed a compromise whereby each ally would take reparations from the zone they occupied. This was far less than Stalin wanted, as the part of Germany that he controlled was poorer than the rest and had much less industry. As a result, the Western Allies agreed that the USSR could have a quarter of the industrial equipment from the Western zones, but stated that they would have to pay for much of this with East German raw materials such as coal.

The atomic bomb

Truman attempted to assert his authority during the Potsdam Conference. He believed that America possessed the ultimate weapon in the atomic bomb and therefore, in Churchill's words, 'generally bossed the whole meeting'. Truman believed that the atomic bomb was 'the master card' in the Potsdam discussions. It gave America the power to destroy entire enemy cities without risking a single American life.

Stalin refused to be pushed around. Truman later remarked that when Stalin was informed about the bomb he 'showed no special interest'. However, Stalin was well aware of the significance of the atomic bomb and had, as early as 1940, instructed Soviet scientists to develop their own. News of the American bomb made Stalin more determined than ever to protect the interests of the USSR. Stalin's plan was to protect the USSR by creating a 'buffer zone' – a communist area in Eastern Europe between the USSR and the capitalist west.

Poland

Truman's arrogance and Stalin's determination soured the relationship at the centre of the Grand Alliance. Their relationship was further strained by the USSR's actions in Poland. Stalin had agreed to set up a government in Poland that included both communists and capitalists. However, by the time of the Potsdam Conference it was evident that he had broken his word.

Although the Potsdam Conference finished with a show of unity, insiders at the conference were aware that there were bitter divisions between

America and the USSR, which some thought would lead to a new war.

Greece

An early battleground for these tensions was found in Greece. The German retreat in 1944 left two groups fighting to rule the country: monarchists and communists. In 1945 British troops were sent in to support the monarchists under the claim of restoring order and supervising free elections. The USSR complained to the United Nations and a civil war erupted. When the British decided to pull out, in 1947, the US stepped in to prop up the king's government.

Build Better Answers

Explain one **effect on the relations between the USA and the Soviet Union of the Potsdam Conference.** (4 marks)

Paper 1 part (b) questions will ask about the effect of one event on another.

■ **A basic answer (level 1)** will give a consequence, or effect, but no supporting detail. For example, *Stalin and Truman disagreed about important issues.*

● **A good answer (level 2)** will make a statement giving a consequence and then develop this statement by giving extra detail or explanation. For example, *Stalin and Roosevelt (US President before Potsdam) had managed to work together. At Potsdam, Truman and Stalin disagreed on the future of Germany, which made relations between the two countries worse. Stalin wanted very heavy reparation payments, while Truman argued for lighter payments and giving Germany the chance to recover economically. Stalin was more concerned that Germany paid and that it never got powerful again.*

Activities

1 Divide the following conference aims into those belonging to the USA, those belonging to the USSR, and those shared by both:
   - a 'sphere of influence' in Eastern Europe
   - reparations from Germany
   - governments representing working people
   - a peaceful and prosperous Germany
   - governments elected by the people
   - prosecution of Nazi war criminals
   - a communist government in Poland
   - democratic governments across Europe.

2 The three conferences – Tehran, Yalta and Potsdam – form the background to the Cold War. During this period it became clear that relations between the USSR and America were uneasy. This activity will help you to understand how these relationships developed.
   - On a large piece of paper, draw the following axes:

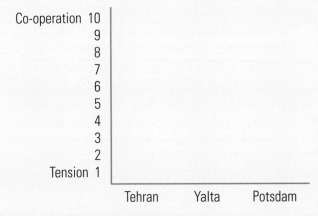

   - For each conference, make two lists: a) evidence that the 'Big Three' were co-operating, and b) evidence that there was tension in their relationship.
   - Use the information on your lists to reach a judgment about the extent to which the 'Big Three' were co-operating at each conference. Give the 'Big Three' a mark out of 10, where 10 represents complete co-operation and 1 represents great tension.
   - Plot the scores for each conference on your graph.
   - In what ways did the relationship between the 'Big Three' change during this period?
   - Make a list of reasons why the relationship between the 'Big Three' changed between the Tehran Conference in 1943 and the Potsdam Conference in 1945.

Fear of war

Learning objectives

In this chapter you will learn about:

- the divisions between the USSR and the USA in 1946
- the origins of the Truman Doctrine.

The war of words

During 1946 it became increasingly clear that Europe had been divided between capitalism in the west and communism in the east. Stalin, representing the East, and Churchill, representing the West, responded with a 'war of words', showing that the former allies now viewed each other with tremendous suspicion. This suspicion became an important part of the Cold War.

> From Stettin in the Baltic to Trieste in the Adriatic, an iron curtain has descended across the continent. Behind the line lie all the capitals of the ancient states of Central and Eastern Europe… all these famous cities and the populations around them lie in the Soviet sphere and all are subject, in one form or another, not only to Soviet influence but to a very high and increasing measure of control from Moscow.

Source A: *Churchill's 'Iron Curtain' speech, March 1946.*

> Essentially, Mr Churchill now adopts the position of the warmonger, and in this Mr Churchill is not alone. He has friends not only in Britain but in the United States of America as well. A point to be noted in this respect is that Mr Churchill and his friends bear a striking resemblance to Hitler and his friends.

Source B: *Stalin's response to Churchill's speech, March 1946.*

Churchill gave his speech during a trip to America, and everyone understood that President Truman supported what he had said. Clearly, both sides had started to view each other as opponents rather than allies.

Secret telegrams

Truman and Stalin were concerned about the breakdown of their alliance and the threat of a new war. Both men asked for secret reports from their embassies to help them to understand how their opponents were thinking. Both reports were sent as telegrams.

The Long Telegram (1946)

Truman received worrying news in the 'Long Telegram', a secret report from Kennan, America's ambassador in Moscow. The telegram reported that:

- Stalin had given a speech calling for the destruction of capitalism
- there could be no peace with the USSR while it was opposed to capitalism
- the USSR was building up its military power.

Novikov's Telegram (1946)

Novikov, the Soviet ambassador to America, sent a telegram to Stalin which was equally concerning. It reported:

- America desired to dominate the world
- following Roosevelt's death, the American government was no longer interested in co-operation with the USSR
- the American public was being prepared for war with the USSR.

Following these secret telegrams, both governments believed that they were facing the possibility of war. Indeed, the government of the USSR came to believe that war with America was inevitable. In America, some soldiers who had fought in the Second World War and entered politics when they returned home called Stalin 'the new Hitler'. Their point was simple: Stalin, like Hitler, was preparing for war and must be stopped.

On the verge of the Cold War

By the end of 1946, the alliance was all but over. America had come to believe that the USSR was planning world domination and many in the USSR feared that America was planning the same. At the beginning of 1947, Truman addressed the American government, setting out his belief that America must stand against communism. This speech, setting out the 'Truman **Doctrine**', can be seen as the unofficial declaration of the Cold War (see page 74).

Source C: *President Truman making the Truman Doctrine speech in March 1947.*

 Watch out!

Do not confuse Churchill's 'Iron Curtain' with the Berlin Wall! The 'Iron Curtain' is a metaphor for the division of Europe, whereas the Berlin Wall was an actual barrier, put up in 1961 that divided Berlin (see pages 92–93).

 Top Tip

Your exam will contain one source in part (d). It is important to use your own knowledge as well as the source in your answer. Answers which only use information from the source can only get 2 of the 10 marks available for the question.

 Build Better Answers

Why had the wartime alliance between the USA and the Soviet Union broken down by the end of 1946?

(8 marks)

■ **A basic answer (level 1)** will give a generalised reason.

● **A good answer (level 2)** will give two or more factors and will include relevant supporting detail.

▲ **A better answer (level 3)** will include relevant supporting detail and explain why two or more factors caused the event in the question.

▲ **An excellent answer (full marks)** will be the same as a very good answer, but also show how the different factors link together. If possible show how the reasons combined to produce the outcome.

Activities

1 Copy and complete the following sentences:

   a The Long Telegram increased US fears of the USSR because...

   b Novikov's Telegram increased...

2 Look at the Build Better Answers question above. Take one of the following factors:

   ● Churchill's 'Iron Curtain Speech'

   ● the Long Telegram

   ● Novikov's Telegram

   Rather than writing the whole essay, write a paragraph based on your chosen factor that is accurate, detailed and really explains why the alliance between the USA and the Soviet Union had broken down by the end of 1946.

The development of the Cold War: the Truman Doctrine and Marshall Aid

> ### Learning objectives
>
> In this chapter you will learn about:
> - the key features of the Truman Doctrine and the Marshall Plan
> - America's reasons for offering Marshall Aid.

The Truman Doctrine (1947)

Following the 'Long Telegram' (see page 72), Truman asked the American military to assess the strength of the USSR's army. He learned that the USSR was in no position to wage a war. Nonetheless, Truman believed that the USSR had a second strategy that would allow it to conquer more and more territory without having to declare war: Stalin would encourage communist revolutions across Europe. After the Second World War, much of Europe was devastated and citizens in countries such as Italy, France, Greece, Turkey and the United Kingdom were suffering great hardships. In these conditions communism was highly appealing because communists believed that the wealth of the richest people should be shared out among the poor. To address this threat, in 1947 Truman set out a new policy that soon became known as the 'Truman Doctrine'.

The Truman Doctrine stated that:

- the world had a choice between communist tyranny and democratic freedom
- America had a responsibility to fight for liberty wherever it was threatened
- America would send troops and economic resources to help governments that were threatened by communists
- communism should not be allowed to grow and gain territory.

The significance of the Truman Doctrine

The Truman Doctrine was important because it suggested that America, rather than the United Nations, had a responsibility to protect the world. This marked a reversal of the USA's traditional policy of '**isolationism**' by which America had stayed out of international affairs. It was also significant because it divided the world according to ideology: it stated clearly that capitalism and communism were in opposition.

This suggested that there could be no further co-operation between East and West due to their ideological differences, and in this sense it marked the unofficial end of the old United Nations and the beginning of the Cold War. Finally, it set a realistic goal for American foreign policy: Truman was committed to '**containment**'. This implied that although America would not invade the USSR, it would make every effort to stop the spread of communism.

The Marshall Plan (1947)

Truman described containment and the Marshall Plan as 'two halves of the same walnut'. By this he meant that America had a dual strategy for dealing with communism. First, containment aimed to beat communism through military force. Secondly, the Marshall Plan of 1947 committed $13 billion of American money to rebuild the shattered economies of Europe. By encouraging prosperity, the Marshall Plan would weaken the attraction of communism. To those suffering economic hardship following the Second World War, the promise of sharing resources equally under communism had great appeal. If people were wealthy, however, the idea of sharing resources would have less appeal. In order to qualify for American money, European countries had to agree to trade freely with America. In this way, the Marshall Plan also helped the American economy.

> ### Did you know?
>
> The United Nations (UN) is an organisation created in 1945 to maintain international peace. The first meeting of the UN, in 1946, was attended by 51 nations. Today, the UN is made up of 192 nations.

Initial reaction to the Marshall Plan

European leaders met at the Paris Conference of 1948 to discuss the American offer. Many European countries were keen to receive Marshall Aid. However, representatives from the USSR walked out of the conference claiming that the Americans were attempting to split Europe into 'two camps'. They argued that Marshall Aid was the first step in creating a military alliance that would wage war on the Soviet Union. Stalin also insisted that Eastern European countries in the Soviet 'sphere of influence' refuse the help offered by America. By contrast, 16 countries including Britain and France welcomed the offer, seeing it as a way of rebuilding their economies and defeating communism in their own countries.

Source A: *A British newspaper cartoon from June 1948 showing the 'Iron Curtain' and Marshall Aid. The figure on the right is Stalin. The figure looking over the 'Iron Curtain' is Tito, the communist leader of Yugoslavia. Although Tito was a communist, he did not see eye-to-eye with Stalin and found some aspects of Western Europe very attractive.*

Build Better Answers

Explain one **effect of the Marshall Plan on the relations between the USA and the Soviet Union.**

(4 marks)

Paper 1 part (b) questions will ask about the effect of one event on another.

■ **A basic answer (level 1)** will give a consequence, or effect, but no supporting detail. For example, *It made relations between the USA and the Soviet Union far worse.*

● **A good answer (level 2)** will make a statement giving a consequence and then develop this statement by giving extra detail or explanation. For example, *... the Marshall Plan made relations worse by giving aid to European countries. The USA was, in its view, stopping them from coming under pressure from the USSR to become communist. The USA thought it was helping these countries to make a choice between communism and capitalism freely. However, the USSR saw this as simple bribery to not become communist. So the USSR saw the Marshall Plan not as help offered to suffering countries, but as an act of aggression against the USSR.*

Activity

Copy this spider diagram. Below it, make notes on each of the words or phrases.

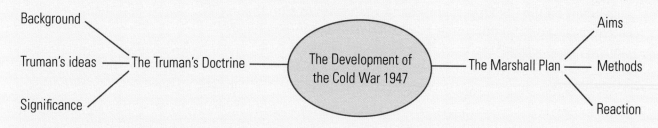

The development of the Cold War: satellite states

What is a satellite state?

A satellite state is a country that is officially independent, but is in reality controlled by another country. Between 1947 and 1949, the USSR extended its influence over Eastern Europe, turning countries such as Czechoslovakia, Hungary and Poland into satellite states.

Why did Stalin set up satellite states?

Stalin described the Marshall Plan as 'dollar imperialism': he believed that the Americans were trying to buy influence over Europe, as any country that accepted Marshall Aid would effectively become an American ally. To prevent this, Stalin extended his control over Eastern Europe, creating a series of satellite states.

How did Stalin take control of them?

This emerged from the 'spheres of influence' discussed at the Tehran, Yalta and Potsdam conferences. At Yalta and Potsdam, the USSR agreed to free elections in these countries. It hoped at first that people would naturally choose communism in the free elections that the West wanted them to have. Some did, but most did not. So the USSR pushed for new 'free' elections that they fixed as much as they could. Once in power, they got rid of opposition parties and made each country a single-party state.

The USSR kept control by:

- making sure the Communist Party in each state had leaders that would obey Moscow
- creating an atmosphere of fear and mistrust so that it was difficult for people who wanted to oppose Soviet rule to trust each other enough to work together
- ruthlessly using the police and army in these states to stamp on any kind of opposition
- arranging the economies of these countries so that they were dependent on the USSR by 'rationalising' industries to stop the satellites being self-sufficient (e.g. Poland did all the shipbuilding, Hungary produced all the trucks).

Yugoslavia

Communists, led by Marshall Tito, took over Yugoslavia in 1945, while the war was still going on. At first, Tito worked well with the USSR, but he wanted to run Yugoslavia himself, not follow orders as a satellite state. Relations worsened and Tito split from the USSR in 1948. He even took aid under the Marshall Plan.

Albania

Communists took over in Albania in 1945, while the war was still going on. It had the least opposition to becoming a satellite state.

The Baltic States

Estonia, Latvia and Lithuania became part of the Soviet Union after the war, as did what had been eastern Poland and part of Romania. There was no pretence of them being separate from the USSR, as there was with the satellite states. They were treated as part of the USSR.

East Germany

East Germany was the part of Germany that the USSR was given to administer when Germany was divided into zones at the end of the war. In 1949, after supposedly 'free' elections, it announced it was a separate country from the other three, Western controlled, zones. It became the communist German Democratic Republic. In June 1953, demonstrations broke out across East Germany against communist policies, but the protests were crushed by Soviet tanks. Thousands were arrested and hundreds wounded.

Bulgaria

Late in 1944, while the war was still going on, a coalition of left-wing parties, including communists, took over in Bulgaria. In November 1945, they held 'free' elections which the communists won by intimidation. They then abolished all other political parties and executed anyone who looked able to oppose them, including many non-communists who had managed to get elected despite communist pressure.

Hungary

In 1945, free elections were held. The communists won some seats, but not enough to come to power. In 1947, after supposedly 'free' elections that they managed by intimidation, the communists were elected.

Poland

In free elections in 1945, a coalition of left-wing parties, including communists, came to power. Britain and the USA urged Stalin to take some Poles who had been in exile in London during the war into the government. He did so but, in 1947, after supposedly 'free' elections that they managed by intimidation, the communists took over entirely. The London Poles were either executed, imprisoned or fled.

Romania

In 1945, as soon as the war ended, a coalition of left-wing parties, including many communists, took over in Romania. In February 1945, the king was forced to take a communist prime minister. By June, the communists were in control of the government. 'Free' elections in 1947 gave the communists complete control.

Czechoslovakia

In free elections in 1945, a coalition of left-wing parties, including communists, came to power. In 1946, the government was dominated by communists. But they could not win complete control in fair elections and began to lose, not gain, support. So, in 1948, they used the army to take over, having removed any officers who might object to doing so. Many non-communists were arrested, some were imprisoned, some executed.

Cominform: The Communist Information Bureau (1947)

In order to extend his control, Stalin established Cominform in 1947. Cominform was an international organisation that represented Communist Parties across Europe and brought them under the direction of the USSR.

The first Cominform Conference rejected the Marshall Plan. Consequently, Eastern European governments refused to accept Marshall Aid and Communist Parties in Western Europe were encouraged to organise strikes and demonstrations against the American plan. In France, for example, 2 million workers, sympathetic to the communists, went on strike in the winter of 1947, demanding that the French government reject Marshall Aid.

Cominform was also used to ensure the loyalty of Eastern European governments. It did this by investigating government ministers and employees, and removing those who were not loyal to Stalin. This process was often violent. In Hungary, for example, 5% of the population was in prison by 1953. In this way, Cominform **consolidated** the power of the USSR through Eastern Europe by stamping out opposition and ensuring the loyalty of Eastern European governments.

Comecon: The Council for Mutual Economic Assistance (1949)

Comecon was Stalin's answer to the Marshall Plan. Stalin was aware that the Marshall Plan was very attractive to some Eastern European governments. Having ordered his satellite states to **boycott** Marshall Aid, he needed to set up a communist alternative. Therefore, in 1949 he established Comecon. In the first year, Comecon comprised the USSR, Bulgaria, Czechoslovakia, Hungary, Poland and Romania. Albania and Eastern Germany joined in 1950. Comecon aimed to encourage the economic development of Eastern Europe. It also attempted to prevent trade with Western Europe and America. This had political and economic implications.

- Politically, it would minimise American influence in Eastern Europe and the USSR.
- Economically, it ensured that the benefits of economic recovery in Eastern Europe remained within the Soviet 'sphere of influence'.
- It also meant that Eastern Europe did not have access to the prosperity of Western Europe.

'Two camps'

The USSR and America both recognised that, following the Potsdam Conference, Europe had divided into 'two camps'. This division had hardened as a result of Marshall Aid, which brought Western Europe into America's camp, and Cominform and Comecon, which established a Soviet camp in the East. In 1945, there had been two unofficial 'spheres of influence' in Europe. Marshall Aid and Comecon turned these 'spheres of influence' into two official economic alliances.

Watch out!

Do not confuse Cominform with Comecon. Remember Comecon is economic, and Cominform is political.

Build Better Answers

Why did Stalin launch Comecon in 1949? Explain your answer.
(8 marks)

Paper 1 part (c) questions expect you to explain why something happens.

■ **A basic answer (level 1)** will give a generalised answer.

● **A good answer (level 2)** will provide detail to support the reason(s). For example, *Stalin launched Comecon in response to America's Marshall Plan. He had told countries in the Soviet 'sphere of influence' not to accept Marshall Aid and instead established Comecon to provide economic support for countries in Eastern Europe.*

▲ **A better answer (level 3)** will show how these were linked. For example, *Stalin launched Comecon in response to the America's Marshall Plan. He had ordered countries in the Soviet 'sphere of influence' not to accept Marshall aid to stop them taking help from the USA. This meant that he needed to provide economic support for them.*

Activity

Complete the following table, summarising the key features of Cominform and Comecon.

	Cominform	Comecon
Full name		
Date established		
Aims		
Effects		

The development of the Cold War: first confrontation

> **Learning objectives**
>
> In this chapter you will learn about:
> - the division of Germany into East and West
> - the impact of the Berlin Blockade
> - the formation of NATO and the arms race.

Germany: Unfinished business

Following the Second World War, Russia and America were unable to agree about the future of Germany. There were four key issues.

- Should a reunited Germany be part of the Soviet 'sphere of influence', the American 'sphere of influence', or should it be neutral?
- Should a reunited Germany have a communist or a capitalist government?
- Should a reunited Germany receive Marshall Aid?
- Should troops from America and the USSR be allowed to remain in a united Germany?

Bizonia

By 1947, the British and American zones were essentially operating as one, and therefore became known as 'Bizonia' (meaning two zones). The relationship between Bizonia and the French zone was also very good, and therefore the three western zones were referred to as 'Trizonia'.

Although Germany's capital, Berlin, was deep within the Soviet zone, it too was divided into four regions, with the western section under American, French and British control.

The division of Germany after the Second World War.

East and West Germany

The future of Germany was still the subject of intense negotiations between East and West. However, in 1948 the Western Allies started to develop a policy for western Germany that was at odds with Russia's plans. First, Britain, France and the USA agreed to set up a German assembly to create a German constitution. Secondly, they introduced a new currency – the Deutschmark – which would become the official currency for Trizonia.

Stalin had not been consulted about these developments and believed they were the first steps to creating a permanently divided Germany. He opposed the division of Germany for the following reasons.

- He was reluctant to allow America to have further influence over Germany.
- He did not want American troops to remain stationed in Germany.
- He realised that Germany's most valuable economic resources were in the west and feared that they would be used to wage war on the USSR.

The Berlin Blockade (1948–49)

In order to prevent the establishment of a separate state in western Germany, Stalin set up a military **blockade** around West Berlin in June 1948. His plan was to cut western Germany off from its capital (Berlin) so that the new government, based in Berlin, could not control its territory in western Germany. Stalin hoped that this would prove that a divided Germany could not work in practice.

President Truman responded with the 'Berlin Airlift'. Allied planes transported supplies to West Berlin around the clock. Initially, America committed 70 large cargo planes and airlifted between 600 and 700 tonnes of food and supplies every day. This had increased to 1000 tonnes a day within a couple of weeks. The British authorities maintained a similar system and, at its height, the airlift provided over 170,000 tonnes of supplies during January 1949.

The airlift prevented the blockade from succeeding. What is more, Truman's response was peaceful and made Stalin's military blockade appear highly aggressive.

The Berlin Blockade was a **propaganda** success for the Americans, and an utter failure for the USSR. In May 1949, Stalin ended the blockade, and in September 1949, West Germany (officially called the Federal Republic of Germany, or FDR) was officially created as an independent state. One month later, the USSR established a second independent state – East Germany (officially known as the German Democratic Republic, or GDR).

Source A: *An aircraft participating in the Berlin airlift in 1949.*

The Formation of NATO (1949)

The Berlin Blockade was the first military confrontation of the Cold War. It raised the possibility of a war in Europe. As a result, Western European nations tried to establish an alliance in order to 'keep the USA in, and the USSR out'. In April 1949, NATO (the North Atlantic Treaty Organisation) was established as an alliance between America and many of the countries in Western Europe. NATO members agreed that if any NATO country came under attack, all members of NATO would come to their defence.

The creation of NATO marked a significant development in the Cold War. The Marshall Plan had created a trading alliance but NATO went further. It was a military alliance with the specific aim of defending the West against communism.

The Warsaw Pact

In 1955, the USSR responded by creating the Warsaw Pact, a military alliance of Eastern European countries which mirrored NATO.

The Pact was signed by eight countries including Poland, Czechoslovakia, Hungary and Romania. First, the countries who signed the Pact agreed to respect each other's independence. Secondly, in the event of war these countries agreed to defend one another.

The arms race

The arms race was an important feature of the Cold War. It included both a continuing commitment to maintaining a large army, navy and air force, and the development of ever-more-deadly nuclear weapons. In 1945, the USA became the first country to develop and use a nuclear bomb. By 1949, the USSR had caught up – it had developed and tested its own nuclear bomb. This prompted the Americans to develop hydrogen bombs – a second generation of more powerful nuclear weapons. By 1953, both countries had hydrogen bombs, and during the 1950s and 1960s both countries competed to create large numbers of nuclear weapons.

Why was the arms race significant?

The arms race was significant because it prevented a war in Europe. The USSR had 3 million troops and could easily capture Western Germany. However, the Soviet leaders would never order an invasion because they feared an American nuclear retaliation. One atomic bomb could turn an entire city into ashes and kill hundreds of thousands of people in a few seconds. Soviet leaders had paid close attention to the American bombings of Hiroshima and Nagasaki at the end of the Second World War and understood the awesome power of the new weapons.

Did you know?

America and Russia named their nuclear bombs. Two of America's first nuclear bombs were named 'Fat Man' and 'Little Boy'. Russia named a bomb 'Layercake'.

Effects

The Berlin Blockade

The Berlin Blockade led to:

- propaganda success for the USA
- failure for the USSR
- increased fears of war in Europe.

This contributed to:

- increased tension
- the setting up of the FDR and the GDR
- the setting up of NATO, a military (not economic) alliance.

This led to:

- the setting up of the Warsaw Pact
- the arms race.

Cartoon A

Cartoon B

Activities

1 a Make a timeline starting in 1947 and ending in 1955. Read through this chapter, add the key events to the time line and highlight them.

   b Below the timeline, make bullet pointed notes on each event you have marked, explaining what happened and why it was important.

2 Cartoons A and B are from British newspapers published during the Berlin Blockade.

   Copy and complete the following sentences:

   a Cartoon A suggests that the West is helping the people in West Berlin by...

   b Cartoon B suggests that the USSR is working against the West using...

3 Cartoon B likens the Berlin Blockade to a game of chess between Stalin and President Truman. Stalin's chess pieces are labelled 'Eastern Block' and 'Berlin Blockade'. Truman's chess pieces are labelled 'Berlin Airlift' and 'Atlantic Pact' (a reference to NATO). Write a paragraph to explain how the Berlin Airlift and NATO were important factors in the struggle.

The Korean War

The causes of the Korean War

Following the Second World War, Korea had been divided between North and South. The division ran along the 38th line of latitude, known as the 38th parallel. North Korea established a communist government and became an ally of the USSR. South Korea became a democratic country and allied itself with the USA. The North Korean leader, Kim Il Sung, wanted to unite North and South Korea under communist rule. On 25 June 1950, he sent 90,000 communist troops into South Korea.

America's reaction

President Truman was alarmed by events in Korea. In 1949, China, which bordered Korea, became communist. Truman felt he had to stop communism spreading in Asia. He declared that the Truman Doctrine applied to Asia as well as Europe. He asked the UN for support. By the end of June UN troops, mainly American and led by US General McArthur, had been sent to Korea.

The outcome of the Korean War

Initially, the war went badly for the UN. By September 1950, North Korea had conquered almost all of the Korean Peninsula. However, under General MacArthur, UN troops turned the war around. By May 1950, the communist army had been forced back to the 38th parallel, and by November 1950, they were pushed back close to the Chinese border. However, at this point China entered the war forcing the UN forces to retreat. After three years of fighting, an armistice was agreed which re-established the border between North and South Korea along the 38th parallel. Although the armistice was never signed, the fighting ceased.

Korea, 1950–53.

Legend:
- Northern limit of MacArthur's advance
- Ceasefire line
- Limit of Chinese advance
- Limit of N. Korean advance

Did you know?

About 90% of the troops that went to Korea were US troops, but they fought as a UN force, even though the leader of that force was American.

Activity

Copy and complete the following table giving the steps to war in Korea.

Step	What happened
1	Korea was divided into North and South Korea after the Second World War.
2	North Korea became
3	
4	

The impact of the Korean War

The impact of the Korean War was threefold. First, it demonstrated America's commitment to containing communism anywhere in the world. Secondly, the involvement of Russia and China in the Korean War persuaded the American government to increase defence spending. Indeed, defence spending increased by almost 400% following the war. Finally, America changed the nature of Marshall Aid. Money from the programme had initially been used to support economic growth in Europe. Following the war, this money was diverted to defence spending in Western Europe. In this sense, the Korean War led to **rearmament** throughout the western world.

Source A: *When the North Korean advance was at its fullest extent (see map), General MacArthur chose to attack them from the rear, by landing an army at Inchon. This would not have been possible without the massive American naval forces he could use.*

Examination question

Study Source B and answer the question that follows. Use the source and your own knowledge to explain why there was a war in Korea from 1950–53.   **(10 marks)**

America's first response to the invasion of South Korea was to rush military supplies to South Korea. Then, on 27 June the United States proposed a resolution in the United Nations calling for military action against North Korea. The resolution was passed and three days later Truman ordered American troops into Korea.

Source B: *From a modern textbook.*

Hungary under Soviet rule: liberation and oppression

Learning objectives

In this chapter you will learn about:

- the causes of the Hungarian uprising of 1956
- the events of the Hungarian uprising
- the effects of the Hungarian uprising.

Hungary under Stalin

Stalin claimed that Soviet troops had liberated Hungary from the Nazis. However, in 1949, Cominform imposed an oppressive regime on Hungary.

- Hungarian land was redistributed to other Eastern European countries.
- Hungarian coal, oil and wheat were shipped to Russia while Hungarian citizens were deprived of food.
- Non-communist political parties were abolished.
- Russian officials controlled the government, the police and the army.
- Cominform began a reign of terror, executing popular political leaders and their supporters.
- Matyas Rakosi was appointed as Hungary's **dictator**.

Matyas Rakosi

Rakosi was Hungary's dictator from 1949 to 1956. He described himself as 'Stalin's best pupil' but the people of Hungary nicknamed him 'the bald butcher'. He developed what were known as 'salami tactics' for dealing with his opponents 'slice by slice', meaning he got rid of opposition by dividing it bit by bit. His oppressive regime imprisoned 387,000 and was responsible for more than 2,000 deaths.

De-Stalinisation

Stalin's death in 1953 was a turning point in the Cold War. Stalin's style of government, which is known as 'Stalinism', was extraordinarily oppressive. For example, it is believed that Stalin was responsible for the deaths of around 20 million people during his time in power. Russia's new leader, Nikita Khrushchev, opened the way for a more liberal approach to governing the USSR and Eastern Europe. In 1956, he gave the 'Secret Speech'. This speech, which did not remain secret for very long, promised an end to Stalinism throughout the entire Soviet sphere of influence through a policy of 'peaceful co-existence'.

Source A: *Matyas Rakosi.*

Top tip

In this section you have learned about three American presidents and two Russian leaders. The examiners will know which leaders are relevant to each question – you cannot get away with guessing. Make sure that you know who was in charge and when.

Top tip

Examiners reward detailed answers more highly than answers that are vague. Use names and dates wherever you can. For example, **don't** say *'The American President encouraged the Hungarian uprising'*; say *'In 1956 the American President, Eisenhower, encouraged the Hungarian uprising.'*

Nagy's programme of reform

Hungary's people were clearly dissatisfied with Soviet rule. Following Khrushchev's 'Secret Speech', students rioted and attacked Soviet troops with petrol bombs and grenades. It was illegal to demonstrate in Hungary but enormous demonstrations took place in Budapest, Hungary's capital. These soon became violent. The police lost control of the situation and similar protests started in Hungary's other major cities. In response, Khrushchev agreed to the appointment of a more liberal leader, Imre Nagy. Nagy proposed the following reforms.

- Hungary should leave the Warsaw Pact and become neutral.
- Communist government in Hungary should end.
- Hungary should become a Western-style democracy with free elections.
- Hungary should ask the UN for protection from Russia.

The government split over Nagy's proposed reforms. He believed that the UN and the USA would help Hungary. Others did not want to break away from the USSR. Janos Kadar, a member of the government, set up a rival, pro-USSR, government in eastern Hungary.

Khrushchev responds to Nagy

Nagy's reforms ended Hungary's alliance with the USSR. Khrushchev believed that the reforms were unacceptable and that if Hungary was allowed to leave the Warsaw Pact, other Eastern European countries would soon follow. Indeed, Khrushchev had access to secret intelligence reports which indicated that discontent with communism was widespread across Eastern Europe. These reports reinforced his view that allowing greater freedom for these discontented countries could mean the end of Soviet dominance in Eastern Europe.

Khrushchev responded with a decisive show of force. In November 1956, 200,000 Soviet troops were sent to Hungary to crush the new government. After two weeks of bitter fighting Khrushchev finally defeated Nagy's government.

- About 2,500 people were killed by Soviet troops, and about 20,000 were wounded.
- Almost 200,000 Hungarians fled to the West.

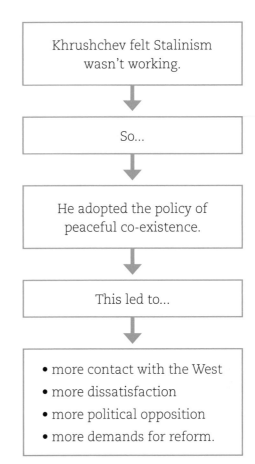

Effects of Khrushchev's policy of peaceful-co-existence.

Activities

Answer the following questions in full sentences:

1 Who was Rakosi?
2 Why were Hungarians dissatisfied with life under Rakosi?
3 Describe Rakosi's relationship with Stalin.
4 What was Stalinism?
5 Who was Khrushchev and what did he promise in his 'Secret Speech'?
6 How did the Hungarian students respond to the 'Secret Speech'?
7 What did the Hungarian students demand and how did Khrushchev respond?
8 How did Nagy propose to reform Hungary?
9 How and why did Khrushchev stop these reforms?

- About 650 Soviet troops were killed and about 1,250 were wounded.

The trouble rumbled on into 1957, with strikes in various parts of the country and outbreaks of fighting. But the revolution was really ended in November.

Nagy's trial and execution

Nagy sought protection in the Yugoslavian embassy. The Yugoslavian ambassador agreed with Khrushchev that Nagy was free to leave Hungary. However, as soon as Nagy left the embassy, he was arrested by Soviet troops. Nagy was accused of treason and, in a trial overseen by Khrushchev, was found guilty. He was hanged in June 1958. Following his execution, Khrushchev stated that Nagy's fate was 'a lesson to the leaders of all socialist countries'.

The international reaction

America had encouraged the Hungarian uprising but had stopped short of offering military help. Indeed, the American government believed it was 'a matter of highest priority to prevent the outbreak of a war', which would lead to the nuclear annihilation of Hungary and the rest of the world. Nonetheless, America did offer $20 million worth of food and medical aid to the Nagy government, and the American President, Dwight D. Eisenhower (1953–61), praised the bravery of the Hungarian people and encouraged them to fight on. Similarly, the UN officially condemned the Soviet invasion, but did nothing more. Spain, the Netherlands and Sweden boycotted the 1956 Olympics in protest at the Soviet invasion. Thousands of people, in many different European countries, resigned their membership of the communist party.

America's failure to support the Hungarians proved that its commitment to liberating Europe from communism did not include offering military support. Consequently, radicals in Eastern Europe were discouraged from following Hungary's example.

Activity

It is November 1956. Kadar has been in power for one month. The people below are reflecting on how the events in Hungary have affected them and changed the balance of power in the Cold War. Complete their thought bubbles to show what they are thinking.

Eisenhower   Khrushchev   Kadar   a Hungarian revolutionary

Reasserting Soviet control

Following the Soviet invasion, Khrushchev appointed Janos Kadar as the new Hungarian leader. Initially, Kadar had no real power as Hungary was under the control of the Soviet army. Nonetheless, Kadar published his Fifteen-Point Programme setting out the new government's direction. Kadar's programme included:

- re-establishing communist control of Hungary
- using Hungarian troops to stop attacks on Soviet forces
- remaining in the Warsaw Pact
- negotiating the withdrawal of Soviet troops once the crisis was over.

The Hungarian people soon accepted Kadar's new government. They really had no choice.

Activities

1   Copy and complete the following sentences:

   a   Khrushchev agreed to let Nagy leave Hungary because....

   b   Khrushchev then had Nagy arrested, tried, found guilty of treason and executed because....

   c   The USA had helped Nagy by...

   d   One effect of US failure to send Nagy armed help was...

2   Using your notes and the textbook, make a timeline of the changing relationship between Russia and America in the period 1945-56.

3   Select three events that you feel led to a change in the relationship between Russia and America and highlight them. Write a short paragraph explaining how each of these events changed the relationship.

Build Better Answers

Study these events that occurred in the years 1945–62.
The Berlin Blockade, the Potsdam Conference, the Hungarian Uprising, the Truman Doctrine, the Yalta Conference.
Write these events in the correct chronological sequence.

(3 marks)

Paper 1 part (a) questions expect you to put a sequence of events in the correct chronological order.

■   **A basic answer (level 1)** will list the events with two in the correct sequence.

●   **A better answer (level 2)** will list the events with three in the correct sequence.

▲   **An excellent answer (worth 3 marks)** will list the events with four or five in the correct sequence.

Here are three sample answers. Read them an award them a mark using the exam guidance sequence.

Answer 1
The Yalta Conference, the Potsdam Conference, the Berlin Blockade, the Truman Doctrine, the Hungarian Uprising.

Answer 2
The Potsdam Conference, the Yalta Conference, the Truman Doctrine, the Berlin Blockade, the Hungarian Uprising.

Answer 3
The Yalta Conference, the Potsdam Conference, the Truman Doctrine, the Berlin Blockade, the Hungarian Uprising.

The Berlin Crisis: a divided city

Learning objectives

In this chapter you will learn about:

● the refugee crisis facing the East German government

● Khrushchev's response to the crisis

● the Khrushchev and Kennedy summit meetings.

 Watch out!

The Berlin Crisis can be very confusing if you forget Germany's geography. During the Cold War, West Berlin was in East Germany (see insert on map).

Following the Second World War, the Allies had been unable to agree on how to govern Germany. It was divided into four zones, one controlled by each power. These zones became two countries, West Germany (British, American and French zones) and East Germany (Soviet). The city of Berlin caused problems. As Germany had been divided into four zones, so Berlin was divided into four zones, one controlled by each power. The problem was that Berlin was not on the border between East and West Germany; it was right in the middle of East Germany.

Refugee problems

The East German government was extremely unpopular, so many East Germans fled to West Germany. West Germany was highly attractive because its citizens enjoyed greater freedom and wealth than those of East Germany. Indeed, between 1949 and 1961, 2.7 million East German **refugees**, many of whom were highly skilled, escaped to West Germany. Berlin was the centre of East Germany's refugee problem because it was easy for East Germans to cross from East to West Berlin, and from there to West Germany.

Khrushchev's challenge

In response to the refugee crisis, Khrushchev declared that the whole of the city of Berlin officially belonged to East Germany and demanded that the USA withdraw its troops. US president Eisenhower was unsure how to respond. He did not want to lose West Berlin, nor did he want to start another war. Consequently, it was agreed to hold an international meeting in order to discuss Berlin's future.

Two summits

Khrushchev and Eisenhower met in Geneva in the summer of 1959 but were unable to agree a solution to the problem. They did, however, agree to keep talking and met for a second summit at Camp David, Eisenhower's presidential retreat, later that year. The Camp David meeting also failed to agree a future for Berlin.

East Germany's economic recovery after the war was far slower than West Germany's. Shops were drab and it was difficult to buy consumer goods. Jobs were hard to come by because industry was struggling to get going again.

Source A: *From a modern textbook.*

Activities

1 a Draw a timeline of the key events mentioned in this section.

   b Under it, copy the name of each event; explain what happened and how it changed the relationship between the USA and USSR.

2 Copy and complete the following sentences:

   a Refugees wanted to cross from the East to the West because...

   b This was a problem because...

   c Summit talks between the USA and ther USSR failed because...

   d The U2 incident increased Cold War tensions because...

3 Use Source A and your own knowledge to write an extended answer explaining why East Germany had problems with people leaving in the 1950s.

The U2 incident

Since 1956, the American air force had sent U2 spy planes into Russian airspace to gather information about the Soviet military. The Soviets condemned this, but could do nothing to stop it because the USA consistently denied the flights were happening. Finally, in May 1960, the Russians shot down a U2 plane and captured its pilot.

Khrushchev used this incident to expose America's spying programme. Eisenhower claimed the plane was merely studying the weather, but Khrushchev played his trump card, producing the US pilot Gary Powers, who confessed that he was spying.

Two more summits

Against this background, the 1960 Paris Conference looked doomed to fail. Khrushchev was enraged by America's spying and demanded that Eisenhower punish the leaders of the U2 programme. Eisenhower refused, and Khrushchev walked out of the conference on the first day. Finally, at the Geneva Conference of 1961, Khrushchev challenged the new American president, John F. Kennedy, to withdraw American troops from Berlin within six months or to declare war. Kennedy refused to remove American troops from German soil. He also started preparing America for war, committing the US government to an additional $3.2 billion of defence spending. More worrying still was Kennedy's decision to spend an extra $207 million on building nuclear fallout shelters.

The main map shows how Berlin was divided into American, Soviet, British and French zones. The insert map shows how Germany was divided and the location of Berlin within Germany.

The Berlin Crisis: the Berlin Wall

Learning objectives

In this chapter you will learn about:

● the reasons for the construction of the Berlin Wall

● the impact of the Berlin Wall on East–West relations and Germany.

Building the wall

Khrushchev knew that the USSR could not win a nuclear war. In 1961, America had almost 20 times more nuclear weapons than the USSR. What is more, American nuclear weapons were able to reach the USSR, whereas Soviet weapons could not reach America. Kennedy's refusal to retreat called Khrushchev's bluff, forcing the Russian leader to back down.

Khrushchev could not force the Americans to leave West Berlin but he still had to solve the refugee problem. His solution was to build a wall separating East and West Berlin, making it impossible for East Germans to escape to the West.

On the night of 12 August 1961, East German troops secretly erected a barbed wire fence around the whole of West Berlin. The next morning, Berliners awoke to a divided city. In the coming months the fence was reinforced and eventually became a heavily guarded wall. Kennedy commented 'it's not a very nice solution, but a wall is a hell of a lot better than a war'.

The impact of the Berlin Wall

The Berlin Wall was significant for the following reasons:

● it stopped East Germans escaping to the West and therefore ended the refugee crisis

● it allowed Khrushchev to avoid war with America while still appearing strong

● it became a powerful symbol of the division of Germany and the division of Europe.

Did you know?

There were numerous attempts to cross the Berlin Wall, many of which ended in tragedy. Peter Fechter, for example, planned to cross the wall to West Germany in 1962. He jumped from a window into the 'death strip' between the East and West sides of the wall. However, during his attempt to climb into West Berlin, he was shot. He fell back into the 'death strip', where he lay screaming for help for almost an hour while he bled to death. Guards on the Western side of the wall were unable to help him as they knew this would trigger further violence from guards on the East.

Source A: *The building of the Berlin Wall.*

Kennedy's visit to Berlin

Kennedy was unable to prevent the wall's construction. However, in 1963 he toured West Berlin expressing his feelings of solidarity with its people. Crowds of West Germans lined the streets shouting 'Kenne-dy – Kenne-dy!' In a famous speech, Kennedy said 'All free men, wherever they live, are citizens of Berlin and therefore as a free man, I take pride in the words *Ich bin ein Berliner*'.

Source B: *Kennedy making a speech during his visit to Berlin, 1963.*

Unit 2 A World Divided: Superpower relations, 1945–62

Examination question

Why did the USSR build the Berlin Wall in 1961? Explain your answer.　**(8 marks)**

Activities

1 Copy and cut out the cards on the right.

2 Group the cards into those that describe causes of the building of the Berlin Wall, and those that describe consequences of the building of the Berlin Wall.

3 For each group, decide which cause/consequence was the most important and write a sentence explaining why.

The USSR realised it could not win a nuclear war.	The East German economy lost skilled labourers.	The problem of the division of Berlin was solved.
Refugees were unable to leave East Germany.	Many people from East Germany escaped to West Germany.	Khrushchev avoided war with America.
The East German government was unpopular.	Kennedy refused to back down.	Peter Fechter was killed.
An important symbol of the Cold War was created.	Kennedy showed solidarity with the people of West Berlin.	Kennedy increased the USA's defence budget.

The Cuban Missile Crisis: origins

Learning objectives

In this chapter you will learn about:

- the arms race and the USSR's reasons for stationing missiles on Cuba
- Fidel Castro's relationship with the USA and the USSR.

The arms race

America was the clear winner of the arms race in the 1940s and 1950s. America had an early lead and was the first country to develop an atomic bomb. By 1961, America had almost 20 times as many nuclear missiles as the USSR. What is more, America had specially equipped B52 bombers that were capable of dropping nuclear weapons on the Soviet Union.

The USSR had relatively few missiles and no way of dropping them on American soil. Nonetheless, the US government was extremely worried about the Soviet Union's nuclear capabilities. In 1957, Russian scientists launched Sputnik 1 – the world's first man-made satellite. By 1960, the Russians had even landed a robotic spacecraft on the moon. Khrushchev boasted that the Americans were 'sleeping under a red moon'. This demonstrated the sophistication of Soviet technology, and many Americans believed that the rockets used to put satellites in space could be used to launch nuclear missiles at America.

However, the USSR was simply not wealthy enough to mass-produce missiles and Khrushchev's claim that the USSR was 'producing missiles like we are producing sausages' was an empty boast.

Did you know?

Communism is associated with the colour red. One symbol of communism is the red star and the flag of the Soviet Union was red. Throughout the Cold War period Americans often referred to communists as 'reds'.

Build Better Answers

Explain one **effect on the relations between the USA and the Soviet Union of the arms race.** **(4 marks)**

Paper 1 part (b) questions will ask about the effect of one event on another.

■ **A basic answer (level 1)** will give a consequence, or effect, but no supporting detail. For example, *It worsened the relationship between the USA and the USSR*.

● **A good answer (level 2)** will make a statement giving a consequence and then develop this statement by giving extra detail or explanation. For example, *The arms race made the relationship between the USA and Russia less stable especially when Khrushchev chose to station missiles on Cuba in order to compete with America's nuclear capabilities.*

Causes

The arms race

The USA and the USSR had an arms race because:

- the USSR wanted to catch up with the USA
- neither side trusted the other
- both feared war was about to break out
- each wanted military superiority.

These things became both causes **and** effects as they spiralled out of control, linked together and setting each other off.

Did you know?

The largest nuclear bomb ever tested was detonated in 1961. The Russian *Tsar Bomba* was eight metres long and weighed 27 tons. The bomb was over 100 times more powerful than the American weapons detonated in Japan at the end of the Second World War. When it was tested, it created a fireball 8 kilometres (5 miles) in diameter.

Source A: *The Tsar Bomba.*

Activities

1 Copy the table below.

2 Use the information in 'The arms race' section of this chapter to complete the second column of the table, explaining why America was in a stronger position than it thought.

America is worried that…	But the real situation is that…
… Sputnik 1 proves that the USSR has very powerful missiles.	
… the USSR can land a spaceship on the moon, therefore it could put nuclear missiles in space.	
… Khrushchev has said that the USSR is producing missiles as fast as it is producing sausages.	

The Cuban Revolution

Cuba had traditionally been an ally of the USA. American presidents believed that Cuba's friendship was important because it was only 145 kilometres (90 miles) away and therefore part of the American sphere of influence.

The Cuban Revolution of 1959 overthrew Cuba's pro-American government. The new revolutionary regime, led by Fidel Castro, wanted greater independence from the United States. As part of this policy, Castro's new communist government took over American property located in Cuba. In response, America banned the import of Cuban sugar. This threatened to bankrupt the Cuban economy.

Cuba turned to the USSR for help. Khrushchev was delighted to have an ally deep in America's sphere of influence. Consequently, he agreed to offer economic aid to Cuba in order to help his new ally industrialise.

The Bay of Pigs incident

President Eisenhower had believed that the best way to solve the Cuban problem was for the Central Intelligence Agency **(CIA)** to assassinate Castro. President Kennedy, who took over from Eisenhower in 1960, hatched a new plan for a CIA-backed revolution to overthrow Cuba's communist government and replace it with a capitalist government sympathetic to America.

Kennedy believed that Castro's government was very unpopular and therefore he assumed that when his small, well-trained force attacked the government, the Cuban people would join the revolution and overthrow Castro. Kennedy instructed the CIA to train and equip a group of Cuban refugees. They invaded the Bay of Pigs in April 1961, but Kennedy had miscalculated: the people of Cuba fought bravely in support of Castro's government. The American-backed force was defeated within two days.

Effects

The Bay of Pigs

The Bay of Pigs invasion led to:

- failure on the part of USA-backed rebels
- success for Castro's government
- propaganda failure for the USA – they could no longer suggest that the people of Cuba did not support Castro
- fear of another US invasion.

This led to:

- Castro asking for help from the USSR
- a plan to put Russian missiles on Cuban soil.

This led to:

- The Cuban Missile Crisis.

Source B: *Fidel Castro and Nikita Khrushchev in Red Square, Moscow, May 1964.*

Map showing Cuba in relation to the USA.

On the map: CANADA; Seattle; San Francisco; Las Vegas; Los Angeles; UNITED STATES OF AMERICA; Chicago; New York; Washington DC; Atlanta; Dallas; New Orleans; Miami; PACIFIC OCEAN; ATLANTIC OCEAN; Range of short range missiles (1,000) miles; Range of long range missiles (2,000) miles; MEXICO; Gulf of Mexico; Havana; CUBA; Caribbean Sea

Missile bases

In spite of his victory, Castro felt vulnerable and feared another American attack. He therefore asked Khrushchev to help him defend Cuba. In August 1961, Khrushchev devised a plan that would solve the problems of both Cuba and Russia. He decided to station Russian nuclear weapons on Cuban soil. This would deter America from attempting another invasion. It would also place Russian nuclear missiles within striking range of America. This meant that Khrushchev could attack America without spending large amounts of money developing inter-continental ballistic missiles.

Activities

1   Copy each statement below.

 a Say whether it is true or false.

 b Find as many facts as you can from the text to support the statement, or to prove it is false.

 ● The USA was the clear winner of the arms race in the 1940s and 50s.

 ● America was worried about Soviet rocket technology in the late 1950s.

 ● America welcomed Castro's new Cuban government in 1959.

 ● Castro was pro-American.

 ● Castro was pro-Soviet.

 ● The Bay of Pigs invasion was a success for the USA.

 ● The plan to place Soviet missiles on Cuba was just to keep Cuba safe from another invasion.

2   Draw a diagram like the one on page 87 to show the effects of the Cuban Revolution up to the end of 1961.

The Cuban Missile Crisis: the 'Thirteen Days'

Learning objectives

In this chapter you will learn about:
- how America learned of Khrushchev's plan
- the 'hawks and the doves'
- the events of the 'Thirteen Days'.

Top Tip

When answering a question about *why* an event such as the Cuban Missile Crisis occurred, you should avoid telling the story of what happened. The examiner wants you to explain the causes rather than describe the event.

The Thirteen Days

The 'Thirteen Days' was the period at the height of the Cuban Missile Crisis during which there seemed to be the greatest threat of nuclear war.

The events of the 'Thirteen Days':

16 Oct	Kennedy is informed of Khrushchev's plans to place nuclear missiles on Cuba.
20 Oct	Kennedy decides to impose a naval blockade around Cuba to prevent further missiles reaching Cuba.
22 Oct	Kennedy gives a public address officially declaring the blockade and calling on Khrushchev to recall his ships.
23 Oct	Khrushchev sends a letter to Kennedy stating that Soviet ships will break through the blockade.
24 Oct	Khrushchev issues a statement that the USSR is prepared to launch nuclear weapons if America goes to war.
25 Oct	American and Soviet armed forces are on the highest level of alert – they are told to prepare for war. Kennedy writes to Khrushchev asking him to withdraw missiles from Cuba.
26 Oct	Khrushchev responds to Kennedy's letter, saying that he will withdraw Soviet missiles in return for a guarantee that the USA will not invade Cuba.
27 Oct	Khrushchev receives intelligence that the USA is planning to invade Cuba in 24 hours. He proposes a deal: the USSR will withdraw missiles from Cuba if the USA will agree never to invade Cuba and withdraw its nuclear missiles from Turkey. An American spy plane is shot down over Cuba. American 'hawks' demand retaliation. Robert Kennedy (Kennedy's brother and chief advisor) approaches the Russian ambassador accepting Khrushchev's deal but demands that the withdrawal of American missiles from Turkey is kept secret.
28 Oct	Khrushchev accepts this secret deal.

Khrushchev's plan is revealed

On 25 September 1962, Khrushchev sent 114 Soviet ships to Cuba. The ships carried a secret cargo, including nuclear warheads and long-range missiles, that would be used to construct nuclear bases on Cuba. For a long time, Khrushchev's plan remained secret. But by mid-October American spy planes had discovered what was going on. On 22 October Kennedy addressed the American people and told them of the Soviet plans to build nuclear missile bases on their doorstep.

Source A: *Images taken by US spy planes of nuclear missile bases being built in Cuba. The images were released in 1962.*

Kennedy's news shocked the world. Many Americans panicked and started building nuclear shelters in preparation for nuclear war.

'Hawks and doves'

During the crisis, Kennedy and Khrushchev's advisors were split into two groups: hawks and doves. The 'hawks' on both sides wanted an aggressive policy. Some American generals, for example, believed that a nuclear war between the USA and the USSR was inevitable and therefore Kennedy should go to war because, as things stood, America had a good chance of winning. The 'doves', on the other hand, advised caution, recommending diplomatic strategies, which they felt offered the best chance of peace.

Activities

1 Copy and complete the table below, explaining how the statements apply to the USA, the USSR or both.

	USA	USSR	Both
Ways in which the outcome of the Cuban Missile Crisis was a success			
Ways in which the outcome of the Cuban Missile Crisis was a failure			

2 Copy and complete the following sentence. I think the most serious crisis point of the Thirteen Days was … because…

3 Write a paragraph that explains who gained most from the Cuban Missile Crisis. Make sure that you back up your point with detailed examples.

The Cuban Missile Crisis: immediate and long-term consequences

The immediate consequences of the Cuban Missile Crisis

The first consequence of the Cuban Missile Crisis was the reduction in Khrushchev's authority. Because the removal of American missiles from Turkey remained secret, it seemed to many that he had backed down and betrayed his allies in Cuba.

The Cuban Missile Crisis had highlighted the fragility of international peace and the difficulties of negotiation between Russia and America in a crisis situation. As a result, the superpowers agreed to the introduction of the following measures:

- the 'hotline' – in June 1963, a direct communications link was set up between the American President in Washington and the Russian Premier in Moscow
- the Limited Test Ban Treaty – in August 1963, the USA and USSR agreed to ban the testing of all nuclear weapons in space, in the sea and above ground. Underground nuclear tests were still permitted.

President Kennedy signalled his commitment to working with the USSR in a speech of June 1963, in which he argued that both superpowers needed to focus on their 'common interests'. This speech was the beginning of a policy called 'détente': a relaxing of tension in the relationship between the USA and the USSR. Initially, moves to détente were slow but détente became a key feature of superpower relations during the 1970s.

OPERATION RENDEZVOUS

" *Right a bit, Nikita.*"   " *Left a bit, Jack.*"

Source A: *A 1962 cartoon, commenting on the early talks about disarmament.*

The long-term consequences of the Cuban Missile Crisis

The leaders of the Soviet Union were determined never again to be pushed around by America. Therefore, the Soviet government made every effort to catch up with America in the arms race. By 1965, the USA and the USSR were on an equal footing in terms of their nuclear capability. This created greater stability in the relationship between the two superpowers. American and Russian leaders realised that any nuclear war was bound to destroy both countries. This idea, known as the doctrine of Mutually Assured Destruction (MAD), gave both superpowers an excellent reason for avoiding war.

Another long-term consequence of the Cuban Missile Crisis was the French decision to leave NATO. In the event of a nuclear war between America and Russia, the members of NATO would be obliged to fight alongside America. French President Charles de Gaulle was appalled at the thought that France would be destroyed in this way. Therefore, in 1966, France ended its military alliance with America and began to develop its own nuclear missiles.

Did you know?

The 'hotline' between the American President and the Soviet Premier is sometimes known as the 'red telephone'. Despite this, it was originally a teleprinter system. It was first used in 1967, and in 1971 it was upgraded and became an actual telephone. It is still used today, and is tested every hour of every day.

Build Better Answers

Source: *From a modern textbook.*

> After the Cuban Missile Crisis, Kennedy worked with Khrushchev to set up a hot line. This would allow the Kremlin and the White House to be in direct contact. The aim of the hotline was to ensure that the two leaders could discuss their differences and therefore avoid war.

Use the source, and your own knowledge, to explain the effects of the Cuban Missile Crisis of 1962.
(10 marks)

The number of statements that you make will affect your mark. In this question, answers that only give one consequence of the Cuban Missile Crisis will not get more than 7 marks. Answers that discuss two or more consequences can achieve up to 10 marks.

■ **A basic answer (level 1)** will make simple generalisations with little support from own knowledge. For example, ... *both sides wanted to avoid getting that close to war again.*

● **A good answer (level 3)** will explain one example, with detail from their own knowledge and the source. For example, *They set up the hotline to get in touch quickly. During the Cuba crisis, they had had to use letters, telegrams or messages through other people and they wanted a more immediate, more rapid, way to get in contact. This way, they hoped to be able to negotiate sooner and not get so close to nuclear disaster.*

▲ **An excellent answer (level 4)** will give more than one supported example and show how they are linked. If possible show how the reasons combined to produce the outcome. **At least two examples must be used.**

Activity

Copy this spider diagram.

a Add any things you think are missing.   **b** Below it, make notes on each of the words or phrases.

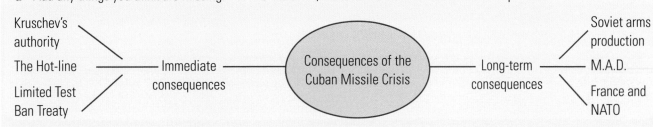

In the Paper 1 final examination you will have to answer questions on the two different options you have studied. You will have to answer four questions. Question (a) is on chronology, (b) asks you to explain effects, (c) asks about causation and (d) is an essay using a source and own knowledge.

You have about 45 minutes to answer the four sub-questions on each theme (the exam is one hour 30 minutes in total), so the examiners are not expecting you to write huge amounts. The number of marks helps you to judge how much to write. For Question (a) allow 5 minutes, Question (b) 8 minutes, Question (c) 12 minutes and Question (d) 15 minutes, with 5 minutes to read over your answers.

Build Better Answers

Question (a)

Examiner's tip: Part (a) questions will ask you to place a series of events in the correct chronological order. This is only worth 3 marks so allow about 5 minutes for this question.

Let's look at an example.

Study these events, which occurred in the years 1945–60.
Write these events in the correct chronological sequence.   **(3 marks)**

the U2 incident	the Hungarian Uprising	the Potsdam Conference	the Marshall Plan	the Korean War

- As part of your revision, ensure you make a timeline of your own showing the key events in superpower relations in the years 1945–62. This will not only help you with Question (a) but with the other three questions in this section. It will ensure that you put events in the correct sequence or order.

- Cut out the events and dates separately and test yourself by matching the dates to the events and putting them in chronological order. Here is an example:

1945	The Yalta Conference The Potsdam Conference	1947	The Truman Doctrine The Marshall Plan
1946	Churchill's 'Iron Curtain' speech	1948	Bizonia The start of the Berlin Blockade

Student answer	**Examiner comments**
The Potsdam Conference, the Marshall Plan, the U2 incident, the Hungarian Uprising, the Korean War.	This would be awarded 1 mark as the candidate has the first two in the correct sequence, the Potsdam Conference and the Marshall Plan.

Let's rewrite the answer with all the events in the right sequence.

The Potsdam Conference, the Marshall Plan, the Korean War, the Hungarian Uprising, the U2 incident.	The candidate has all five events in the right chronological order and would be awarded full (3) marks.

Build Better Answers

Question (b)

Examiner tip: Question (b) will pick two of the five events from question (a). It will ask you to choose one of these events and use your knowledge to explain its effects. This is only worth 4 marks, so allow about 7 minutes for this question. An effect means the results or the consequences of an event – in other words, what the event led to. For example, one effect of the U2 incident was that Khrushchev walked out of the Paris Summit Conference. One effect of the Potsdam Conference was that Germany was divided into four zones.

Let's look at an example.

Choose **either** | The U2 incident | **or** | The Potsdam Conference |

Explain one effect on relations between the USA and the Soviet Union of the event you have chosen. **(4 marks)**

- Choose **one** of the events and stick with your choice. Some candidates, half way through writing their answer on the first event, decide to write about the other event. This wastes valuable time.
- Focus on the question. It is about one effect, so begin your answer with *One effect was…*. Do not just tell the story.
- Give the effect and explain it. Using the word because helps you to give a developed description.
- One paragraph is enough because it is only worth 4 marks.

Student answer	**Examiner comments**
A U2 American spy plane was brought down over the USSR by a Soviet missile. The pilot, Gary Powers, was captured by the Russians. Films and tapes were recovered from the plane.	This student tells the story rather than focusing on one effect and describing it. This would be marked in Level 1.

Let's rewrite the answer and focus on one effect.

| **One effect** of the U2 incident was to worsen relations between the UA and the Soviet Union. This was <u>because</u> Khrushchev demanded an apology from Eisenhower, the American President, for allowing the U2 plane to fly over and to spy on the USSR. <u>As a result</u> of Eisenhower's refusal to apologise, Khrushchev walked out at the start of the Paris Summit Conference. <u>Therefore</u> the Summit Conference, which was to discuss Berlin and international disarmament, was abandoned. | The student immediately focuses on the question by giving the effect. There is a developed explanation of the effect using links words and phrases such as 'because' and 'as a result'. This would be marked in Level 2. |

Build Better Answers

Question (c)

Examiner tip: Part (c) questions will ask you to use your knowledge to explain why something happened. In other words, this is a question about causation. Causation means explaining the reasons why an event happened. In the example given below, you are being asked to explain reasons why there was a crisis over missiles in Cuba in 1962. You will always need to explain at least two reasons and these reasons should be linked. It is worth 8 marks, so allow about 12 minutes for this question.

Let's look at an example.

Why was there a crisis over missiles in Cuba in 1962? Explain your answer. **(8 marks)**

There are several reasons that you could write about for this question. These include:

- Castro removes American influence from Cuba
- Closer relations between Cuba and the Soviet Union
- Khrushchev's decision to place missiles on Cuba
- The US discovery of Soviet missile bases on Cuba and Kennedy's actions.

Remember to:

- Focus on the question. It is about causation, so ensure you write about the reasons why something happened. Do not just tell the story.
- Write a separate paragraph for each reason. At the beginning of each paragraph give the reason and then fully explain it. Using the word '*because*' helps you to give a developed explanation.
- Two paragraphs or explained reasons are enough to achieve the top level.
- For the highest marks you also have to make links between each reason, and if possible show how the reasons combined to produce the outcome. This means explaining how one reason led to the next. For example, a paragraph on Khrushchev's decision to place missiles on Cuba could be linked to the US discovery of these bases. For example, *The Soviet decision to place missile bases on Cuba meant that the Soviet threat to the USA was now on an island very close to the American mainland. Moreover, this threat became real when, on 14 October 1962, an American U2 spy plane flew over Cuba and took detailed photographs of the Soviet missile sites in Cuba.*

You would then write a paragraph giving an explanation about the US discovery of the bases.

Link words or phrases often help to achieve this. Here are some examples: *this led to, as a result, moreover, furthermore, as a consequence, in addition.*

- Write a conclusion confirming how the two factors combined to produce the outcome.

Here is a grid to help you plan your answer to this question.

First reason	Give the reason. Fully explain it.
Link	Make a link with the second reason.
Second reason	Give the reason. Fully explain it.
Conclusion	Sum up the two reasons stressing the links between them.

Build Better Answers

Student answer

Relations between Cuba and the Soviet Union grew closer. Castro agreed that the Soviet Union could build missile bases on Cuba. This would stop the USA from invading Cuba and would place Soviet missiles close to the USA. An American spy plane flew over Cuba and took photographs of these sites. President Kennedy now decided to take action and to blockade Cuba.

Examiner comments

The candidate knows the reasons. For example, mentions the Soviet decision to build missile bases on Cuba and gives some supporting detail. The discovery of the bases and USA reaction are mentioned, but there is little supporting detail. In addition, there is no attempt to show links between the two reasons. This would be marked in Level 2.

Let's rewrite the answer with the details added and links shown between the reasons.

The first reason for the Cuban Missiles Crisis was the closer relations between Cuba and the Soviet Union. Castro feared a second US invasion, following the Bay of Pigs in 1959, and agreed to allow the Soviet Union to build missile sites on Cuba. This would deter an American invasion and, at the same time, meant that Khrushchev could attack America without having to spend large sums of money developing inter-continental ballistic missiles. The Soviet decision to place missile bases on Cuba meant that the Soviet threat to the USA was now on an island very close to the American mainland.

Moreover, this threat was confirmed when, on 14 October 1962, an American U2 spy plane flew over Cuba and took detailed photographs of the Soviet missile sites in Cuba. More reconnaissance followed over the next two days which confirmed that some sites were nearly finished while others were being built. American planes also reported that 20 Soviet ships were currently on the way to Cuba, carrying missiles. As a result of these discoveries, four days later, 20 October 1962, Kennedy decided to impose a blockade around Cuba to prevent missiles reaching Cuba. This was the beginning of a 13-day crisis. The Cuban Missiles Crisis was due to the Soviet decision to build missile sites on Cuba. When this was confirmed by US spy planes, Kennedy had no choice but to take action to remove this threat.

Now we have two clearly explained reasons. Notice how the candidate immediately focuses on the question at the start of the first paragraph. Furthermore, the answer makes links between the first factor, the Soviet decision to build the missiles, and the second factor, the reaction of the USA. This link is reinforced by the conclusion which explains how the factors combined to cause a crisis over missiles in Cuba in 1962. In addition, the answer gives supporting details for the second reason, the US reaction.

Build Better Answers

Question (d)

Examiner tip: Part (d) questions will ask you to use a source and your knowledge to describe or explain cause, effect or change. It is worth 10 marks, so allow about 15 minutes for this question. If the question is about change, you must show change either by comparing the situation before and after the development, or you must show how it developed during the period. Let's look at an example.

Study the source and then answer the question that follows.

Source A: *From a modern textbook.*

> The Berlin Blockade was a <u>propaganda success</u> for the Americans and a <u>failure</u> for the Soviet Union. In May 1949, Stalin <u>called off</u> the blockade. In September 1949, <u>West Germany</u> was officially created as an independent state, followed one month later by <u>East Germany</u>. In addition, the USA set up the <u>North Atlantic Treaty Organisation</u>.

Use the source and your own knowledge to explain the changes to relations between the USA and the Soviet Union brought about by the Berlin Blockade of 1948–49. **(10 marks)**

- It is also asking you to use your own knowledge. Use the source to stimulate your own knowledge by underlining key names, events or dates in the source. This is shown in Source A where the candidate has underlined <u>propaganda success</u>, <u>called off</u>, <u>West Germany</u>, <u>East Germany</u> and <u>NATO</u>. Once you explain these in more detail, you are using your own knowledge.

- Focus on the question. It is about change, so ensure you write about changes. Do not just tell the story.

- At the beginning of each paragraph, give the change and then fully explain it. Using the word 'because' helps you to give a developed explanation.

- Two paragraphs or explainations are enough to achieve the top level.

- For the highest marks you also have to make links between each factor. This means explaining how one change led to the next. Link words or phrases help to achieve this. Here are some examples: *this led to, as a result, moreover, furthermore, as a consequence, in addition.*

- Write a conclusion confirming how the two factors combined to produce the outcome.

Here is a grid to help you plan your answer to this question.

The source	Underline or highlight key words, events, people in the source that you can write more about.
First factor	Give the first factor mentioned in the source. Fully explain it.
Link	Make a link with a second factor mentioned in the source.
Second factor	Fully explain the second factor.
Conclusion	Sum up the two factors stressing the links between them.

Student answer

The Berlin Blockade was a propaganda success for the USA but a failure for the Soviet Union when Stalin had to call off the blockade. After the Berlin Crisis, West Germany was set up and East Germany not long after that. In the same year the USA set up the North Atlantic Treaty Organisation (NATO) in order to stop further Soviet expansion.

Examiner comments

This answer summarise or paraphrases the source. There is little own knowledge except a hint of support about NATO. It would be awarded Level 1.

Let's look at an answer where the student has used some of his or her own knowledge.

The British and Americans turned the Berlin Blockade into a propaganda success by airlifting supplies into West Berlin with an average of 1000 tonnes per week. The airlift prevented the blockade from succeeding. It showed that the West, especially Truman, were prepared to act in a peaceful way. This was a contrast to Stalin, who was seen as a bully because of his original decision to set up the blockade of West Berlin.

This time the student has used own knowledge but made no direct reference to the source or to the idea of change. In addition, the answer only explains one factor, US propaganda, and cannot show links to a second factor. This would be awarded a Level 2 mark.

Let's re-write the answer to include the sources and own knowledge and two linked factors focused on change.

The Berlin Blockade **changed** relations between the US and the Soviet Union by making them worse. **As the source suggests**, the blockade was a propaganda success for the USA but a failure for Stalin and the Soviet Union. The British and American airlift of supplies into West Berlin (an average of 1000 tonnes a week) prevented the blockade from succeeding. It showed the West, especially Truman, in a good light. In contrast, Stalin was seen as a bully because of his decision to set up the blockade. Moreover, **as suggested in the source, as a result of** the threat to Berlin caused by the blockade, the Superpowers to made further **changes** to Germany, dividing it into two nations. In May 1949, the British, French and American zones became the Federal Republic of Germany, or West Germany. The communist eastern zone was formed into the German Democratic Republic or East Germany in October 1949. Furthermore, **as mentioned in the source**, to strengthen their position in West Germany, the US set up the North Atlantic Treaty Organisation. NATO was set up in April 1949 as an alliance between the USA and countries in Europe in which NATO members agreed to help any member that was attacked. This **changed** superpower relations because it committed the USA to the <u>military</u> defence of Western Europe and worsened relations with Stalin, who believed that NATO was aimed against the Soviet Union. Six years later, the Soviet Union set up its own military alliance, the Warsaw Pact. Overall, there was much **change** in relations between the superpowers as a result of the Berlin Blockade. It worsened relations between the USA and the USSR who strengthened their hold over West and East Germany. The USA committed itself to the military defence of Western Europe.

This candidate has used the source and own knowledge and explained two changes and has ensured that the answer focuses on change. Furthermore, the answer links the first change to the second as well as showing how these combined to produce the outcome in the conclusion.

The period between the end of the Second World War and 1974 was a time of division and protest in the USA. A significant number of people were divided by their age, their sex, their race and their politics. At the start of the period, many people in the USA feared a communist takeover of Europe, the USA and the world. The USA was swept up in a 'Red Scare' which resulted in the persecution of Americans who were thought to be communist. As the period passed, more and more groups protested to change the way American society worked. Black people wanted the civil rights that they were legally entitled to, but seldom allowed to exercise. Young people thought their parents' ideas were out of date. Women wanted more equality than they had. Many people across the various divides wanted America out of the war in Vietnam. The period ended with a political scandal – Watergate. President Nixon was found to have acted illegally during his re-election campaign, then lied and tried to cover up what his staff had done.

In this section you will study:

⊙ McCarthyism and the Red Scare
⊙ Civil Rights in the 1950s
⊙ the impact of Martin Luther King and Black Power
⊙ protest movements: students, women, Vietnam
⊙ Nixon and Watergate.

The exam

This page shows you exactly what your Paper 1 exam paper will look like. This is a topic from Group C. You answer the two questions on Paper 1 that relate to the options you have studied.

There are four questions, parts (a), (b), (c), and (d). **You must answer all four.**

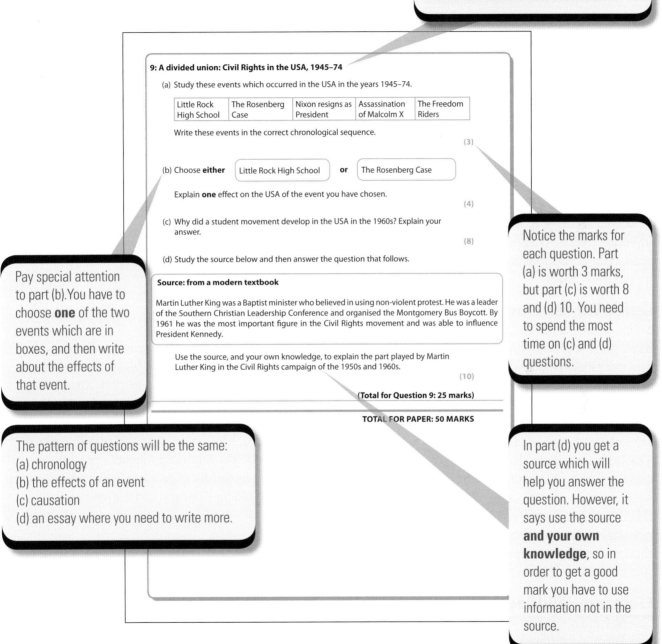

9: A divided union: Civil Rights in the USA, 1945–74

(a) Study these events which occurred in the USA in the years 1945–74.

Little Rock High School	The Rosenberg Case	Nixon resigns as President	Assassination of Malcolm X	The Freedom Riders

Write these events in the correct chronological sequence.

(3)

(b) Choose **either** [Little Rock High School] **or** [The Rosenberg Case]

Explain **one** effect on the USA of the event you have chosen.

(4)

(c) Why did a student movement develop in the USA in the 1960s? Explain your answer.

(8)

(d) Study the source below and then answer the question that follows.

Source: from a modern textbook

Martin Luther King was a Baptist minister who believed in using non-violent protest. He was a leader of the Southern Christian Leadership Conference and organised the Montgomery Bus Boycott. By 1961 he was the most important figure in the Civil Rights movement and was able to influence President Kennedy.

Use the source, and your own knowledge, to explain the part played by Martin Luther King in the Civil Rights campaign of the 1950s and 1960s.

(10)

(Total for Question 9: 25 marks)

TOTAL FOR PAPER: 50 MARKS

Notice the marks for each question. Part (a) is worth 3 marks, but part (c) is worth 8 and (d) 10. You need to spend the most time on (c) and (d) questions.

Pay special attention to part (b). You have to choose **one** of the two events which are in boxes, and then write about the effects of that event.

The pattern of questions will be the same:
(a) chronology
(b) the effects of an event
(c) causation
(d) an essay where you need to write more.

In part (d) you get a source which will help you answer the question. However, it says use the source **and your own knowledge**, so in order to get a good mark you have to use information not in the source.

Reasons for the Red Scare

Learning objectives

In this chapter you will learn about:

● how the Cold War developed, 1945–50

● reasons for the Red Scare.

The **communist** Soviet Union and the **capitalist** West fought on the same side in the Second World War. But after the war was over, their political differences caused mistrust and tensions almost at once. Both sides wanted the nations of the world to accept their political system. The struggle between them became known as the Cold War. Cold War fears drove much US policy, at home and abroad, for many years. People were especially fearful of possible nuclear war, and the USA was desperate to keep the secret of making **atomic bombs** out of Soviet hands. Their determination to find and prosecute communists in the USA became known as the Red Scare.

Cold War tensions

Many of the countries the Soviet Union occupied during the war soon had communist governments and became 'satellite states' of the USSR. The British Prime Minister, Winston Churchill, referred (in a speech in the USA) to Europe being divided by an 'Iron Curtain'. The USA feared a communist takeover of Europe that would spread worldwide. The US government decided to send aid to Europe, suffering badly from the war, to help keep them non-communist. The Marshall Plan, set up by the US government, gave thousands of millions of dollars in aid to European countries, providing money, food and equipment. The Soviet Union saw this as a bribe to keep these countries capitalist.

Germany divided

The Soviet Union, Britain, France and Germany all controlled different parts of Germany after the war. The plan was to work together to re-unite Germany. Cold War tensions led to both sides making plans without consulting the other, and a growing spiral of mistrust developed.

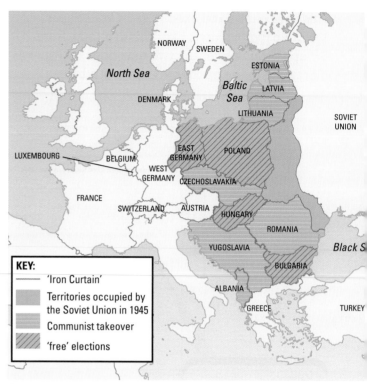

Soviet expansion in Europe by 1950.

KEY:
— 'Iron Curtain'
Territories occupied by the Soviet Union in 1945
Communist takeover
'free' elections

The hostility between Russia and the West which began in 1917, when Russia became communist, was only temporarily buried in 1941. The extension of Soviet power in Eastern Europe after 1945 alarmed American statesmen: was this the first step in Moscow's well-known plan to conquer the world? The continued American presence in Europe was equally worrying to Stalin: why were they rebuilding Germany, and distributing dollars so freely?

Source A: *From a modern textbook.*

Today, nearly every nation must choose between opposing ways of life. I believe the US must support peoples resisting attempted control by armed minorities or outside pressures. I believe our help should be mainly economic aid to restore economic stability and orderly political progress.

Source B: *From a speech made by US President Truman on 12 March 1947. It set out the Truman Doctrine – the idea that the USA should help other countries to resist communism.*

The Berlin Crisis

Berlin was in Soviet-controlled Germany but, as the capital city, was divided into four sectors run by the Soviet Union, the USA, Britain and France. The Soviet Union pressed all Berliners to vote to become communist in 'free' elections (that the Soviets would run). In June 1948 the Soviet Union cut off transport links to Berlin, stopping the British, French and Americans from getting supplies to their sectors. It would also cut West Germany off from its capital, Berlin, disrupting government. So the Western powers flew in supplies, despite the possibility that the Soviets would shoot the planes down. In April 1949 the British, French and Americans united their zones as the Federal Republic of West Germany. The Soviets then set up the communist German Democratic Republic. Berlin (and Germany) was split in two.

The Korean War

Korea, like Germany, was occupied by US and Soviet troops after the war. It, too, split into two. North Korea elected a communist government, South Korea elected a non-communist one. In 1950 North Korea invaded South Korea and war broke out. The United Nations Council sent in about 600,000 troops, led by US General Douglas MacArthur. About 90% of these were American, although troops from 15 other countries also took part, including Britain. The Soviet Union supported the North. The war dragged on until 1954 and ended with the country still divided. But, at the end of the war, the USA was no longer just promising economic aid, advice and supplies (as the Truman **Doctrine** said). It sent troops, too.

Source C: *The front cover of a magazine sold and given away free by a church group in America in the 1940s and 50s.*

Top tip

When explaining the effect of an event on people or governments, give exact details to get top marks. If asked what effect the Cold War had on US government policy don't just say *'It made the US want to stop countries becoming communist'*. Add an example of what it did – refer to the Marshall Plan, the Berlin Airlift or helping the South Koreans.

Activities

1   Copy and complete the table below.

Beliefs	Government	Economy
Soviet Union (communist)		
USA (capitalist)		

2   Use Source A and your own knowledge to write an extended answer explaining why the Cold War developed in the late 1940s.

3   Write a paragraph explaining what each crisis was, and how it might have made some Americans feel their way of life was under threat from communism:

   a   the Berlin Crisis

   b   the Korean War.

Villains or victims?

> ## Learning objectives
>
> In this chapter you will learn about:
> - the activities of HUAC
> - the Hollywood Ten
> - the Hiss and Rosenberg cases.

The Red Scare was fuelled by the belief that American communists were working with the Soviets to overthrow the US government. The Federal Bureau of Investigation (FBI) built up files on communists. The House Committee on Un-American Activities (HUAC), set up by the government, questioned more and more people in a search for Soviet agents. One woman, Elizabeth Bentley, admitted to spying. She gave the FBI names of 150 other agents, 40 of whom were government workers. The HUAC investigations, grew, fuelled by the allegations of Senator Joseph McCarthy (see pages 112–113). HUAC began with government workers, but the investigations spread.

The Hollywood Ten

HUAC investigated Hollywood, fearing communists might use the film industry to spread propaganda. Ten Hollywood writers refused to give evidence to HUAC, saying that the US Constitution gave them the right to their own political beliefs and free speech. Some film stars, such as Humphrey Bogart, supported the Ten, who were imprisoned for not giving evidence. Then HUAC began to investigate the Ten's supporters. The FBI set up 'loyalty boards' to investigate government workers – over 200 were force to resign.

The Hiss case

In 1948 Alger Hiss, who had been an adviser to President Roosevelt, was accused of being a communist. He had been accused before, but this time HUAC sent him to trial. During the trial, the Soviets tested their first atom bomb, increasing fears of nuclear war and Soviet spy rings. The evidence in the Hiss case was complicated and confused. He was found guilty of lying to the court (not spying) and sent to prison. The guilty verdict meant many people thought he had been a spy. Congress passed the McCarran Act denying communists US passports and limiting the work they could do. All communist organisations had to be registered and their members were investigated.

Watch out!

Acronyms like HUAC are usually made up from the first letter in each word of a name. For example, the FBI is the **F**ederal **B**ureau of **I**nvestigation. However, HUAC does not take the letters in the correct order. Make up a phrase to help you get the correct order. Some people call it House Un-American Activities Committee, but that is not its original name.

Build Better Answers

Chose either **the Hiss case** or **the Rosenberg case. Explain** one **effect of the Red Scare on the event you have chosen.** **(4 marks)**

Paper 1 part (b) questions will ask about the effect of one event on another.

■ **A basic answer (level 1)** will give a consequence, or effect, but no supporting detail. For example, *People were scared of American communists helping the Soviets take over the country.*

● **A good answer (level 2)** will make a statement giving a consequence and then develop this statement by giving extra detail or explanation. For example, *The Hiss case was just after the first Soviet atom bomb test, so fears of that would affect the verdict making it harsher...* OR *The Rosenberg trial was just after war broke out in Korea and the judge said that affected his verdict because he felt what they did set off the Korean War.*

The Rosenberg case

On 18 July 1950 Julius and Ethel Rosenberg were arrested for passing atomic bomb secrets to the Soviets. The evidence against them, like much of the evidence in communist conspiracy trials, was not clear. It depended greatly on the evidence of others arrested in the case, including Ethel's brother. It also depended on identifying Julius and Ethel from code names in Soviet telegrams. The case against Ethel was especially weak.

Unfortunately for the Rosenbergs, the arrest came after the Korean War broke out, as the Red Scare was reaching new heights. Many people blamed the Rosenbergs for the Soviets learning to make atom bombs, the invasion of South Korea and many other problems in the USA. They were found guilty and sentenced to death. The spy who gave the Soviets the most useful atom bomb information lived in the UK, where anti-communist feeling was less. He was sentenced to 14 years in prison.

The huge contrast between his sentence and the Rosenbergs' (added to the confused evidence and the fact the Rosenbergs had two young sons) led to mass demonstrations against a death sentence for them. However, they were executed on 19 June 1953.

The Rosenbergs got an unusual amount of public support. The HUAC investigations, the number of prosecutions and the growth of anti-communist hysteria meant that Americans became more suspicious of their neighbours and co-workers, less willing to talk politics and less likely to support someone accused of communism. They did not want to be accused themselves and maybe lose their jobs or homes, or end up in prison.

> I believe your conduct, in putting the secrets of the atom bomb into the hands of the Russians has already caused, in my opinion, the communist aggression in Korea with the resulting casualties exceeding 50,000. Who knows how many millions of people will pay the price of your treason.

Source A: *From the judge's summing up in the Rosenberg case, just days before he passed the death sentence on 5 April 1951.*

Activities

1. Complete the following sentences:
   a. HUAC investigated Hollywood because … .
   b. The Hollywood Ten were prosecuted because … .
   c. The timing of the Hiss case was bad for Hiss because… .
   d. The Red Scare affected the outcome of the Rosenberg case because … .

2. Draw two diagrams or write two paragraphs to show how the factors below affected the Hiss and Rosenberg cases:
   a. fear of communism
   b. current events
   c. confused evidence.

3. Write a paragraph giving three reasons for the high level of public support for the Rosenbergs.

Source B: *Just a few of the people taking part in a demonstration to change the death sentence against the Rosenbergs on 18 June 1953.*

The role of McCarthy

Learning objectives

In this chapter you will learn about:
- the methods used by McCarthy
- the growth of opposition to McCarthy.

In October 1949 China became communist. As anti-communist hysteria rose, Joseph McCarthy, senator for Wisconsin, made a speech saying he had the names of 205 communists who were working 'and shaping policy' in the government. The next day, he changed the number to 57. Ten days later, he told the Senate he could name 81. Despite this random series of numbers, the Senate felt under public pressure to follow up his accusations. It set up the Tydings Committee to investigate his accusations. Communist-hunting had a new name: McCarthyism. In the years following his accusations 25 US states passed anti-communist laws. Anti-communist groups formed to beat up 'suspected communists' and hound them out of their jobs and homes. In 1951 McCarthy led the next wave of HUAC investigations.

McCarthy's methods

McCarthy deliberately played on Red Scare fears. In speeches, interviews and TV appearances over several years, he stressed he had evidence to show there were communists in government (later in the army too). But when the Tydings Committee heard his evidence, it was very weak. The three Democratic members of the Committee signed a statement on 20 June 1950 calling the charges 'a fraud and a hoax, the most wicked campaign of half-truths and untruths in this country's history.' The two Republicans (McCarthy was a Republican) refused to sign. McCarthy's reaction was to accuse Senator Tydings of having communist sympathies. He made more and more accusations, many of them now aimed at his personal and political enemies, including journalists who had spoken against him.

McCarthy's accusations grew wilder, his evidence more obviously faked. For example, he produced a photo said to show Senator Tydings with a communist leader, Earl Browder. The photo was made up from one of Browder taken in 1950 and one of Tydings taken in 1938.

Opposition to McCarthy

In January 1953 the new president, Eisenhower, set up an investigation into communist beliefs among government workers to 'clear the air of unreasoned suspicion that accepts rumour and gossip as evidence'. McCarthy was moved to a committee where it was hoped he might have less publicity. But McCarthy, who still had a lot of public support, continued his anti-communist campaign. Then he went too far. By September 1953 he had begun to hunt communists in the army. The hearings were on TV and the public saw McCarthy at his worst: bullying army officers such as General Zwicker, a war hero. McCarthy's popularity dropped sharply. First the media, then the Senate and the public, turned against McCarthy. On 2 December 1954 the Senate voted to censure him for 'improper conduct' by 67 votes to 22. McCarthyism clearly damaged those who were blacklisted, but it also affected almost all Americans. Many people feared being seen as 'radical'. HUAC was still communist-hunting. The Communist Party (banned in 1954) had lost thousands of members by then. Unions, in order to survive, seldom called strikes. Politicians were less likely to campaign for 'socialist' reforms, such as welfare schemes. USA world politics stayed firmly anti-communist.

Some have argued that McCarthy's end justifies his methods. Not one of the hundreds of people accused by McCarthy was ever actually convicted of spying, but no one dared to speak out against his bullying and his lies. Eventually, McCarthyism burned itself out. By 1955, the Korean War was over. When the proceedings of the Un-American Activities Committee were televised, people were shocked at McCarthy's rudeness and bullying. He lost the public's support.

Source A: *From a modern textbook.*

Source B: *Senator McCarthy presenting photographic evidence against the Secretary of the Army, Robert Stevens, in April 1954. The photo was later proved to be faked.*

Activity

Copy and complete the following diagram explaining the reasons why opposition to McCarthy grew in the 1950s.

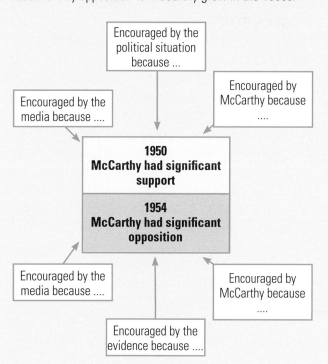

Encouraged by the political situation because ...

Encouraged by the media because ....

Encouraged by McCarthy because ....

1950 McCarthy had significant support

1954 McCarthy had significant opposition

Encouraged by the media because ....

Encouraged by McCarthy because ....

Encouraged by the evidence because ....

Top tip

When asked why something happened, you should give more than one reason. Do not just give a list of reasons. Show how the reasons combined to produce the outcome, using words and phrases such as *consequently* or *this led to* or *however*.

Examination question

Why did opposition to McCarthy grow to a point where he was censured by the Senate? Explain your answer.

(8 marks)

Segregation and discrimination

> **Learning objectives**
>
> In this chapter you will learn about:
> ● segregation and discrimination.

Discrimination

By 1890, the USA had abolished slavery and given black people equal rights as American citizens. The Fourteenth Amendment of the **Constitution** (1866) made black people full US citizens. However, black people, especially in the South, still faced **racism**, **segregation**, **discrimination** and violence. They were often prevented from voting.

In the North, discrimination denied black people equality. Black people often lived in the worst areas and were 'last hired, first fired'. Groups such as the National Association for the Advancement of Colored People (NAACP) and the Congress of Racial Equality (CORE) campaigned for black people's civil rights. During the Second World War millions of black people fought in the US armed forces and worked on the home front making war supplies. Yet, when the war ended, there was no real change in white attitudes towards black people. More and more black people joined groups such as the NAACP, CORE and local organisations (often set up by churches) to campaign for their rights and fight segregation laws in the Southern states.

Segregation

Under segregation, laws forced black people to live in separate areas with separate, usually worse, facilities for everything from education to healthcare. These laws became known as '**Jim Crow**' laws, after a white singer who did racist impressions of Jim Crow, a black man. Because states were allowed to make their own laws, they could pass Jim Crow laws despite the fact that the Constitution gave black people equal rights. In 1947, President Truman told the Committee on Civil Rights that it was time to make sure that civil rights were enforced – the federal government could overturn state laws if they were shown to be against the Constitution. So it should have been easy to overturn Jim Crow laws. It wasn't, because the federal government was often forced to compromise with the Southern states. In 1896 the Supreme Court, in the case of *Plessy v. Ferguson*, had ruled that individual states could impose segregation as long as the separate schools, hospitals and so on were 'separate but equal'. They seldom were.

> ### Did you know?
>
> The Supreme Court was set up to interpret federal laws and to overturn state laws if there was an appeal against them that claimed the state law was denying people their rights under the Constitution. The Supreme Court tried not to overrule state laws too often, while still preserving rights. The *Plessy v. Ferguson* ruling was an attempt to make sure black people had rights while keeping the southern states happy.

> ### Watch out!
>
> Students can get confused about some civil rights terms. **Segregation** is keeping black and white people separate – its supports are sometimes called separationists. **Integration** is having black and white people living in the same areas and using the same facilities.

> The North did not need to have an official system of segregation because there were few enough blacks in the North to be kept in place by discrimination: white employers would not hire them, white trade unionists would not admit them to membership, white residents would not have them as neighbours. In this way they were kept out of all but the lowest-paid unskilled jobs and confined to slum housing.
>
> **Source A:** *From a modern textbook.*

Voting rights

Most civil rights groups agreed that one of the most important things to do was to get black people registered to vote and to get them to vote in elections. They knew that politicians would be more likely to think about civil rights issues if black votes could help them into, or out of, power. This was hardest to achieve in the South.

There were no Jim Crow laws to stop black people from voting in the South. But they were stopped from voting all the same. Firstly, the registration rules had literacy tests for a person wanting to register to vote. Black people were given difficult passages to read to prove they could read, or simply told they had not passed the test. They were also threatened with violence and the loss of their jobs or homes if they went to register to vote.

Activities

1 Write a paragraph explaining what Jim Crow laws were.

2 Copy out the practices listed below under one of two headings: Segregation and Discrimination.

   a Preventing black people from registering to vote.

   b Making black people use 'coloureds only' water fountains.

   c Having separate schools for black and white children.

   d Having a company where black people are 'last hired, first fired'.

3 Add one item of your own to each of the lists you made to answer Question 2.

4 Use Source A and your own knowledge to write an extended answer explaining why black people felt the need to demonstrate for civil rights in the 1950s.

Source B: *A NAACP demonstration in Houston, Texas, in 1947.*

The Montgomery Bus Boycott

Learning objectives

In this chapter, you will learn about:

- the causes, events and results of the Montgomery Bus Boycott
- the key events of the boycott
- the role of Martin Luther King.

On 1 December 1955, Rosa Parks, a black woman, was riding home from work in the sixth row of seats on a bus in Montgomery, Alabama. Montgomery buses were segregated. The front five rows were for whites only. Black people had to clear any whole row for a white person to sit – even if it emptied the rest of the row. The bus filled up. The driver told Mrs Parks and three other black people to clear a row for a white person. The others moved. Mrs Parks refused, even when the driver threatened her with arrest for breaking the law. The driver stopped the bus and called the police who arrested her.

Rosa Parks' trial was on 5 December. Members of the NAACP (Rosa was also a member) worked with church and college organisations to set up a one-day **boycott** of Montgomery buses on that day. The court found Rosa guilty and fined her $10. That evening, protesters set up the Montgomery Improvement Association (MIA) to improve **integration** – beginning with the buses. They chose Martin Luther King as chairman. The MIA asked all black people to boycott Montgomery buses. About 70% of bus users were black, and most black bus users joined the boycott. The MIA planned and organised the boycott very carefully. They organised lifts and asked black taxi firms to charge less during the boycott.

Some employers sacked workers who took part in the boycott. Boycott leaders were arrested (there was a 'no boycott' law in Alabama) and they and their homes were attacked. The boycott went on for 381 days. It worked because almost every black person carried on supporting it (as did some whites) and because the MIA organised good support for it. The bus company lost a lot of money and Montgomery got a lot of bad publicity, both nationally and worldwide.

Because the state government would not change the law, the Supreme Court had to act. On 19 December 1956, it ruled segregation on buses **unconstitutional** and, as of 21 December, black people rode the buses again. The ruling was unpopular with many white people in Montgomery and elsewhere.

A Negro woman has been arrested and thrown in jail in Montgomery for refusing to give up her seat on the bus for a white person. It is the second time since the Claudette Colvin Case [when, 9 months before, a 15 year-old black girl was arrested in Montgomery] that a Negro woman has been arrested for the same thing. This must be stopped. The next time it may be you, or your daughter, or your mother. This woman's case comes up on Monday. We are asking every Negro to stay off the buses Monday in protest of the arrest and trial. Please, children and grown-ups, don't ride the bus on Monday.

Source A: *From a leaflet about the arrest of Rosa Parks, handed out by Jo Ann Robinson, a teacher and head of a group of professional black women in Montgomery. It urged a boycott of buses on the day of her trial. Think about the language she used to get the message across.*

Source B: *Martin Luther King and other members of the MIA ride a bus in Montgomery on 21 December 1956, once the Supreme Court ruling was passed.*

Effects

The Montgomery Bus Boycott

The Montgomery Bus Boycott worked because:

- almost all black people boycotted the buses
- the organisers arranged alternative transport
- people kept the boycott up for over a year.

This led to:

- publicity for the campaign
- the bus company losing a lot of money
- desegregation of the buses.

The Montgomery Bus Boycott had effects beyond Montgomery because:

- its success encouraged more civil rights actions by various civil rights groups (e.g. the Tallahassee Bus Boycott, 1956–58)
- Martin Luther King gained a following that raised the levels of civil rights awareness and numbers of campaigners
- more racist whites joined anti-integration groups like the Ku Klux Klan
- prominent civil rights campaigners, such as King and Ralph Abernathy, had their homes firebombed
- violence against civil rights campaigners increased with their rising numbers and rising success.

Build Better Answers

Why did the black people of Montgomery boycott the buses for 381 days in 1955–56? Explain your answer.
(8 marks)

Paper 1 part (c) questions expect you to explain why something happened.

■ **A basic answer** will make simple generalisations.

● **A good answer** will give reasons supported by detail (more than one would get a higher mark). For example, *They wanted to stop segregation. There had been earlier arrests there for sitting in the wrong place on the buses. It would hurt the bus company as 70% of bus users were black.*

▲ **An excellent answer** will be the 'better' answer from above with more than one factor showing how they were linked. For example, *... they wanted to stop segregation and there had been previous arrests for sitting in the wrong place on buses, so the buses seemed a good protest target and also 70% of bus passengers were black – so it would be a visible point.*

Examination question

Why did the Montgomery bus boycott succeed?

(8 marks)

Activities

1. Make a timeline (showing day, month and year where possible) to put the following events in the Bus Boycott into chronological order:

   - segregation of buses ruled unconstitutional
   - arrest of Claudette Colvin
   - bus boycott begins
   - Rosa Parks arrested
   - black people rode the buses again.

2. Write a paragraph explaining the effects of the Montgomery Bus Boycott.

3. Plan an answer to the examination question on this page using the Build Better Answers box as a guide.

Integrating schools

Learning objectives

In this chapter you will learn about:

- the importance of court cases: *Brown v. Topeka* (1951) and *Brown v. the Board of Education* (1954)
- key events and importance of Little Rock (1957).

Brown v. Topeka

The *Plessy* ruling (1896) that allowed 'separate but equal' facilities for black and white people meant black children in many states had to go to all-black schools. These schools often had poor funding; buildings were not well-maintained, and there was a shortage of books and equipment. In June 1951 Oliver Brown brought the case *Brown v. Topeka* in the Topeka State Court to integrate elementary schools in Topeka, Kansas. It was rejected because of *Plessy*. The NAACP urged Brown to try again in the Supreme Court, combining his case with four others into *Brown v. the Board of Education of Topeka*. The other cases were in Washington DC, Delaware, South Carolina and Virginia.

On 17 May 1954 the Supreme Court ruled that all school segregation was unconstitutional. However, it did not give a date for integration. A year later it made another ruling, saying integration had to be done 'with all deliberate speed'. This still left the speed of integration up to individual states, weakening the force of the law. After the *Brown* case, schools did integrate – some peacefully, some less so. Some whites in the South reacted to the ruling by forming White Citizens Councils to stop integration.

We conclude that the idea of 'separate but equal' has no place in state education. Separate educational facilities are inherently unequal. Therefore, we hold that the plaintiffs [the black people who brought the case] are, by reason of the segregation complained of, deprived of the equal protection of the laws guaranteed by the Fourteenth Amendment.

Source A: *From the Supreme Court decision on* Brown v. the Board of Education, *17 May 1954.*

Taking cases to court was risky. It relied on the court being fair, rather than biased against black people. If the campaigners won, the decision still had to be enforced. In 1954 judges in the Supreme Court in the *Brown v. the Board of Education* case said school segregation was illegal. Some Southern states urged schools to ignore this. Some schools desegregated anyway. But in most cases black people had to bring court cases in each state to send their children to 'white' schools.

Source B: *From a modern textbook.*

Activities

1. Write these events in the correct chronological sequence: *Brown v. Topeka*; *Plessy v. Ferguson*; Little Rock Nine attempt integration; *Brown v. the Board of Education*.

2. Write a note from an NAACP official explaining why, having lost his case at state level, Brown should take *Brown v. Topeka* to the Supreme Court.

3. Schools in Little Rock did not have a significant level of integration until the 1970s. Write a paragraph explaining why you think this was. Give more than one reason.

 Watch out!

The 1954 Supreme Court ruling to integrate schools was a ruling in the case *Brown v. the Board of Education of Topeka*. Questions about *Brown v. Topeka* refer to this federal case, brought in 1951, not the state case that was overturned earlier in that year.

Little Rock schools were technically integrated after 1959. However, a significant level of integration was not really achieved until the 1970s. Governor Faubus maintained his opposition to integration and did not step down as governor until 1967.

A small group of whites bothered us every day. They called us names, tripped us in hallways and pushed us down stairs without fear of the teachers telling them off. We couldn't fight back, we couldn't even say anything that might cause a fight, because then we might be expelled. There was a screaming mob outside the school every day.

Source C: *This photo of Elizabeth Eckford walking to school on the first day became famous for summing up the problems of integrating schools in the South.*

Source D: *From an interview with Elizabeth Eckford in 1962.*

Integrating Little Rock

In 1957 school officials in Little Rock chose nine black students to integrate Central High School. The governor of Arkansas, Orville Faubus, opposed integration. He called out the Arkansas National Guard on the first day of school to 'protect the school' by keeping the black students out. The NAACP had arranged for the children to arrive together, but a mix up meant that one student, Elizabeth Eckford, arrived alone. The mob was terrifying, but she managed to reach the soldiers thinking they would get her into the school and safety. They turned her away. She had to go back through the mob that was shouting '**lynch** her!'

There was worldwide shock when photos of her ordeal were published. President Eisenhower felt he had to act. He sent in federal troops to guard the 'Little Rock Nine', as the students became known. Then he took the Arkansas troops under federal control and had them guard the students.

The guards had to make sure the students got into school and between classes safely. They could not make white teachers or students treat them equally (and some did not). They didn't guard the students' homes, or stop the hate mail and threatening phone calls.

At the end of the year the oldest of the Little Rock Nine, Ernest Green, graduated with the rest of his year. There was an empty seat either side of him at the ceremony because no one would sit next to him. Martin Luther King came as a guest of the Green family. Governor Faubus then closed the school for a year while the state court and the Supreme Court argued over delaying integration. A state judge, Harry Lemley, argued that black students might have a constitutional right to attend white schools, but 'the time has not come for them to enjoy that right'. The Supreme Court did not agree. The school reopened in 1959; integration continued. Faubus made a speech against it and demonstrations against the students continued.

Martin Luther King

Learning objectives

In this chapter you will learn about:

- Martin Luther King's significance
- Martin Luther King's methods.

Martin Luther King is one of the most famous civil rights campaigners ever. He was born in 1929, the son of a Baptist minister. He went to segregated schools. He studied to become a minister and went to Boston University. He was a member of NAACP. In 1954 King became minister of a Baptist church in Montgomery. His work during the bus boycott there (pages 118–119) led to him working with groups such as the Southern Christian Leadership Conference. He won black and white supporters for civil rights, including the politician John F. Kennedy (see page 128). King joined local protests in many Southern towns and cities, often getting arrested and imprisoned (e.g. the campaign in Birmingham, Alabama, in 1963, where he and Ralph Abernathy were arrested along with many other campaigners).

Methods

King's Christian faith and his admiration of the Indian leader Mahatma Ghandi's non-violent protests meant he believed in non-violent **direct action** – protesting peacefully in a highly visible way to produce maximum publicity. He knew such publicity would embarrass the US government, which told the world it supported freedom. Protests included:

- **picketing** (standing outside a segregated shop or diner and asking people not to use it)
- **boycotts** (not using any service that discriminated against black people)
- **sit-ins** (sitting at a 'whites only' lunch counter waiting to be served)
- **jail-ins** (deliberately getting arrested and filling jails)
- **mass marches**.

King was an inspiring speaker. He convinced many people to join demonstrations, boycotts and sit-ins despite the threat of arrest, imprisonment or attack. He urged his supporters not to be afraid of resisting because 'what we are doing is within the law'. For publicity that left no doubt as to 'who were the oppressors and who were the oppressed', protestors had to be non-violent at all times, no matter what. This was hard, because opponents of civil rights were only too ready to use violence, or to try to provoke black protestors into fighting back.

> Privileged groups rarely give up their privileges without strong resistance. So the basic question confronting the world's oppressed is: How to struggle against the forces of injustice? The alternative to violence is non-violent resistance. The non-violent resister protests by non-cooperation or boycotts to shame his opponent.

Source A: *From an interview with Martin Luther King in* Christian Century Magazine *in 1957.*

Civil rights campaigners used public, non-violent direct action, such as sit-ins and boycotts.

↓

So...

↓

- the police moved them on, often roughly
- their opponents were often violent, too.

↓

This led to...

↓

- positive publicity for the campaigners
- negative publicity for their opponents
- pressure for change.

Effects of the use of non-violent direct action.

Top tip

When you answer Section A part (b), part (c) and (part d) questions, you will only get a good mark if you use detailed examples. Generalisations will earn a maximum of 2 marks. The best answers for part (c) and part (d) questions will show links between examples.

Source B: *Martin Luther King speaking on a tour in 1966 to encourage black people to register to vote.*

Voting rights

King was passionate about urging black people to vote. He knew how hard this was to do in the South, where they were prevented from registering to vote by violence, intimidation and discriminatory qualification systems. But he also knew that black people would get their demands taken more seriously if politicians knew there were enough black people voting in elections to help (or hinder) them getting elected.

King's importance

King was important because he was an excellent and convincing speaker for civil rights. Many people joined the civil rights campaign who would not have done so without his lead. His stress on highly visible campaigning gained him worldwide recognition (he won the Nobel Peace Prize in 1964). He appealed to white politicians because he stressed non-violent action and seemed willing to work with them for progress. This became less the case after reaction to the new civil rights laws made it clear to King that progress was still going to be too slow.

Activities

1. Write a paragraph to explain how each of the factors below made King acceptable to some white politicians:
   a. his education
   b. his job
   c. his methods.

2. Write a paragraph to explain how each of the factors below made King seem dangerous to some white politicians:
   a. his education
   b. his job
   c. his methods.

3. Why did King think voter registration was important?

4. Write a letter of reply from King to a protester who had written asking why their protests always have to be non-violent.

Sit-ins and freedom rides

Learning objectives

In this chapter you will learn about:

- the importance of sit-ins
- the problems facing freedom rides.

Sit-ins

In February 1960 four black students in Greensboro, North Carolina, decided to hold a sit-in to integrate a local lunch counter. Sit-ins were not a new form of protest. But the Greensboro sit-ins set off a wave of them, across North Carolina, then the rest of the South. Most of the protesters were students, including some who travelled from campuses in the North to join in. In April, students in Raleigh, North Carolina, set up the Student Nonviolent Co-ordinating Committee (SNCC, pronounced 'snick') to co-ordinate this growing movement. The SNCC held courses for the protesters, giving them tips about how to remain non-violent in the face of aggression and actual violence.

Through all their efforts at desegregation and protest, one of the hardest things for the black people involved was having to be non-violent. If they fought back, their leaders said, they could be removed from the school, the bus or the restaurant. They would have lost. There were no such constraints on the whites who opposed them. Black and white protestors were beaten, threatened and even bombed. Their lives were at risk.

Source B: *From a modern textbook.*

The Freedom Riders' victory set the tone for the great civil rights campaigns that followed. Not for the first time during these climactic years, a free press forced Americans to take a cold, hard look at the reality of racial oppression.

Source C: *From* Free at Last, *a book published by the US government's Bureau of International Information programs in 2008.*

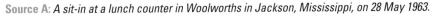

Source A: *A sit-in at a lunch counter in Woolworths in Jackson, Mississippi, on 28 May 1963.*

Effects

The sit-ins:

- produced positive publicity for the civil rights movement
- were easier and quicker to organise than large demonstrations, and so helped the movement spread and got more people involved
- drew in student support, black and white, from universities all over the USA
- led to the setting up of SNCC, which became an important civil rights organisation.

Freedom riders

In December 1960 the Supreme Court ordered the desegregation of all bus station facilities. CORE and the SNCC set up 'freedom rides'. Buses drove through the South 'testing' the facilities in bus stations to make sure they were integrated. They were not expecting this to be the case and were expecting a hostile response, especially as both black and white protesters rode together. They wanted to create a crisis that would get worldwide publicity to give America negative publicity abroad. They hoped this would force the government to act more decisively to enforce the law.

They got their crisis. The first two buses were attacked and the riders were beaten up at several stops. At Anniston, Alabama, one of the buses was firebombed and the people leaving the bus were beaten up. White riders were often beaten more severely than black riders, because of what was seen by the attackers as their 'betrayal'.

The next week, more buses set off. The riders were imprisoned in Birmingham and beaten up in Montgomery. Over the summer, more than 400 freedom riders were arrested. A much larger number were beaten up. Three were killed. The riders kept riding. On May 29, 1962, the government told the Interstate Commerce Commission that it had to make strict rules about integration on buses moving between state lines. It did. Buses, trains and their facilities along the interstate routes desegregated. However, internal state routes were slower to do so. The government, as was often the case when they were forced to act by bad publicity, did only as much as they had to do to make the publicity die down.

Activities

1 Copy and complete the sentences below:
   a Non-violent direct action aimed to …
   b So protesters could never …
   c For it to work their protest had to be highly … and get worldwide …
   d When this happened, the government did …
   e However, the government usually …

2 Write a paragraph explaining what made the Greensboro sit-in so important.

3 Produce an 'effects' box like the one on page 124 for the effects of the freedom rides.

Build Better Answers

Use Source C and your own knowledge to describe the main effects of the non-violent direct action tactics used in the civil rights campaigns of the 1960s. **(10 marks)**

Paper 1 part (d) questions expect you to use a source and your own knowledge to explain something.

■ **A basic answer (level 1)** will make simple generalisations. For example, *they got the campaigners noticed.*

● **A good answer (level 2)** will give examples, with detail from their own knowledge and the source (more than one will get a higher mark). For example, *they got the campaigners publicity. So they did the rides to show that the laws weren't being enforced. They knew there would probably be violence against them which would get publicity. The publicity from them made people really think about racism.*

▲ **An excellent answer (level 4)** will be the 'good' answer above with more than one factor showing how they combined to produce the outcome. At least two factors must be used. For example, *The sit-ins (where they often got food and drink poured on them and shouted at or hit) and all their other non-violent protests aimed at the same thing – showing themselves as the oppressed and their white opponents (and often the police) as oppressive.*

Examination question

Study these events which occurred in America in the years 1954–61: *the Montgomery Bus Boycott; the Anniston bus bombing; Brown v. the Board of Education; the first Greensboro sit-in; the first attempt to integrate Central High School, Little Rock.*

Write these events in the correct chronological sequence. **(3 marks)**

Marching for change

Learning objectives

In this chapter you will learn about:
- the Birmingham civil rights protests
- the March on Washington
- the effects of these marches.

Birmingham

Despite the campaigns and legislation, many places in the South had not carried out any desegregation. One of these was Birmingham, Alabama. Its chief of police, 'Bull' Connor, was said to have given the Ku Klux Klan 15 minutes to beat up the Freedom riders who stopped there in 1961, before moving in to protect them as the government had ordered. In 1963, civil rights campaigners targeted Birmingham for a full-scale non-violent desegregation campaign.

The campaigners began marching on 3 April. Many people were arrested, including Martin Luther King. Children were trained in non-violent tactics, to take the place of the arrested adults. The first big children's demonstration was on 2 May. By the end of the day, 956 children were in jail. The next day, more children marched. The police turned fire hoses and dogs on them. The stories and photos were published worldwide, causing President Kennedy to say 'I feel ashamed'. On 10 May, the mayor and protest leaders met to discuss desegregation. The next day the governor of Alabama sent in troops disrupting the talks. On 12 May, President Kennedy sent in federal troops to restore calm. The mayor passed desegregation laws. Lunch counters and shops desegregated. Black people were able to apply for jobs they had previously been banned from.

Did you know?

Many of the children in the children's marches were teenagers – but younger children took part too. Audrey Faye Hendricks was nine years old. She was in jail for seven days. Her parents had no idea where she was for all that time. All the jails were full, so the police had to use other public buildings as jails. They refused to give any information to those asking about their children.

Source A: *William Gadsden was not even marching on 3 May. He was just trying to cross the road when these police dogs were set on him.*

The march on Washington

The success of the Birmingham campaign set off civil rights actions all over the USA. Kennedy promised to ask Congress to commit itself to enforcing civil rights. But opposition groups such as the Ku Klux Klan reacted against rising support for the civil rights movement. They continued to murder black people and bomb black homes, churches and businesses. Black people felt increasingly threatened by the violence, and ignored by the government. Despite Kennedy's speeches, the federal government was slow to act to preserve black rights in states, because they did not like interfering in state issues. There were riots in many towns and cities. A Civil Rights Bill was being discussed, but making slow progress.

Civil rights groups organised a march on Washington, to convince Congress the Civil Rights Bill had a lot of support. Estimates of the number of marchers who reached Washington range from 250,000 to 500,000. The march was reported world-wide and it was one of the first events to be broadcast live around the world by the newly-launched Telstar satellite. Many people sang and spoke to the crowds.

Martin Luther King gave the last speech. It became instantly famous, as the 'I have a dream' speech. In it he spoke of his dream that his four children would be judged not by the colour of their skin, but by their character. Support for the civil rights movement rose. The government saw that there was a huge amount of public support for the civil rights movement. But violent opposition to civil rights was also set off by the march. Two weeks after the march, four young black girls were killed when a church in Birmingham was bombed. On 2 July 1964, the Civil Rights Act was passed and an Equal Opportunities Commission was set up to investigate discrimination.

Activities

Copy and complete the diagram below.

> Publicity for the events at Birmingham gained the civil rights movement …
>
> ↓
>
> The government began to consider…
>
> ↓
>
> Opponents of the movement reacted by …
>
> ↓
>
> The march on Washington aimed at …
>
> ↓
>
> Opponents of the movement reacted by …
>
> ↓
>
> The government …

Build Better Answers

Choose either the Birmingham campaign or the March on Washington. Explain one **effect on the civil rights campaign of the event you have chosen.**

(4 marks)

Paper 1 part (b) questions will ask about the effect of one event on another.

■ **A basic answer (level 1)** will give a consequence, or effect, but not supporting detail. For example, *After the march on Washington, civil rights issues got more support.*

● **A good answer (level 2)** will make a statement giving a consequence and then develop this statement by giving extra detail or explanation. For example, *After the march on Washington civil rights issues got more support. Politicians saw that civil rights had a lot of support, because of the numbers at the march. So they saw it as an issue that they could get votes for supporting. King's 'dream' speech affected a lot of ordinary people and got them thinking about the issue.*

Civil rights legislation of the 1960s

Learning objectives

In this chapter you will learn about:
- civil rights legislation pre-1964
- the 1964 Civil Rights Act
- the 1965 Voting Rights Act.

In 1947 President Truman said it was time to enforce civil rights laws. He had little luck, nor did his successor Eisenhower. They needed the support of senators (and voters) from the Southern states, many of whom fiercely opposed civil rights. So laws were usually only enforced in crises, making no one happy. In 1960 Massachusetts Senator John F. Kennedy became president with 75% of all black votes. Kennedy supported civil rights and admired Martin Luther King. Were things about to change?

James Meredith

James Meredith, a black student, was turned down by the University of Mississippi in 1961 because he was black. The NAACP fought for a federal ruling to admit him and won; the university was told to admit him in 1962. On his first day, he was refused entry by the university authorities and the governor of Mississippi. President Kennedy had to send in 3,000 troops to stop riots against his admission and to get him in. Despite continual threats and harassment by many of the students, he stayed, got his degree and continued to fight for civil rights.

Kennedy and civil rights

Kennedy talked a lot about civil rights, gave a few black people key government jobs and set up committees to work out how to improve education, housing and work for black people. But he had to keep the South happy, so he did not act decisively. Then, in 1963, he met various African leaders at the White House. The worldwide publicity of growing violence against black people in the USA (especially in Birmingham, Alabama, where the targets were children) was embarrassing. The March on Washington had shown how many different groups in America supported the idea of a civil rights bill. So, in June, Kennedy committed himself to get a new Civil Rights Act passed and enforced. He was assassinated in November 1963, before the law was passed.

The Civil Rights Act

On 2 July 1964 the new president, Johnson, signed the new Civil Right Act. It banned discrimination in education, work and public places. An Equal Opportunities Commission was set up to investigate discrimination. Discriminatory state laws became illegal and voter registration tests had to be the same for everyone. However, laws only work if they are enforced, and the Southern states continued to resist, especially over voter registration. So civil rights leaders organised a march in Alabama, from Selma to Montgomery, to highlight the problem. On 7 March 1965 they were stopped at Edmund Petus Bridge by state troopers with tear gas, clubs and electric cattle prods.

Top tip

Part d) answers ask you to use a given source and your own knowledge. Make sure you use **detail** from the source and your own knowledge. Using relevant detail from both is what will get you into the top level.

Did you know?

In the state elections that followed the 1965 Voting Rights Act, 75% of the black population of Mississippi were registered to vote. After the elections Mississippi had the highest number of black state officials in the USA. This seems to show the act working. However, in Alabama, so few black people were registered to vote (the state worked deliberately slowly) that Martin Luther King said, in exasperation, that it would take over a hundred years to register all those qualified to vote in just one part of the state. So state obedience was patchy.

The Voting Rights Act

After the violence in Selma, President Johnson forced through another civil rights bill. The Voting Rights Act, signed on 6 August 1965, set up a national literacy test for blacks and whites registering to vote. It also set up a group of federal examiners to go into states and check that black people were not being discriminated against when they registered to vote. In 1966 many Southern states had to set up registration points in halls and even shops because of the number of black people registering to vote.

James Meredith, the first black student at the University of Mississippi, set up a march through Mississippi to encourage voter registration. The march resulted in about 3,000 voters registering. During the march Meredith was shot (but not killed). In all, about 250,000 new black voters registered, but still faced violent opposition.

Activities

1 Write an article about black voting rights for a local newspaper in 1966 explaining:

 • why so few black voters were registered to vote in the 1950s and early 1960s, especially in the South (linked to the reasons that stopped them voting)

 • why the federal government was slow to help

 • how the 1965 Voting Rights Act changed things

 • if this helped the situation.

 Make links between each separate section.

2 The Selma to Montgomery march of 1964 and the James Meredith march of 1966 both met violent opposition. Write a slogan to persuade civil rights protesters to keep marching.

Source A: *President Johnson shakes hands with Martin Luther King after signing the 1964 Civil Rights Act.*

Malcolm X and the Nation of Islam

Learning objectives

In this chapter you will learn about:
- reasons for growth of black militancy
- Malcolm X and the Nation of Islam.

Separate but equal

As non-violent protests put growing pressure on the government and states to give black people their rights, protestors became the target of increasing levels of violence. Some groups, like the Nation of Islam (NOI or the Black Muslims), demonstrated against integration. They said ending segregation would not stop discrimination. They argued that black people would be better off living separately – but with the same facilities as whites. Some groups, such as the Back to Africa movement, argued that blacks would be better off if they left the USA.

Meet violence with violence

Other groups argued that violence should be met with violence. At first people who said this, such as Malcolm X, pointed out they were only suggesting self-defence, not starting violence. Malcolm X became the voice of many angry black people who felt non-violent action had failed. Malcolm X first came to public attention in the late 1950s when he left prison and made speeches for the NOI and produced the newspaper *Muhammad Speaks*. Many black Muslims used 'X' instead of their family surnames, often given to their ancestors by white slave-owners.

Source A: *Black Muslims demonstrating against the NAACP in Harlem in 1961.*

Did you know?

MALCOLM X

Born: Malcolm Little, 19 May 1925

Father: Baptist preacher

Education: good student, wanted to be a lawyer; told by his favourite teacher that this was 'no realistic goal for a nigger'

Turned to crime: in Boston and New York

Arrested: 1946, served 7 years of a 10-year sentence; joined Nation of Islam (NOI) in jail.

Released: 1953 became NOI preacher and campaigner – rise in numbers from 500 in 1952 to 30,000 in 1963.

Left NOI: March 1964

assassinated: 21 February 1965.

Did you know?

NATION OF ISLAM (NOI)

Set up: July 1930

By: W D Fard Muhammad, who claimed to have had a vision of Allah and is seen by NOI as both the Bible's Messiah and Islam's Mahdi.

Aims: freedom, justice and equality for black people, a superior race to white people. If this cannot be achieved, separation from them. Non-involvement in civil rights activities and white politics.

⚠ Watch out!

Don't confuse the Nation of Islam with the religion Islam. NOI is an American movement that uses some Islamic ideas (Ramadan, fasting, not drinking alcohol) but has fundamental differences of beliefs (black superiority, black people creating both the Bible and the Qu'ran).

At first, the differences between Malcolm X and Martin Luther King were clear. King believed in working with the government to gain civil rights; Malcolm X said, 'The government of America is responsible for the oppression and exploitation of black people in this country'. King believed in non-violent protest; Malcolm X made speeches saying things like, 'If we don't get to cast a ballot [vote], then we're going to have to cast a bullet'. King focused on voter registration and integration in the South; Malcolm X focused on the inequalities faced by black people all over the USA.

However, by 1965 King and Malcolm X had both changed their positions. Malcolm X left the NOI in March 1964 after a series of angry disputes over his involvement in civil rights issues. He set up Muslim Mosque Inc. as a radical civil rights group. He travelled the world and returned more open to the idea of working within the system. He began to talk about the importance of voter registration. King, meanwhile, made a speech in March 1965 saying black people were not 'begging' for the ballot, but 'demanding' it. There was still a huge divide between them: the difference between King's non-violence and Malcolm X's belief that it was wrong to teach someone who was being attacked not to defend themselves. His work had a significant effect on black thinking – especially among young black people (see Source B). Any chance there might have been that they could negotiate this and work together was ended by the assassination of Malcolm X in February 1965.

Source C: *The only meeting between Malcolm X and Martin Luther King, on 26 March 1964.*

> More than anyone else, Malcolm X was responsible for the growing awareness and militancy among black people. His clear words cut the chains on black minds like a giant blowtorch. He didn't want to wake America's conscience about black rights. He knew America had no conscience.

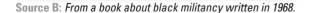

Source B: *From a book about black militancy written in 1968.*

Activities

1 Copy and complete the following table on the views of Martin Luther King, Malcolm X and the NOI.

Views on:	M L King	Malcolm X	NOI
Publicity			
Separation			
Non-violence			
Working with the system			

2 Write a paragraph explaining the effect of Malcolm X's work.

Rising anger

> **Learning objectives**
>
> In this chapter you will learn about:
> - the Black Panther movement
> - race riots.

As more black people registered to vote, they needed a party that supported civil rights to vote for. In 1965 Stokely Carmichael and other SNCC workers in Lowndes County, Alabama, set up the Lowndes County Freedom Organisation political party to get people to go out and vote. Its symbol was a black panther and its slogan was 'vote for the panther, then go home'.

The SNCC, along with other civil rights groups that had been non-violent, changed their emphasis, especially after the violence on the Meredith march of 1966. The South was still violently resisting civil rights; the government was still slow to act decisively. The old methods weren't working quickly enough. So groups changed. White people were less welcome. Non-violence was no longer stressed. Slogans such as 'Freedom Now' changed to 'Black Power'.

The Black Panthers

In October 1966 in Oakland, California, Huey Newton and Bobby Seale set up the Black Panther Party. The group had a ten-point plan, aimed at improving living and working conditions for black people. The media paid most attention to their demand for the monitoring of police brutality and the fact they carried guns for self-defence (which was legal in California, as long as the guns were not concealed). The Panthers had a uniform: black jacket and trousers, blue shirts and a black beret. Some people saw them as a more efficient community police than the state police force. They also organised community projects, such as free healthcare in poor black areas. Not surprisingly, the government saw them as a threat, especially as the movement spread. By 1968, 25 US cities had Black Panther groups.

> **Did you know?**
>
> THE BLACK PANTHER TEN-POINT PLAN
>
> (simplified; what they wanted for 'black and oppressed' communities)
>
> 1. Freedom to run their own communities
> 2. Full employment
> 3. An end to capitalist exploitation of these people
> 4. Decent housing
> 5. A decent education
> 6. Free healthcare
> 7. An end to police brutality
> 8. An end to all wars of aggression
> 9. All those in prison to be released
> 10. Land, bread, housing, education, clothing justice, peace and control of technology.

Source A: *A Black Panther poster from 1970.*

Race riots in the late 1960s

From 1965 on, waves of race riots swept the USA. They were not the result of action by the Black Panthers or any other **militant** group. They were not organised. They were mostly in towns and cities in the North, and they mostly broke out in the summer months. They were often set off by an act of police brutality – so that different cities had major riots in different years.

The riots were not just a reaction to police brutality. They were a reaction to the long-term problems of city living for black people: unemployment, overcrowding and poor services. In 1967 Martin Luther King said: 'Everyone underestimated the amount of rage the Negroes were feeling (but holding back) and the amount of prejudice that white people were hiding'.

There were major riots in New York (1964), Los Angeles (1965), Chicago and Cleveland (1966), Newark and Detroit (1967) and Washington and Cleveland (1968). The rioting in the Watts district of Los Angeles lasted from 11–17 August. It followed the arrest of a young black driver for drunk driving. Over 14,000 Californian National Guardsmen enforced a 45 mile curfew zone. Almost 4,000 people were arrested; thousands were injured; hundreds of shops were looted and damaged and 34 people died. There were smaller riots in other towns and cities. For example, in the first nine months of 1967 more than 150 cities reported riots.

On 4 April 1968 Martin Luther King was assassinated by a white gunman (see pages 134–35). The violence that followed was worst in Washington and Cleveland, but there were riots in over 100 US towns and cities over the week that followed.

It took over 55,000 soldiers to stop the riots. The riots caused $45 million worth of damage and 46 people (41 of them black) died. Thousands were injured and 27,000 were arrested. The US government was shaken by the level of violence, and many people who had previously supported the civil rights movement turned against it. The image of innocent, non-violent black people being persecuted by white police was replaced in the minds of many with the image of an angry young black man with a petrol bomb.

President Lyndon Johnson appointed a Commission of Enquiry headed by Governor Kerner of Illinois to find out what was causing the riots. The resulting report found that the riots were brought on by a sense of frustration among black people at the way they were being treated and concluded: 'The nation is rapidly moving towards two increasingly separate Americas.'

Source B: *From a modern textbook.*

Examination question

Study Source B on this page and then answer the question which follows.
Use the source, and your own knowledge, to explain why there were race riots in the late 19 60s. **(10 marks)**

Activities

1 Copy and complete the following sentences:
'Black Power' was different from earlier civil rights protests because...
The idea of Black Power gained support because ...

2 Chose the word below you think best sums up the Black Panther aims as simplified on page 132. Write a paragraph to explain why.
reasonable/unreasonable/idealistic/achievable/unachievable

3 Plan, then write, your answer to the examination question above.

The assassination of Martin Luther King

Learning objectives

In this chapter you will learn about:

● Martin Luther King's assassination

● King's significance.

During the 1960s several important US political figures, black and white, were assassinated. President Kennedy (November 1963) was followed by Malcolm X (February 1965), Martin Luther King (April 1968) and Robert Kennedy (June 1968). King was shot by a white gunman outside a motel in Memphis on 4 April. The instant reaction of one of his companions was to say to Ralph Abernathy, another important civil rights leader, 'Oh God, Ralph, it's over.' Abernathy got angry and replied, 'Don't you say that. It is not over.' But to many people King's death seemed like the end of the movement they felt he had held together.

King's death caused widespread mourning all over the USA and worldwide. It also sparked off an explosion of riots in many American towns and cities. The damage was huge, not only in terms of damage to the towns and cities themselves, but also to the image of the civil rights movement. Civil rights leaders such as Ralph Abernathy, who had been working to keep things going, were seen by many people, including politicians, as not being able to control the situation.

Four weeks after King's assassination, Abernathy led a group of marchers to Washington to continue the Poor People's campaign that King had set up. They built a camp, Resurrection City, near the Lincoln Memorial in Washington to make the poor visible to the government. It ran for about two months. It rained almost continuously and the atmosphere was disorganised and despairing. People fought among themselves. The National Guard broke the camp up with tear gas attacks.

Build Better Answers

Why was the assassination of Martin Luther King such a blow to the civil rights movement? Explain your answer. (8 marks)

Paper 1 part (c) questions expect you to explain why something happened.

■ **A basic answer (level 1)** will make simple generalisations. For example, *He'd campaigned hard for civil rights.*

● **A good answer (level 2)** will give reasons supported by detail (more than one would get a higher mark). For example, *He was a good organiser (as in the Montgomery Bus Boycott) and good at getting publicity (march on Washington). He was a good speaker, so lots of people did as he suggested.*

▲ **An excellent answer (level 3)** will be the 'good' answer from above with more than one factor showing how they combined to produce the outcome. For example, *He was just right as a leader of the movement. He was an excellent speaker and very good at getting people on his side. This made him a good organiser (as in the Montgomery Bus Boycott, where he had to get the free rides organised and things like that to make the boycott work for so long AND he had to get people to keep not riding the buses). He was good at getting publicity (as in the march on Washington) and it was publicity that pulled civil rights into the spotlight.*

Source A: *A poster from the 1970s, urging black Americans to register to vote and to vote.*

Various civil rights groups poured money into keeping Resurrection City running, but they found that far fewer people were now willing to give money to support the movement. This was not just because of the death of Martin Luther King, although he had been an excellent fundraiser. It was as much about the changing image of black civil rights – the increasing violence, the increasing unwillingness to accept help from whites. King had always stressed that non-violence was vital to the civil rights movement. His view was that black people, in order to get support, clearly had to be seen as the victims of injustice. It seemed that he was right. As support fell away, groups were less able to stage big demonstrations. Civil rights became just one issue of many that the US government had to face. The biggest of these was the growing protest about the war in Vietnam (see pages 137–39).

(see pages 137–39)

Build Better Answers

Paper 1 part (a) questions ask you to put five events from the unit into chronological order. This question is only worth three marks, so you need to be able to answer it quickly. Build up a timeline of the key events as you go along and read it over from time to time, to keep the order fresh in your mind.

Activities

1 Copy and complete the following sentences:

Martin Luther King's assassination was a huge blow to the civil rights movement because...

Resurrection City failed because...

People were less willing to support the civil rights movement because...

2 Copy and complete the diagram below.

> The assassination of Martin Luther King sparked off ...

↓

> [ ]

↓

> Many people thought the civil rights leaders ...

↓

> [ ]

↓

> This view was strengthened when Resurrection City ...

Reasons for protest

Learning objectives

In this chapter you will learn about:

- reasons for growth of protest movements
- the Vietnam War.

The 1960s were a time of protest, especially among students and other young people. This happened across Europe as well, not just in the USA. Why?

Expectations

When the Second World War ended, people hoped for a return to prosperity. In the USA the prosperity came, but mostly for WASPs (White Anglo-Saxon Protestants) and mostly for men. When Kennedy was elected president in 1961, he promised a fairer, more equal society. It didn't happen. And people noticed, and protested.

A new generation

For the first time, large numbers of young people rejected the values of older generations. Many were children of WASPs, but said they did not want to 'buy into' their parents' privileged lives at the expense of others. Some 'dropped out' and set up a counter-culture with its own values and social organisation. Many more experimented with parts of this counter-culture and protested about the issues that mattered to them, including:

- civil rights
- injustice and social inequality
- the power held by 'the establishment' (politicians, police, banks)
- the war in Vietnam
- the rights of women.

A counter-culture

The counter-culture that emerged in the 1960s had its own rules, often summed up by a phrase used by one of its leaders, Timothy Leary, in 1966: 'Turn on, tune in, drop out'. One of the most influential 'drop-out' groups was the hippie movement, which horrified the older generation by its emphasis on peace, free love, communal living and the use of drugs such as LSD.

Did you know?

The University of California, Berkley, had strict rules about political activities on campus. Students could only campaign or raise money for the Democratic or Republican parties. Students had protested about this from as early as 1958. In September 1964, students campaigned for the Congress of Racial Equality (CORE), despite the rules. Campus police intervened and a rising spiral of arrests and sit-ins developed. The protests began to cover all aspects of rights on campus and attracted speakers and others from outside, such as the famous folk-singer Joan Baez. In January 1965 the university gave students wider campaigning rights in some parts of the campus.

Build Better Answers

Use Source B and your own knowledge to explain why protest movements were so active the 1960s.
(10 marks)

Paper 1 part (d) answers expect you to use a source and your own knowledge to explain something.

■ **A basic answer (level 1)** would make simple generalisations. For example, *Protesters, especially young people, wanted a fairer society.*

● **A good answer (level 2)** would give reasons supported by detail from their own knowledge and the source (more than one would get a higher mark). For example, *People were reacting to things they felt were wrong or unfair. They wanted the war in Vietnam to stop. They wanted black people to have their civil rights. They wanted women to be treated more equally to men.*

▲ **An excellent answer (level 4)** would be the 'better' answer from above with more than one factor showing how they combined to produce the outcome. For example, *Different groups protested about different things. However, they were all against government actions they saw as unfair. So, many different people protested against the war in Vietnam because of the cost, or because young men were drafted (even before they could vote) or because they didn't want the USA involved in wars abroad. The civil rights movement had black and white protesters who wanted black people to have the equality the law gave them.*

Source A: *Robert Talmonson, aged 19, burns his draft card as a protest in 1966.*

The Vietnam War

The war in Vietnam, which the USA entered in 1955, drew together many different kinds of protester, especially as US involvement increased from 1965 and more US money and soldiers were committed to it. US military tactics, such as chemical bombing of areas the enemy were said to be hiding in, were widely condemned. TV images of burning villages and terrified villagers damaged the government's image at home and abroad, showing the USA as the oppressor. Millions of people marched. It was especially damaging when returning soldiers formed groups to protest against the war, including Veterans and Reservists to End the War and Vets for Peace. These soldiers burned their discharge papers and gave back their medals. Some demonstrators even burned the US flag. Some carried banners actively supporting the enemy. By fighting its war against communism, the government seemed to be producing support for it.

The war that dominated the USA in the 1960s was the anti-communist war in Vietnam. The US government could call up men as young as 17 years to fight in Vietnam for two years. Those same young men were not seen as responsible enough to vote until they were 21.

Source B: *From a modern textbook.*

 Watch out!

Be careful not to treat the events in Unit 3 as if they happened in chronological order – the Red Scare, the civil rights movement, then other protest movements. They overlapped, and affected each other. If you keep one big timeline or timechart for all the major events in each section, you will be able to see the overlap.

Activities

1   Copy out these slogans used in the 1960s and write next to them what the protest was about, **and give reasons for your choice** (if you think it could be used in more than one type of protest, explain each one you think it could be used it):

   a   Hell No! We Won't Go!
   b   Power to the People
   c   We March for First Class Citizenship Now!
   d   Independence Not Dependence
   e   Equal Pay for Equal Work
   f   Hey! Hey! LBJ! How many kids did you kill today?

2   Copy and complete the following:

   In the 1960s, young people, especially students, protested about a number of issues, such as...

   'Dropping out' was...

   Many older people objected to the hippie lifestyle because...

Student protest

Year	All students	Women (per cent)
1947	2,338,226	29%
1950	2,281,298	32%
1955	2,653,034	35%
1960	4,145,065	38%
1965	5,920,864	39%
1970	8,580,887	41%

Source A: *Student enrolment in American universities, 1947–70, from official statistics.*

The numbers of students grew in the 1960s. Students also became more dissatisfied. They wanted to change society. Their attitude to their parents' generations was summed up by badges warning: 'Don't trust anyone over 30'. At first, students protested peacefully, using non-violent methods. However, when this had little effect, many talked of violent revolution. Student protest had an impact because many of the students involved were middle-class, educated and white.

SDS

One of the most important activist groups was Students for a Democratic Society (SDS), set up in 1960. In 1962, it drew up the Port Huron Statement that laid down its aims. The statement contrasted the values the students had been brought up to approve of (the Declaration of Independence's 'all men are created equal') with the reality of life in the USA (the situation of black people). It aimed to campaign against 'racial injustice, war and the violation of human rights'. By the end of 1967 it had about 30,000 members.

The SDS and other student groups began by using the direct non-violent protest methods used by civil rights groups. They organised sit-ins and other protests over issues ranging from student involvement in university decision-making to the war in Vietnam. They broke laws they saw as wrong and got themselves arrested. As the 1960s progressed, student protests became more organised, more large-scale and more violent. The language of protest became more confrontational – with the police called 'pigs' and chants like 'Ho, Ho, Ho, Chi Min, the NLF [who were fighting the USA in Vietnam] are gonna win!'.

SDS publications began to fill with images of guerrillas waving automatic weapons. The dangers of the politics of confrontation were clear to some leaders of the Left, but they were powerless to stop it. Lee Webb, an SDS member in 1965, said: 'SDS now influences its membership to become more militant. Calls to stand in front of a troop train or burn a draft card have replaced analysing and understanding the situation.' But it was militant action, not debate, which increased membership of the SDS.

Source B: *From* America Divided: the Civil War of the 1960s, *by Maurice Isserman and Michael Kazinin, published in 2000.*

Examination question

Study these events which occurred in the USA in the years 1945–74.

Nixon resigns; Montgomery Bus Boycott; Senate censures McCarthy; SDS set up; assassination of Martin Luther King

Write these events in the correct chronological sequence.

(3 marks)

Berkeley 1964	sit-ins, marches, passive resistance
Columbia 1968	more people involved: sit-ins, marches, occupations of buildings
Kent State 1970	more people involved: sit-ins, marches, occupations of buildings, destruction of papers, burning buildings

How protest changed 1964–70.

Key features

Most campus protests in the 1960s followed a similar pattern. They:

- began with a small, often radical, group of students
- lasted several days
- often targeted several issues, for maximum support
- used many of the disruption tactics learned from civil rights protesters (although they also used their own tactics, such as burning the draft cards for the war or going on strike).

Often, after some negotiation, the campus authorities called the police and there were arrests.

The Kent State shootings

On 1 May 1970, students at Kent State University in Ohio protested against the escalation of the war in Vietnam by burying the Constitution and some draft cards. Over the weekend there were demonstrations and some violence. The National Guard were called in to keep the peace. On 4 May they killed four unarmed students and seriously wounded nine more while trying to break up a protest.

Causes

Student protest

Student protest became locked in an escalating spiral of violence because:

- the marches and passive resistance actions needed police intervention
- the police became less patient
- the students became more violent and there were more people involved
- some students saw provoking violence as a way to radicalise more students and so gain support.

When there was significant fighting between police and protesters the state governor usually called in the National Guard, and they were trained as soldiers.

Activities

1 **a** Write a paragraph outlining how student protest changed from 1964 to 1970.

   b Write a second paragraph to explain why you think this happened.

2 Read Source B and study Source C. Use them and your own knowledge about student protest in the 1960s to explain why the government felt so threatened by student protest.

Source C: *An anti-Vietnam demonstration in Washington in 1967. The face on the red placard is Che Guevara, who fought for Cuban independence from a government backed by the USA. The placard next to it reads: 'Crush the Draft'.*

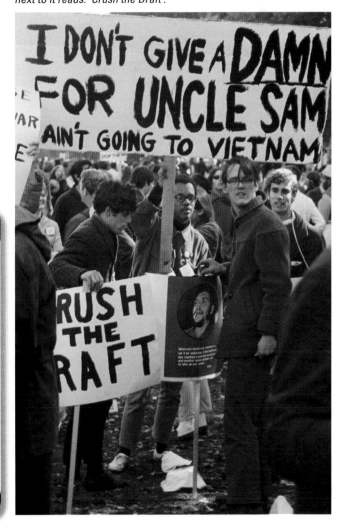

The position of women in the early 1960s

Learning objectives

In this chapter you will learn about:
- views of the role of women in the 1950s and early 1960s
- position of women in the workforce
- the importance of Betty Friedan.

In the 1950s and early 1960s, most people expected women to be homemakers. The general feeling was that single young women could work while waiting to 'catch' a husband and leave work to start a family. But that was all. Many people did not want to employ women in 'career' jobs (with more responsibility and better pay). They argued that women, no matter how capable, didn't need careers – work was a temporary thing. Women's organisations, such as the Federation of Business and Professional Women (set up in the 1920s), were largely ignored. Even people fighting other forms of prejudice (such as racial prejudice) often had a prejudiced view of women. Female civil rights campaigners, and women in other radical groups, were expected to do the secretarial work, not lead or make speeches.

Campaigning for change

Some people fought the idea that women were just homemakers. Eleanor Roosevelt, the wife of Franklin D. Roosevelt (president 1933–45), campaigned for equality for women before the war. During the war, she pressed for childcare for women working on the home front. Her position meant she could encourage women working by, for example, holding press conferences for women journalists only. She also pressed her husband (and later presidents) to give jobs to women. Roosevelt and Kennedy did this. Her campaigns made the idea of working women more acceptable to many people. Newspapers employed women to gain access to her press conferences and the White House employed more, too. She continued to campaign for women's rights until her death in 1962. She made speeches, wrote articles and spoke on radio about the right of women to work. Just one year later, *The Feminine Mystique*, by Betty Friedan was published. Friedan asked the women she had graduated with in 1942 about their lives, what they were doing and if they were happy with their circumstances. Most of the women were either housewives or in low-paid jobs and felt unhappy about their lives. So she interviewed younger women too, and found the same thing. The book was a bestseller and changed the way a lot of people thought about the role of women.

During the Second World War, Eleanor Roosevelt encouraged women's employment in the defence industries. She urged women to volunteer for civil defence work and the military. She defended women in the military who wanted to do more than type, file, and clean. She campaigned for legislation to set up on-site day care for defence workers. Her insistence that President Kennedy appoint more women to his administration led him to create a Presidential Commission on the Status of Women and appoint Eleanor Roosevelt as its chair.

Source A: *From an article about Eleanor Roosevelt on a US government website.*

The problem lay buried, unspoken, for many years in the minds of American women. Each wife struggled with it alone. As she made the beds, shopped for groceries, matched furnishing fabric, ate peanut butter sandwiches with her children, drove them to Cub Scouts and Brownies, lay beside her husband at night – she was afraid to ask even herself the silent question "Is this all?" There was no word of this feeling in all the novels, books and articles by experts telling women their role was to seek fulfilment as wives and mothers.

Source B: *From* The Feminine Mystique, *written by Betty Freidan in 1963.*

Source C: *This is an advertisement for a fridge from the 1960s.*

The average SNCC worker finds it difficult to discuss the woman problem because of the assumptions of male superiority. Assumptions of male superiority are as widespread and deep-rooted and every much as crippling to the woman as the assumptions of white supremacy are to the Negro. Consider why, in SNCC, women who are competent, qualified, and experienced, are automatically given the 'female' jobs such as typing, telephone work, filing, library work, cooking, and the assistant kind of administrative work but rarely the 'executive' kind.

Source E: *From a document about the role of women in the SNCC, presented to the SNCC anonymously in November 1964.*

Census information for 1960 shows that:
- 38% of all students at university were women
- 38% of all women went out to work.

Working women made up:
- 98% of those working in other people's homes
- 68% of those doing clerical work, such as filing and typing
- 14% of managers.

Source D: *Information from the US Bureau of Statistics.*

Examination question

Explain **one** effect of *The Feminine Mystique* on women in the 1960s. **(4 marks)**

Activities

1 Using Source A, copy and complete the following sentence: *Eleanor Roosevelt pushed for women's rights by...*

2 In pairs, make a list of at least three features of a woman's role in the early 1960s shown in Source C.

3 Write a sentence explaining why the behaviour of the men in SNCC [Source E] might be seen as surprising.

4 Copy and complete the diagram on the right.

> Women Betty Friedan graduated with told her...
>
> ↓
>
> ↓
>
> So she...
>
> ↓
>
> ↓
>
> Then she wrote...
>
> ↓

Women's liberation movements

Learning objectives

In this chapter, you will learn about:

● groups that campaigned for women's liberation

● legislation aimed at equality.

In 1963, the Equal Pay Act made it illegal to pay women less for doing the same job as men. But it did not abolish discrimination and was unclear about how 'same job' was defined. The 1964 Civil Rights Act made it illegal for employers to discriminate on sexual grounds, as well as religious and racial ones. But the law added that religious and sexual discrimination was allowed if employers proved it was necessary for a particular job.

As with the civil rights movement, passing a law was not enough to change attitudes and behaviour. In June 1966, a group consisting mainly of women, including Betty Friedan, set up the National Organisation for Women (NOW) as a women's civil rights group. Its aim was 'to bring women into full participation in American society now, with all its privileges and responsibilities, in truly equal partnership with men'.

Talk of 'women's liberation' began on campuses all over America. Radical men could be as prejudiced against equal rights for women as anyone else. At one radical meeting in Chicago, the man choosing speakers from the audience ignored women who raised their hands to speak. When a woman tried to take the microphone to speak, he patted her head and said, 'Cool down, little girl, we have more important things to talk about than women's problems.' Women in radical organisations set up local groups that spread ideas and developed their own radical magazines, but they did not form a national organisation. They felt they would work more effectively at a local level.

After university, I wanted to be a journalist and worked unpaid for several months to put together a file of my work. When I went to look for a job as a news reporter, I was told, before they even opened my file, that the 5 per cent quota for women reporters was met, so they did not need a woman. During the next few months of answering job adverts and signing up at employment agencies, I experienced the many subtle and not-so-subtle forms of sex-discrimination for any job paying more than that of a secretary. Time and time again, I was told that, despite my abilities and the need for skilled workers, I could not be offered a good job because I would leave to get married (or have a baby, or just leave). At first, I tried to persuade them that I was different. Slowly, I realised that they didn't want to listen. The fact that I was a woman was all they saw.

Source B: *Jo Freeman, author of* The Politics of Women's Liberation, *describing her attempts to find work after university in 1967.*

Source A: *Betty Friedan talking to reporters in April 1967. She is on a NOW demonstration urging the New York State Assembly to amend their laws to ban sexual discrimination as well as racial discrimination.*

Census information for 1970 shows that:

- 41% of all students at university were women
- 43% of all women went out to work.

Working women made up:

- 96% of those working in other people's homes
- 69% of those doing clerical work, such as filing and typing
- 14% of managers.

Source C: *Information from the US Bureau of Statistics.*

Watch out!

When you are asked to explain the effect of one event on another, don't just give a list of effects or generalise. This will get you some marks (as long as you are accurate), but to get to the top level you need to do more. Make sure that you explain **how** one event affected another, giving details. So don't just say The Feminine Mystique *made people think women weren't happy with their lives.* Add: *It showed that they didn't like being expected just to be wives and mothers, or only do low-paid or part-time work.*

The contraceptive pill let women plan their pregnancies...

Margaret Chase Smith stood for President...

The Equal Pay Act was passed and sex discrimination was put into the Civil Rights Act...

... but they were hard to enforce.

Many cases were brought to court over equal opportunities...

...but she only got 27 votes.

...but only some states allowed its use, and usually only for married women.

President Johnson removed the limit on women in the military...

...but they could still not go into battle.

...but there was still discrimination everywhere else.

Courses of women's history were introduced at some universities...

...but some women lecturers were sacked for teaching female equality.

New York City banned 'men only' public facilities such as bars...

...but many failed (a firm in Indiana was allowed to stop women working on the factory floor because they had to lift over 35 lb – the average weight of a typewriter, which they moved all the time).

Activities

1. Compare Source C with Source D on page 141 (the previous set of census information). Write a sentence saying how things have changed between 1960 and 1970.

2. Read Source A. If Jo Freeman's experience was usual, what is unusual about the reporters in Source B? Do you think the photographer did this on purpose?

3. Read the thought bubbles above. They contain seven sentences split into 'heads and tails'. Match the sentence starters to the correct endings. Write out the completed sentences.

4. Write a progress report for a NOW meeting in 1970 saying whether you think its aims have been achieved.

Opposition to women's liberation

Learning objectives

In this chapter you will learn about:
- reasons for opposition
- the issue of abortion
- the importance of Phyllis Schlafly.

Reasons for opposition

The women's liberation movement faced opposition, for various reasons, from many men and some women. Some opponents objected to everything the movement stood for. Others objected only to some of the changes the movement pushed for. Of all of the issues that provoked controversy, the biggest was abortion.

Abortion

In 1960 abortion was illegal in the USA, although a few states allowed it if the mother's life was at risk. Doctors who were found to have performed illegal abortions were prosecuted and barred from working. Illegal abortions were often carried out by unqualified people and were expensive and dangerous. There are no accurate statistics about how many women died because of an attempted abortion – the fact was often covered up because it was illegal.

Unwanted pregnancy was too often seen as a problem for the pregnant woman to solve. Many women's liberation groups campaigned for the right to abortion, because it was a woman's body and life that were affected by the pregnancy. The issue soon became, and still is, a struggle between those advocating the rights of the pregnant woman and those advocating the rights of the unborn child.

From 1965 on, following pressure by groups such as NOW, some states brought in laws that allowed abortions for more reasons than just to save the mother's life, but they were still very few. Then, in 1973, the case of *Roe v. Wade* was taken to the Supreme Court fighting for a woman's right to have an abortion. The decision was that for the first 12 weeks a woman had the right to choose an abortion, in any state. The abortion had to be done by a registered doctor in medically safe conditions. For the next 12 weeks, the state could allow an abortion, depending on individual cases. For the last 12 weeks of the pregnancy the mother's life had to be at risk. Abortion was now legal – but anti-abortion campaigners did not give up the fight to stop it.

Some opponents wanted women to stick to the role of homemaker. As late as 1970, new organisations such as Happiness of Womanhood were being formed to support the role of woman as homemaker. Others thought that women should be putting their energy into other movements (those against poverty or racism, for example).

Source A: *From a modern textbook.*

Year	Number of reported abortions
1960	292
1962	292
1964	823
1966	1,028
1968	6,211
1970	193,491

Source B: *The number of reported abortions 1960–70, from US Government statistics.*

Effects

Legalised abortion

There is much debate about some of the effects of legalised abortion. It is clear that:

- Abortions became safer. Before 1973, over 23% of all pregnancy complications brought to hospital were because of attempted abortions. The rate began to fall in the same year and fell steadily. It is now under 1%.

- The rift between people in favour of allowing abortion and those against it grew deeper.

One of the most fiercely disputed claims is that it is the cause of a big drop in the crime rate 20 years and more after *Roe v Wade*.

The Equal Rights Bill (ERA)

Every year since 1923, Congress was asked to consider passing an Equal Rights Amendment Bill. Its aim was simple – to pass an amendment to the Constitution stopping any state discriminating against a person because of their sex. The bill seldom reached Congress. Opponents managed to stop it at the committee stage, where the exact wording was considered.

In 1972, thanks to the work of NOW and other women's liberation groups, politicians saw that enough women supported ERA to affect voting results. Holding it up might lose them votes. The Bill was passed by the House of Representatives and the Senate. So Congress had passed the amendment. Now it had to be ratified by at least 38 states by 1980 to become law.

Phyllis Schlafly

By 1972, 30 states had ratified ERA. Then Phyllis Schlafly set up STOP (Stop Taking Our Privileges) to campaign against ERA. Schlafly was a married lawyer who had unsuccessfully run for Congress in 1952 and, in 1964, wrote a book about corruption in presidential elections. She opposed women's lib as damaging to family values. In 1967 she set up the *Eagle Forum*, a conservative, pro-family group. This became STOP in 1972.

Schlafly argued against ERA because she said it would remove privileges that many women wanted (for example, exemption from conscription to the army and 'dependent wife' benefits). She also argued that many poorer women who wanted to be wives and mothers would be disadvantaged by the amendment. Her campaign convinced states that there was considerable opposition to ERA, as well as support for it. Only 30 of them ratified the amendment. It was not passed.

Source C: *Phyllis Schlafly campaigning against ERA at the Illinois State government building in June 1968.*

> ### Top tip
>
> The biggest percentage of the marks given in the exam is given for your ability to recall information (and sometimes also select it from a given source) and use it to answer the question. Always focus on the question. If asked about issues in the period 1960–70, be sure to use detail from that period. Only this detail will be rewarded.

Activities

1 Copy and complete the following sentences:
   a Pro-life campaigners believed...
   b Pro-choice campaigners believed...
2 Use Source A and your own knowledge to write a detailed answer explaining why people objected to the aims of women's liberation groups.

Re-electing President Nixon

> **Learning objectives**
>
> In this chapter you will learn about:
> - reasons for Watergate
> - key events: the break-in, the cover-up, the investigations and Nixon's re-election.

In 1972 President Richard Nixon, a Republican, stood for re-election. The Committee to Re-elect the President (CRP, soon popularly known as CREEP) was set up to raise funds for the campaign. CREEP and other White House groups got information about the Democrats using money from a secret fund run by John Mitchell, the Attorney General. It paid for spying and sabotage. Nixon's aides broke into buildings and bugged them or stole material that might compromise the government or help to smear the Democrats.

The break-in

On the night of 17 June 1972, five burglars were caught in the offices of the National Democratic Committee in the Watergate office building in Washington. All but one, a locksmith, had government connections (see box). From the start, two reporters from the *Washington Post*, Bob Woodward and Carl Bernstein, were suspicious. As they investigated, they found out that it had been a professional job, that the men carried thousands of dollars in cash and that one of them was on CREEP's payroll. The day after the *Washington Post* announced this, Nixon and his chief of staff, Bob Haldeman, secretly discussed forcing the FBI to drop the burglary investigation. Publicly, a White House spokesman refused to comment on 'a third-rate burglary.' From the start, Nixon seems to have thought it was possible to cover up how far he and many senior people in his government were involved in what had happened.

The Watergate tapes

From 1971, well before the break-in, Nixon had been secretly taping conversations and phone calls in his office. He was not the first president to do so. The policy began under Franklin Roosevelt, who came to power in 1933. Very few people knew about this, however – certainly not the American public. It was these tapes, once their existence became known, that allowed investigators to sort out, to an extent, how far the President and his aides were involved in setting up the burglary then trying to cover it up.

> **Did you know?**
>
> ***The burglars***
> **Bernard Barker:** ex-CIA
> **Virgilio Gonzales:** a locksmith
> **James W McCord:** ex-FBI and ex-CIA, working for CREEP
> **Eugenio Martinez:** ex-CIA
> **Frank Sturgis:** ex-CIA
>
> ***Their outside help***
> **Howard Hunt:** ex-CIA and White House
> **G Gordon Liddy:** ex-FBI and White House, advisor to CREEP
>
> ***Part of the cover-up***
> **Richard Nixon:** President
> **John Dean:** White House lawyer
> **John Ehrlichman:** Adviser on Domestic Affairs
> **Bob Haldeman:** White House Chief of Staff
> **Richard Kleindienst:** Attorney General
> **John Mitchell:** head of CREEP, ex-Attorney General

> **Watch out!**
>
> We know that Nixon was involved in the cover-up and that he was forced to resign. But at the time, many people dismissed the *Washington Post* revelations as they came out as unbelievable. This does not make them stupid or prejudiced (although some of them may have been). The scale of the spying scheme, the existence of White House tapes and who was involved in the cover-up only became clear later.

The Washington Post

No one knew the extent of the scandal to start with. Even when the *Washington Post* showed a connection between the burglars and CREEP, many people thought it was supporters of Nixon going too far – they did not believe the White House could be involved. Even most newspapers ignored the story at first. If Woodward and Bernstein had not carried on investigating, the cover-up might have worked. But they were convinced the burglary was part of something bigger and that the White House was involved. So, helped by police sources and a secret FBI source, they went on digging. They had not found enough evidence by November to affect the election. Nixon won, with 60% of the vote.

Watergate events, 1972	
17 June	The break-in
19 June	The *Washington Post* reported that burglars have government connection. This was denied.
1 August	The *Washington Post* reported a $25,000 check, intended for the Nixon campaign, was banked by a Watergate burglar.
30 August	Nixon claimed John Dean had investigated Watergate and found that no-one from the White House was involved. A Grand Jury was set up to investigate.
15 September	The burglars were called to give evidence to the Grand Jury. Also Howard Hunt and Gordon Liddy, said to have helped them.
29 September	The *Washington Post* revealed the existence of John Mitchell's secret fund.
1 October	The *Washington Post* reported that FBI agents discovered the break-in was part of a huge CREEP spying campaign.
11 November	Nixon was re-elected.

Top tip

You do not have to learn all the dates and events in the boxes on pages 147 and 148. The boxes are there to help you to follow the complicated turns of events.

Activity

There were a lot of people involved in the Watergate scandal, and their involvement became clear at different times. Using the 'who was who' box on the left, make a spider diagram with 'The Watergate Scandal' at the centre and the people radiating out from it. You will use the diagram in Question 3 on page 149 as well. Fill in when you think each person is **clearly** linked to the scandal up to the end of 1972.

Source A: *The* Washington Post *gave Watergate front page coverage from the start.*

Watergate events, 1973

8 January	The trial of the Watergate Seven began for conspiracy, burglary and wiretapping.
11 January	Hunt pleaded guilty.
15 January	All the burglars except McCord pleaded guilty.
30 January	Liddy and McCord (who pleaded not guilty) were found guilty.
7 February	The Senate set up the Select Committee on Presidential Campaign Activities.
23 March	Hunt wrote to the trial judge, claiming Dean and Mitchell told the burglars to lie – so beginning the cover-up.
17 April	Nixon denied knowing about the affair beforehand. He appointed a special prosecutor, Archibald Cox, to hold a separate investigation.
30 April	Nixon announced (on TV) his dismissal of Dean and the resignations of Haldeman and Erlichman. Kleindienst resigned the same day.
18 May	Televised Watergate hearings began.
25 June	Dean told the Committee Nixon was involved in the cover-up within days of it happening and gave details of other White House spying activities.
7 July	Nixon refused to testify or hand over any documents.
13 July onwards	Alexander Butterfield (ex-White House) told the Committee about the taping of phone calls and conversations in Nixon's office. A legal battle began over the tapes and documents. Cox and the Senate Committee both demanded the tapes. Nixon refused.
19 October	Nixon suggested a Democratic Senator listened to some tapes and made summaries.
20 October	Nixon's suggestion was turned down. He told the Attorney General to sack Cox. He (and his deputy) refused. They were sacked, as was Cox, by the new Attorney General, who then demanded the tapes anyway.
23 October	Nixon finally handed over some edited transcripts of the tapes.
17 November	Nixon defended himself in a press conference, saying, "I am not a crook".
21 November	A gap of about 20 minutes is discovered on a tape of a conversation between Nixon and Haldeman on June 20, 1972. Electronics experts said there were at least 5 separate cuts.

Watergate events, 1974

January	Public outrage at the scandal led to many people demanding Nixon's resignation. The Senate began to consider impeaching Nixon (putting him on trial for his actions).
6 February	Investigations began to see if there were grounds for impeachment.
16 April	The Prosecutor demanded 64 more tapes.
30 April	Nixon refused to hand over the tapes, but provided edited transcripts. There was public shock at what was said and the bad language used.
9 May	Impeachment hearings began against Nixon for: 1 obstructing the investigation of the break in 2 misuse of power and breaking his oath of office 3 failure to obey the laws requiring him to hand over evidence.
24 July	The Supreme Court ordered Nixon to make the tapes available.
27 July	Nixon found guilty on point 1.
29 July	Nixon found guilty on point 2.
30 July	Nixon found guilty on point 3.
5 August	Nixon released transcripts of three conversations with Haldeman just after the break-in. The 23 June tape revealed Nixon ordered the FBI to abandon its investigation of the break-in.
8 August	Nixon announced on TV that he would resign.
9 August	Nixon resigned.

Why was it a scandal?

What did the president know, and when did he know it? This was the question that occupied everyone's mind. In many ways the thing that most concerned people about Watergate was not the break in but the cover-up and the way Nixon and his most important officials in the White House had lied. The scandal was that they could not trust their president to be truthful or behave honourably. Nixon's initial denial of involvement in the cover-up was undermined by the evidence that the tapes were altered before they were handed over. This was enough for the Senate to **impeach** Nixon. When the 23 June tape (on which he discussed stopping the FBI investigation) was released, it proved he had been involved from the start and that his television appearances and speeches denying involvement had been a lie. This tape was the 'smoking gun' that implicated Nixon in the crime that left him with no alternative but to resign.

> In April 1973, Nixon went on television and told the nation that 'there can be no whitewash at the White House'. He then appointed a special prosecutor to investigate the Watergate affair. The man chosen for this was Archibald Cox.

Source B: *From a modern textbook.*

1974	% who believed in Nixon's innocence
May	75%
Early June	75%
Late June	65%
July	61%
August	53%

Source C: *The percentage of Americans who said they believed Nixon was innocent, May–September 1974.*

Build Better Answers

Choose either Dean's revelations of Nixon's involvement or Nixon's refusal to testify or hand over documents. Explain one effect on the Watergate scandal of the event you have chosen. (4 marks)

Paper 1 part (b) questions will ask about the effect of one event on another.

■ **A basic answer (level 1)** will give a generalised effect. For example, *It just made him look even more guilty.*

● **A good answer (level 2)** will give more explanation, relevant to the question. For example, **either:** *It was bound to make it more of a scandal and make Nixon seem guilty. Here was a senior White House aide saying Nixon knew about the cover-up.* **or:** *It was bound to make Nixon seem guilty of helping, if not ordering, the cover up. Why would he refuse to do these things unless he was part of the cover-up?*

Activities

1 a What does Source B tell you that makes the events of 20 October 1973 significant?

   b What do the events of 20 October suggest about Nixon's involvement in the bugging and the cover-up?

2 a Choose the four events from the timetable that you think were the most significant in Nixon's downfall. List them, explaining the significance of each one.

   b Compare Source B to the timeline and your list. Does this affect your choices? Explain your answer.

3 Complete the diagram you started on page 147. If you are unsure about any of your decisions, put a question mark next to the box.

The impact of Watergate

Learning objectives

In this chapter you will learn about:
- Watergate's impact on Nixon
- Watergate's impact on US politics.

Watergate's effect on Nixon

The most obvious effect of Watergate on Nixon was that he resigned – he lost the presidency. He also faced trial: the Attorney General recommended prosecution. However, on 8 September 1974 the new president, Gerald Ford, granted Nixon a full pardon for any offences committed over the Watergate period. He said he was doing this for the sake of the country, to end the matter, rather than have it dragged out over years in court. Nixon, in his response, came the nearest he ever came to admitting involvement, saying, 'the way I tried to deal with Watergate was the wrong way' and was a burden he would have to carry for the rest of his life. He is remembered by many people only for Watergate, despite the fact that his diplomacy with leaders in the Soviet Union and China had led to a real improvement in relations between those countries and the USA.

Watergate's effect on US politics

Watergate had wide-ranging effects on US politics. In the short term, White House officials and Republican politicians suffered.

- Although Nixon escaped trial, many other White House officials caught up in the scandal were tried and over 30 went to prison.
- In the next round of federal elections, the Republican Party lost 48 seats in the House of Representatives and 8 seats in the Senate.
- In the next round of presidential elections, the public chose Democrat Jimmy Carter as president, a man who was likeable and honest, but not as good at managing the more complicated side of his job, such as international relations.

Watergate had more long-term repercussions, too.

- American politicians felt that their reputation worldwide had been damaged.
- The American people became more cynical about their politicians and less willing to trust what they said.
- The media was less deferential to the government. It was quicker to hunt down, and 'expose' without full evidence, political scandals.

Year	% of trust in the federal government
1958	75%
1964	75%
1966	65%
1968	61%
1970	53%
1974	36%

Source A: *The percentage of Americans who said they would trust the federal government to do the right thing, 1958–74.*

Examination question

Choose **either** the Watergate scandal **or** the integration of Little Rock. Explain one effect on the USA of the event you have chosen. **(4 marks)**

Top tip

When asked, in part b) questions, to choose **one** event and write about its effects, take time to think carefully about which event you can best answer the question on. When you have chosen, stick to your choice. Time taken at the start stops you wasting time by changing your mind half-way through. Remember, the question only asks for **one** effect, too. You will only get marks for one event and one effect of that event.

Source B: *A cartoon published in the New York Post on 14 May, 1973.*

Richard Nixon's Presidency started badly, but his handling of the economy in the early 1970s and his visits to China and Russia made him appear statesmanlike. ... [After Watergate] many Americans were shaken by the admission that a President could be a liar and a cheat. Nixon's successor, Gerald Ford, lost to Jimmy Carter in the November 1986 election. Carter promised an 'open Presidency'. His sincerity and honesty were never questioned, but he was seen as a weak President, unable to deal with Russia over Afghanistan and with the hostage crisis in Iran.

Source C: *From a modern textbook.*

New legislation

After Nixon resigned, Congress pushed through laws to limit the powers of the president. The 1973 War Powers Act stopped him from going to war without the support of Congress. In 1974, the Election Campaign Act set limits to contributions and spending on campaigns, while the Congressional Budget Act controlled the president's use of government money. In the same year the Freedom of Information Act gave people the right to see government documents about them, while the Privacy Act set rules for the government's collection of information about people. The 1978 Ethics in Government Act said government officials had to make the finances of their work publicly available. It also set limits on the work they could do once they left the government. This stopped them taking advantage of things they found out while in government.

Activities

1 List four effects of the Watergate scandal on the USA. Chose one and explain why it had the effect it did.

2 Copy and complete the following sentences:

   a In 1958, 75% of Americans trusted the federal government. In 1974 the percentage had dropped to ...

   b I think this was/was not/was partly [chose one] due to the Watergate scandal, because...

3 List the two main provisions of the 1978 Ethics in Government Act, explaining how it was an effect of the Watergate scandal.

In the Paper 1 final examination you will have to answer questions on the two different options you have studied. Civil Rights in the USA, 1916–74 is one of them. You will have to answer four questions. Question (a) is on chronology, (b) asks you to explain effects, (c) asks about causation and (d) is an essay using a source and your own knowledge.

You have 45 minutes to answer the four sub-questions on each theme (the exam is one hour 30 minutes in total), so the examiners are not expecting you to write huge amounts. The number of marks helps you to judge how much to write. For Question (a) allow 5 minutes, Question (b) 8 minutes, Question (c) 12 minutes and Question (d) 15 minutes.

Build Better Answers

Question (a)

Examiner's tip: Part (a) questions will ask you to place a series of events in the correct chronological order. This is only worth 3 marks, so allow about 5 minutes for this question.

Let's look at an example.

Study these events which occurred in the years 1954–72.

The Montgomery Bus Boycott	Nixon re-elected as President	The Hiss Case	The *Brown v Topeka* Case	The assassination of Martin Luther King

Write these events in the correct chronological sequence. **(3 marks)**

- As part of your revision, ensure you make a timeline of your own showing the key events in the USA in the years 1945–74. This will help you not only with Question (a) but also with the other three questions in this section. It will ensure that you put events in the correct sequence or order.

- Cut out the events and dates separately and test yourself by matching the dates to the events and putting them in chronological order. Here is an example:

1947	The Truman Doctrine The Marshall Plan The Hollywood Ten	1949	Soviet Union tests atomic bomb
1948	Start of Berlin Crisis	1950	The Hiss Case Start of Korean War

Student answer	**Examiner comments**
The Hiss Case, Brown v Topeka, Nixon re-elected as President, Martin Luther King assassinated, the Montgomery Bus Boycott	This would be awarded 1 mark as the candidate has the first two in the correct sequence.

Let's rewrite the answer with all the events in the right sequence.

The Hiss Case, Brown v Topeka, the Montgomery Bus Boycott, Martin Luther King assassinated, Nixon re-elected as President	The candidate has all five events in the right chronological order and would be awarded full (3) marks.

Build Better Answers

Question (b)

Examiner tip: Question (b) will pick two out of the five events from Question (a). It will ask you to choose one of the two of the events and to use your knowledge to describe its effects. This is only worth 4 marks, so allow about 8 minutes for this question. An effect means the results or the consequences of an event – in other words, what the event led to. For example, one effect of the *Brown v Topeka* case was that the Supreme Court became involved in civil rights and ordered the southern states to set up integrated schools. One effect of the Montgomery Bus Boycott was to make Martin Luther King the leading figure in the fight for black civil rights.

Let's look at an example.

Choose **either** | The Montgomery Bus Boycott | **or** | The *Brown v Topeka* Case

Explain one effect on the USA of the event you have chosen. **(4 marks)**

- Choose **one** of the events and stick with your choice. Some candidates, half way through writing their answer on the first event, decide to write about the other event. This wastes valuable time.

- Focus on the question. It is about one effect, so begin your answer with *One effect was…*. Do not just tell the story.

- Give the effect and describe it. Using the word *because* helps you to give a developed description.

- One paragraph is enough because it is only worth 4 marks.

Student answer	**Examiner comments**
The Montgomery Bus Boycott started when Rosa Parks refused to give up her seat on a bus to a white person. She was arrested and then her supporters boycotted the bus company.	This student tells the story rather than focusing on one effect and explaining it. This would be marked in Level 1.

Let's rewrite the answer and focus on one effect.

| **One effect** of the Montgomery Bus Boycott was to **make Martin Luther King the most important figure in the black civil rights movement**. This was **because** King was made the leader of the Montgomery Improvement Association, which organised the boycott against the bus company. <u>As a result</u> of his leadership, the boycott against the bus company was a success, encouraging the Supreme Court to rule that segregation of public transport was unconstitutional. | The student immediately focuses on the question by giving the effect. There is a developed explanation of the effect using links words and phrases such as 'because' and 'as a result'. This would be marked in Level 2. |

Build Better Answers

Question (c)

Examiner tip: Part (c) questions will ask you to use your knowledge to explain why something happened. In other words, this is a question about causation. Causation means explaining the reasons why an event happened. In the example given below, you are being asked to explain reasons for the Red Scare. You will always need to explain at least two reasons and these reasons should be linked. It is worth 8 marks, so allow about 12 minutes for this question.

Let's look at an example.

Why was there a growing fear of communism in the USA in the late 1940s and early 1950s? Explain your answer. **(8 marks)**

There are several reasons that you could write about for this question. These include:

- The early Cold War, 1945–50
- The Hiss Case
- The case of the Rosenbergs
- The actions of Joseph McCarthy.

Remember to:

- Focus on the question. It is about causation, so make sure you write about the reasons why something happened. Do not just tell the story.
- Write a separate paragraph for each reason. At the beginning of each paragraph give the reason and then fully explain it. Using the word *because* often helps you to give a developed explanation.
- Two paragraphs of explained reasons are enough to achieve the top level.
- For the highest marks you also have to make links between each reason. This means explaining how one reason led to the next. For example, a paragraph on the early Cold War could be linked to the Rosenberg Case. For example, *The fear of communism caused by the Cold War intensified when the Soviet Union exploded its first atomic bomb in August 1949, several years sooner than had been expected. Some in the USA became convinced that only spies could have helped them achieve this so quickly, especially with the arrest of the Rosenbergs.*

You would then write a paragraph giving an explanation about the Rosenbergs.

Link words or phrases often help to achieve this. Here are some examples: *this led to, as a result, moreover, furthermore, as a consequence, in addition.*

- Write a conclusion confirming how the two factors combined to produce the outcome.

Here is a grid to help you plan your answer to this question.

First reason	Give the reason.
	Fully explain it.
Link	Make a link with the second reason.
Second reason	Give the reason.
	Fully explain it.
Conclusion	Sum up the two reasons stressing the links between them.

Build Better Answers

Student answer

In 1948 Alger Hiss, a member of the State Department, was accused and tried for spying. There was no evidence to prove Hiss was a spy but he was found guilty of lying. This alarmed many people in the USA, who now believed that there were communist spies in all government departments. Not long afterwards a married couple, the Rosenbergs, were arrested and found guilty of spying for the Soviet Union.

Examiner comments

The candidate knows the reasons. For example, mentions the Hiss Case and gives good supporting detail about the trial and the effect on people in the USA. The answer also mentions the Rosenberg Case but does not give supporting detail. In addition, there is no attempt to show links between the two reasons. This would be marked in Level 2.

Let's rewrite the answer with the details added and links shown between the reasons.

The first reason for the growing fear of communism was the Hiss Case. In 1948 Alger Hiss, a high-ranking member of the State Department, who had been an advisor to President Roosevelt, was accused of being a communist spy. Hiss denied the charge and although never convicted of spying, was, in 1950, found guilty of lying and sentenced to five years in jail. Many people assumed because he was sent to jail, he must have been a spy.

Moreover, this case convinced many Americans that there were Soviet spies in high places in government, which seemed to be confirmed by another spy case, that of the Rosenbergs, which further increased the fear of communism. The Soviet Union developed its atomic bomb in August 1949, and in 1950 Julius and Ethel Rosenberg were arrested and charged with spying. The government claimed that they gave atomic secrets to the Soviet Union. The government case was quite weak, depending on the evidence of others arrested in the case, but the Korean War had just broken out and the Red Scare was reaching new heights. Both were tried, found guilty and executed.

The fear of communism in the USA increased due to the Hiss Case which seemed to suggest there were many Soviet spies in high places. This seemed confirmed by the arrest and trial of the Rosenbergs.

Now we have two clearly explained reasons. Notice how the candidate immediately focuses on the question at the start of the first paragraph. Furthermore, the answer makes links between the first factor, the Hiss Case, and the second factor, the case of the Rosenbergs. This link is reinforced by the conclusion which explains how the factors combined to produce a fear of communism. In addition, the answer gives supporting details for the second reason, the Rosenbergs.

Build Better Answers

Question (d)

Examiner tip: Part (d) questions will ask you to use a source and your knowledge to describe or explain cause, effect or change. It is worth 10 marks, so allow about 15 minutes for this question. If the question is about change, you must show change either by comparing the situation before and after the development, or you must show how it developed during the period. Let's look at an example.

Study the source and then answer the question that follows.

Source A: *From a modern textbook.*

> A number of mainly young black Americans lost patience with the <u>peaceful methods</u> used by Martin Luther King. <u>Malcolm X</u>, for example, wanted to see black Americans create their own state, by force if necessary. Stokely Carmichael was the leader of the <u>Black Power</u> Movement, which also encouraged greater violence.

Use the source and your own knowledge to explain why the campaign for black civil rights in the USA changed in the 1960s.   **(10 marks)**

- The question is asking you to use the source as well as your own knowledge. Ensure that you directly refer to the source in your answer.

- It is also asking you to use your own knowledge. Use the source to stimulate your own knowledge by underlining key names, events or dates in the source. This is shown in Source A where the candidate has underlined <u>peaceful methods</u>, <u>Malcolm X</u> and <u>Black Power</u>. Once you explain these in more detail, you are using your own knowledge.

- Focus on the question. It is about causation, so explain reasons. Do not just tell the story.

- At the beginning of each paragraph give the reason, and then fully explain it. Using the word *because* should help you to give a developed explanation.

- Two paragraphs or explanations are enough to achieve the top level.

- For the highest marks you also have to make links between each factor. This means explaining how one reason led to the next. Link words or phrases often help to achieve this. Here are some examples: *this led to, as a result, moreover, furthermore, as a consequence, in addition.*

- Write a conclusion confirming how the two factors combined to produce the outcome.

Here is a grid to help you plan your answer to this question.

The source	Underline or highlight key words, events, people in the source that you can write more about.
First factor	Give the first factor mentioned in the source. Fully explain it.
Link	Make a link with a second factor mentioned in the source.
Second factor	Fully explain the second factor.
Conclusion	Sum up the two factors stressing the links between them.

Student answer

Martin Luther King believed in peaceful methods such as speeches but many young black Americans lost patience with these methods. Malcolm X wanted a separate state for black Americans and was prepared to use violence. He was followed by the Black Power Movement led by Stokely Carmichael.

Let's look at an answer where the student has used some of his or her own knowledge.

Malcolm X was a member of the Nation of Islam and was a very good speaker. He toured the USA making speeches for the Nation of Islam. In his speeches he attacked the non-violent methods used by Martin Luther King. Malcolm X had a great influence on young black Americans, especially in the cities. He did not want integration with the whites but suggested a separate state for black Americans. He was also prepared to use violence, especially in self-defence, in order to secure a separate black nation.

Let's re-write the answer to include the sources and own knowledge and two linked factors focused on reasons for change.

The methods used to campaign for civil rights <u>changed</u> a great deal in the 1960s, <u>from</u> the peaceful methods advocated by <u>Martin Luther King, to</u> the more violent methods of <u>Malcolm X</u> as well as the <u>Black Power Movement</u>. 'The first reason for change', as suggested in Source A, was that many black Americans lost patience with the peaceful methods used by Martin Luther King and began to support the more violent methods of Malcolm X. As the source suggests, Malcolm X did not agree with King's methods. He was a member of the Nation of Islam and, unlike King, did not believe in integration between black and white Americans. He suggested a separate black state. The other change was in his methods. King would not agree to any violence. Malcolm X, allowed for the use of violence in self-defence. <u>Moreover</u>, although Malcolm X was assassinated in 1965, his views influenced <u>reasons for change</u> in methods as mentioned in **Source A**. The Black Power Movement emerged out of the inner-city riots in the mid 1960s. Its leader, as mentioned in **Source A**, was Stokely Carmichael. Carmichael took the views of Malcolm and further changed the methods of campaigning. He supported violence when necessary and wanted his followers to have a pride in their heritage. Black Power promoted African forms of dress and appearance and adopted the slogan 'black is beautiful'. <u>Therefore</u> the main reason for change in the civil rights movement of the 1960s was the influence of Malcolm X. Not only did he challenge the more peaceful methods of Martin Luther King but his ideas influenced the emergence of the Black Power movement.

On 6 April 1917, the USA joined the Allies fighting the First World War against the Central Powers. The USA had sold the Allies supplies and lent them money from the start (1914). The USA played a big part in winning the war, which ended in 1918, and in building the peace that followed.

The economy of the USA was boosted by war production. The 1920s were a time of prosperity for many Americans; a time where people could buy an increasing range of mass-produced consumer goods, such as washing machines and fridges. It was a time of contrasts. Many Americans took to new ideas and ways of life. However, other Americans showed great intolerance of some groups of people on racial, political or religious grounds.

In this section, you will study:

- the impact of the First World War on the USA
- immigration
- Prohibition and gangsterism
- mass production and the stock market boom
- the Roaring Twenties
- the position of black Americans.

A4: The USA, 1917–29

This question is about the Roaring Twenties. Study Sources A, B, C and D and then answer all the questions that follow.

Source A: A newspaper advertisement for a car in 1927.

Source B: From a speech by Henry Hoover in October 1928.

We have increased home ownership. Today there are almost nine automobiles for every ten families. Seven years ago only enough automobiles were running to average less than four every ten families. Our people have more to eat, better things to wear, and better homes. Wages have increased, the cost of living has decreased. The job of every man and woman made more secure. We have in a short period decreased the fear of poverty, the fear of unemployment, the fear of old age.

Source C: From the *New York Herald Tribune*, early 1929.

Any US citizen willing to get up early enough can look out of his own windows and see a trail of thousands of workmen's automobiles scooting down the boulevards to their factory or new building destination. Even ten years ago this great mass of labour had to live around the corner in a hovel next to the factory or hang on street cars at six o'clock in the morning in order to reach the building site.

Source D: From a history of the USA between the wars, 1987.

By 1920 Americans owned a total of seven million cars. By 1930 the total had risen to nearly twenty-five million. Car ownership brought a major change in people's lives and the success of the car manufacturers ensured the prosperity of other industries too. However, government policies of laissez-faire and protection also stimulated industrial growth.

Study Source A.

(a) What can you learn from Source A about life in the USA during the 1920s?

(3)

Study Sources B and C.

(b) How far does Source C support the evidence of Source B about life in the USA during the 1920s? Explain your answer.

(7)

Study Sources A, B, C and D, and use your own knowledge.

(c) 'The main cause of the boom of the 1920s was the car industry.'

Use the sources, and your own knowledge, to explain whether you agree with this view.

(15)

(Total for Question A4 = 25 marks)

The exam

This page shows you what the Paper 2 Section A exam paper will look like. In Section A of the paper you have two pages with sources and questions. (We have put them together to fit them onto the page.)

The instruction tells you exactly what to do. Study the four sources, **then** answer the questions. Even though the first question is just about Source A, you should do this. Studying the other sources will give you a full picture.

At least one of your sources will be a picture. Make sure you read the caption so you know what you are looking at. Study the picture carefully: sometimes there is useful information in the details.

It is not an accident that the caption, which tells you where and when the source comes from, comes first. It contains important information that helps you to really understand the source.

Part (a) says just use Source A, and part (b) says use Sources B and C. **In these questions you only get marks for what you use from the sources.** Don't tell the examiner lots of things you have learnt. In part (c), though, you need to use your own knowledge as well as the sources.

Remember, you have to answer each of the three questions. The number of marks gives you a clue how much time to spend on each.

Impact of the First World War

Learning objectives

In this chapter you will learn about:
- how the war boosted the US economy
- Europe's dependence on US loans
- how to make inferences from sources.

Europe at the end of the war

When the First World War ended in 1918, the economies of most European countries were in ruins. Some had borrowed huge sums of money from the USA to finance the war. Trade links and production of ordinary goods had been disrupted by the war. In many countries mines, factories and communication links had been destroyed by the fighting. Britain and France were heavily in debt to the USA, and still borrowing – they needed more money to rebuild and start normal life again. Britain's wartime and post-war borrowings added up to a total of $4,277 million; while France owed $3,405 million.

The USA at the end of the war

The USA had no war damage. Just the opposite. Its factories and farms were producing goods and food at full capacity. It was exporting food and all sorts of manufactured goods to Europe. It had won new export markets that, before the war, the Europeans had dominated (such as supplying cotton to Japan). The war gave the USA high productivity and full employment, with good wages for its workers.

Industry

Many industries began to apply the principles of mass production during the war, making their factories more efficient. When the war ended, they were in a good position to produce goods quickly and cheaply, both for the home market and for exports.

Year	Wheat ($ per bushel)
1915	$0.96
1917	$2.04
1919	$2.16
1921	$1.01
1923	$0.92

Source A: *Price of wheat from farming statistics compiled by the US government.*

US international loans (in $ millions)			
	Wartime loans	**Postwar loans**	**Total loans**
To the countries who were allies in First World War	$7,067m	$2,911m	$9,977m

Source B: *From US government figures.*

Activities

1 List three ways in which Europe was damaged by the First World War.

2 List three ways in which the USA benefitted from the war.

3 Draw a diagram to show the percentage of the world's wheat, corn, cotton and petrol the USA was producing in the early 1920s.

4 Write a paragraph saying how much the USA loaned European countries after the war and what they needed the money for.

Agriculture

America's European allies suffered terrible food shortages in the last years of the war. Campaigns like Source D aimed to reduce US consumption, leaving more food to sell to Europe. Farmers played their part too. They expanded their farms, often taking out loans to buy new land and machinery. They also ploughed up land previously used for grazing cattle and sheep and grew wheat instead. Prices rose so high during the war that farmers were confident that they would sell crops at a good profit and repay their loans. In the early 1920s, the USA was producing 30% of the world's wheat, 75% of its corn and 55% of its cotton. It produced 70% of its petrol, too. It saw itself as the world's banker and the world's supplier of necessities.

A time of adjustment

The government, meanwhile, believed in *laissez faire*: letting businesses run their own affairs rather than passing laws to control working hours, prices or wages. *Laissez faire* led to problems immediately after the war, when the prices of crops fell and many employers reduced wages. There was discontent and strikes People lost their jobs. Those who still had jobs found that their hours of work were reduced. But the government felt that all this was part of the economy returning to normal after its huge wartime push. It hoped that falling prices would eventually even things out without government interference.

This is
what GOD gives us
What are you giving
so that others may
live ?
Eat less
WHEAT
MEAT
FATS
SUGAR
Send more to Europe
or they will Starve

UNITED STATES FOOD ADMINISTRATION

Source D: *A US government poster produced in 1918.*

Coolidge [President 1923–29] believed in as little government interference as possible and declared, 'the business of America is business'. Very soon, America was revelling in what became known as 'Coolidge prosperity'. It had very little to do with him and everything to do with the fact that America, after the First World War, was the country the world owed money to. Its undamaged industries achieved miracles of production on the first great assembly lines. It had the highest average income of any country. It made more steel than Europe. And Henry Ford built a car that almost everyone could afford.

Source C: *From* America, *written by Alistair Cooke in 1976.*

Build Better Answers

Paper 2, Section A part (a) is an *inference* question. An inference is something that can be worked out by 'reading between the lines'. It is **not** repeating information in the source. Begin each inference with *Source A suggests...* or *The source also suggests...*

A possible inference from Source D is:

In 1918, many Americans were religious.

This is an inference because it is not directly stated in the source, but the words imply the person reading the poster would feel it was their duty to God to help others.

To achieve the maximum mark for these questions (three), you need to give one or more inferences and support them with evidence from the source.

Reactions to the war

> ## Learning objectives
>
> In this chapter you will learn about:
> - attitudes to the Treaty of Versailles and the League of Nations
> - protectionist policies.

America suffered less from the effects of the war than Europe. Even so, many Americans felt it had been wrong to send 'our boys' to fight. They did not want to get caught up in European politics, or wars, again.

The Treaty of Versailles

The 'Big Three' in the negotiations over the treaties that ended the war were France, Britain and the USA. The US President, Woodrow Wilson, wanted the peace to be based on his Fourteen Points, drawn up before the war ended. It was not. The Treaty of Versailles, between the Allies and Germany, forced Germany to take the blame for starting the war and to pay **reparations** (compensation) to the Allies. Germany was not allowed to take part in the negotiations. Many people felt the treaty was too harsh.

Source A: *A cartoon from 1920 by American cartoonist Winsor McCoy.*

Instead of pursuing a healing policy of reconciliation, which alone was worthy of the agony of war and the great army of dead who fought for a better world, the Treaty of Versailles and the other treaties reflect too much the spirit of vengeance. There are many points in the treaties which can be explained only on the basis of vindictiveness, bad judgment, and unwise compromise.

Source B: *From an article in* The Atlantic, *an American magazine, in October 1920.*

During almost all my public life, I have argued for an agreement between the leading nations of the world to set up the necessary international machinery to end war between civilized nations. I realize no such thing can happen unless every man and every nation approaches the subject with a willingness to compromise, with a willingness to sacrifice some of his own cherished opinions, to bring nations together. Nothing has ever happened in my life in which I felt a deeper interest or for which I would make a greater sacrifice.

Source C: *From a letter to the* Nebraska Times, *written in 1920 by George Norris, Senator for Nebraska. He is discussing the need for a League of Nations.*

 Watch out!

Remember that the Allies made separate treaties with each of the countries they had fought in the First World War. The Treaty of Versailles was the treaty between the Allies and Germany, not any other country.

The League of Nations

At the peace talks, President Wilson pressed for a League of Nations, an international organisation for world co-operation and peace. Eventually the Allies built it into the peace treaties. If a country signed a treaty, it automatically joined the League.

Isolationism

Wilson returned home to find many Americans, and most of the US Senate, did not want to accept the treaties or joint the League. Instead, they wanted to follow a policy of **isolationism** – not becoming involved in world politics. Their first isolationist step was to refuse to ratify (accept) the treaties. The USA did not join the League.

Financial isolationism

The government still had a policy of *laissez faire* – not interfering in business. However, it made some exceptions in the early 1920s to make the USA's economic independence more secure. It introduced laws to keep the government 'living within its budget' and lowered the high wartime taxes. It also introduced trade tariffs – taxes on goods imported into the USA. This pushed up the price of imports, encouraging Americans to 'buy American'.

- **May 1921, Emergency Tariff Act:** increased the import taxes on wheat, sugar, meat, wool and other agricultural products.

- **June 1921, Budget and Accounting Act:** put controls on government spending.

- **November 1921, Revenue Act:** changed taxes, cutting individual tax and the wartime tax on high levels of profit. However, it put in place a rise in the amount of tax paid by business from 1922.

- **September 1922, Fordney and McCumber Tariff Act:** raised tariffs and extended them to industrial goods. It also gave the president the power to raise the tariff yearly, in line with the selling price of these goods in the USA.

These tariffs did encourage Americans to buy American goods. However, they did not help US exports. Other countries retaliated by introducing tariffs of their own, so US exports became more expensive and so less popular.

How shall you keep from meddling in the affairs of Europe or keep Europe from meddling in the affairs of America? I will not, I cannot, give up my belief that America must, not just for the happiness of her own people, but for the moral guidance and greater contentment of the world, be permitted to live her own life.

Source D: *From a speech by William E Borah in the Senate on 19 November 1919. He was urging the Senate to vote against joining the League of Nations.*

Tariffs did nothing to foster cooperation among nations. They quickly became a symbol of the 'beggar-thy-neighbour' policies, adopted by many countries during this time, which contributed to a drastic reduction of international trade once they had taken effect. For example, US imports from Europe declined from a 1929 high of $1,334 million to just $390 million in 1932, while US exports to Europe fell from $2,341 million in 1929 to $784 million in 1932. Overall, world trade declined by some 66% between 1929 and 1934.

Source E: *From a discussion of protectionism on a US government history website in 2009.*

Activities

1 Write a paragraph summing up why an American might object to the Treaty of Versailles.

2 Draw a table to show the terms of the 4 tariff acts of May 1921 to September 1922.

3 Write a paragraph outlining the benefits and problems the tariffs caused for US trade.

4 Write a paragraph about three things you can infer about American attitudes to the League of Nations from Source A. Begin with 'Source A suggests...'.

5 **a** Which source do you think most strongly supports the attitude to the League of Nations suggested by Source A? Explain your answer.

b Which source do you think least strongly supports the attitude to the League of Nations suggested by Source A? Explain your answer.

Immigration

Learning objectives

In this chapter you will learn about:

- American attitudes to immigration
- policies to restrict immigration
- the Sacco and Vanzetti case.

Attitudes to immigration

US isolationism led to the introduction of restrictions on immigration. Previously, the USA had had an 'open door' policy, allowing unlimited immigration. There had always been some people who resented the arrival of immigrants, but several waves of immigrants had, over the years, become part of American society. However, numbers were rising. From 1900 to 1920, despite immigration slowing to a trickle during the war, 12.5m people emigrated to the USA from Europe and 1.5 m from Canada, Asia and Mexico.

Source A: *A cartoon published in a US newspaper on 19 May 1921.*

Top tip

When using sources, always read the captions carefully and think about the information they give you. Captions give you important information that might suggest reasons for the creator of the source to be biased – to take one side or another on an issue, or to want to make you believe one thing rather than another.

For example, a politician who supports a particular policy might say it had a huge amount of public support – that is a statement you would want some supporting evidence for before you believed it.

Examination question

What can you learn from Source A about immigration to the USA in 1921? **(3 marks)**

American institutions rely on good citizenship. New arrivals should be limited to our capacity to absorb them into the ranks of good citizenship. America must be kept American. For this purpose, it is necessary to continue a policy of restricted immigration. I am convinced our present economic and social conditions warrant a limitation of those to be admitted.

Source B: *Part of a speech made by President Calvin Coolidge to Congress on 6 December 1923.*

Quotas

As part of the government's isolationist policy to 'keep America American', it passed laws to cut immigration sharply. Laws set limits based on US census details of immigrants already in the USA. They aimed to reduce migration most from Eastern Europe and Italy. This was because many of the immigrants from those countries were unskilled workers. There was a high level of prejudice in the USA against these immigrants.

The 1921 Emergency Quota Act restricted immigration to 3% of the number of immigrants (from any country) in the US census in 1910. The 1924 Immigration Act reduced this to 2% and set a limit of 150,000 a year. The quota system didn't stop prejudice against immigrants. Some prejudiced reasons given for objecting to immigrants were:

- immigrants were often poor people
- they were often unskilled
- they lived in poor, high-crime areas and did not learn the language
- they often brought bad influences with them (the Italian Mafia and Italian immigrant involvement in gangsterism was an example regularly given)
- they often had communist political ideas.

The Sacco and Vanzetti case

On 15 April 1920 two men were killed and $15,777 stolen in a robbery. On 5 May, two other men were arrested when they picked up a car the police thought was used for the crime. These men, Nicola Sacco and Bartolomeo Vanzetti, were Italian immigrants and also anarchists – members of a political group that believed in the violent overthrow of all governments. The car was similar to the one used in the robbery. Sacco and Vanzetti were carrying guns when arrested; one of these used bullets of the same type as the gun used in the crime. Vanzetti had been convicted of armed robbery before and the police had 61 'eyewitnesses' who identified Sacco and Vanzetti.

But Sacco and Vanzetti had 107 'eyewitnesses' that they were elsewhere, and investigation techniques were not good enough to conclusively identify the car or bullets. Each side accused the other of persuading people to be 'eyewitnesses'; there was no clear evidence. However, the judge at the trial made it clear that he expected a 'guilty' verdict. He got one. There were appeals, petitions and protests, in the USA and abroad. Sacco and Vanzetti were finally executed on 23 August 1927.

> The supreme court of Massachusetts has spoken at last and Bartolomeo Vanzetti and Nicola Sacco, two of the bravest and best that ever served the labour movement, must go to the electric chair. The decision of this capitalist judicial tribunal is not surprising. It fits perfectly with the farcical tragedy of the whole trial of these two absolutely innocent and shamefully persecuted working men.

Source C: *Part of a statement made by Eugene Debs, a famous radical politician who was in prison in Atlanta.*

> We have proved beyond any reasonable doubt that the defendant Sacco fired a bullet from the Colt automatic that killed Allesandro Berardelli and that that some other person, not Vanzetti, shot Frederick Parmenter. We say the defendant Vanzetti, although we have no evidence that he fired a weapon, was actively assisting Sacco and the other man who were doing the killing. This makes him, in law, just as guilty as the defendant Sacco, who is the man we say killed Alessandro Berardelli.

Source D: *From the prosecution summing up in the Sacco and Vanzetti case.*

Activities

1 Where did most immigrants to the USA come from between 1900 and 1920?

2 Give four reasons used by some people to object to Eastern European and Italian migrants.

3 How does the Sacco and Vanzetti case show these prejudices?

4 Write a paragraph comparing how Sources C and D feel about whether Sacco and Vanzetti were guilty.

The Red Scare

Learning objectives

In this chapter you will learn about:
- reasons for the Red Scare
- targets of the Red Scare.

The Sacco and Vanzetti case was part of a wider anti-immigrant reaction as part of the Red Scare. This fear, which gripped the country from 1919 to 1920, was a fear of a communist revolution. Immigrants were the most usual targets, but so were people in workers' unions, or anyone with left-wing ideas. The International Workers of the World union (IWW) and the Socialist Party came under particular suspicion. Newspapers and radio fanned the flames of the Red Scare. It even reached the government. Thousands of people were arrested, imprisoned and deported.

To uphold and defend the Constitution of the United States of America; to maintain law and order; to foster and perpetuate a 100 Percent Americanism; to preserve the memories and incidents of our association in the Great War; to inculcate a sense of individual obligation to the community, state, and nation; to combat the autocracy of both the classes and the masses; to make right the master of might; to promote peace and good will on earth; to safeguard and transmit to prosperity the principles of justice, freedom, and democracy; to consecrate and sanctify our comradeship by devotion to mutual helpfulness.

Source B: *From the Constitution of the American Legion, passed in St. Louis in 1919.*

By the fall, the Legion had 650,000 members, and over a million by year's end. While most of the Legion engaged in such relatively innocuous activities as distributing pamphlets, the patriotic and anti-communist fervour of the Legion led many to engage in vigilante justice meted out against Reds both real and suspected. The Legion's prevalence in the country and reputation for anti-communism was so great that the phrase "Leave the Reds to the Legion" became a common catchphrase.

Source C: *From a US university website.*

Source A: *An American cartoon published during the Red Scare. Attached to the man's hat is a label that says 'Alien slacker', one of the papers another man is carrying says 'Bolsheviki propaganda' and the dog says 'They're going away for their health'.*

Why was there a Red Scare?

The Red Scare blew up for several reasons.

- **Patriotism:** During the First World War the government worked hard to build up patriotism. The USA was fighting Germany in Europe. Many people became suspicious of people of German origin in the USA. They were also suspicious of people who didn't whole-heartedly support the war, including groups like the IWW and the Socialist Party. When the war ended a variety of 'patriotic' groups were formed by returning soldiers. The largest of these was the American Legion, set up in May 1919. They urged the government to pass laws against immigrants, communists and the IWW.

- **Economic problems:** By the end of the war, about 4 million people were in the armed forces and about 9 million people worked in war industries. When the war ended, they became unemployed. Even though the USA suffered less than Europe at the end of the war, this was a huge number of people to get back to work. Some employers began to exploit the situation, lowering wages and putting up working hours.

- **Worker unrest:** Workers began to go on strike in response to their poor working conditions. The first big strike was in the Seattle shipyards. It began on 21 January 1919. On 6 February there was a general strike involving 60,000 workers. Despite the strike being peaceful, it got a lot of publicity, and people, including the government, reacted as if it had been violent. More strikes followed across the country and the press reacted as if they were the start of a communist rising.

- **Violence:** In April 1919 over 30 letter bombs were posted to important people all over the USA, to arrive for 1 May. About half of these exploded. In early June, much larger bombs were set off in eight US cities. These bombings, by anarchist groups, fuelled media hysteria.

Activities

Study Source A. Answer the questions below, using details from the source to explain your answer.

1 What kinds of people are leaving the city?
2 What reason does it suggest they have for going?
3 Who does it suggest is behind their leaving?
4 Does the cartoonist think they should have to go?

Build Better Answers

'The main cause of the Red Scare was a distrust of immigrants.' Use the sources and your own knowledge to explain whether you agree with this view.   **(15 marks)**

■ **A basic answer (level 1)** will make a generalised statement. For example, *No, it was more to do with unions and the economy.*

● **A good answer (level 2)** will use detail from the sources and/or own knowledge to evaluate the statement. Considering arguments for **and** against the view will gain higher marks in the level. For example, *People were against immigrants, but also organisations like the IWW because of its strikes. Source B talks about 100% Americanism and C talks about vigilante justice against Reds – that's communists, not immigrants.*

▲ **An excellent answer (level 4)** will use detail from the sources and own knowledge to produce a balanced evaluation of the evidence for and against the view. For example, *It was a scare about communism, but people saw immigrants as more likely to be communists. People also turned against organisations (like the IWW) that they saw as 'unpatriotic' and 'communist'. The American Legion talks about 100% Americanism (Source B), but people saw it as anti-immigrant too (Source A). Source B talks about its vigilante justice against 'Reds'. It was complicated. It came out of the lack of jobs and strikes and even the patriotism left over from the war as well as anti-immigrant feeling.*

Prohibition and crime

> **Learning objectives**
>
> In this chapter you will learn about:
> - reasons for Prohibition and for its failure
> - organised crime, including Al Capone.

Prohibition

Several groups (such as the Anti-Saloon League, set up in 1895) had been demanding an alcohol ban in the USA for a long time. They said drinking broke up homes and families and led to crime (some claimed it led to insanity, too). Employers complained that drinking made many workers unreliable. By 1917, alcohol was banned in several states. During the war there was also a ban on brewing alcohol from grain, because the grain was needed for food. Congress passed the 18th Amendment to the Constitution, outlawing the manufacture, transport and sale of alcohol in December 1917, and it was ratified in January 1919, coming into effect in January 1920. A new law enforcement group was set up whose officials, prohibition agents, were sent out to catch people making, transporting or selling alcohol.

Millions of people still wanted to drink. It became clear that people would break this law if they could find a place to serve them. The 'speakeasy' was born. Some speakeasies were like private clubs and served food as well as drink. They served 'bootleg' alcohol made illegally in the USA or smuggled from other countries, such as Mexico. Others were simply bars, and alcohol was also sold in gambling dens. The worst places served 'moonshine' – home-brewed alcohol that could be very dangerous to drink.

Organised crime

Organised crime had existed in the USA for a long time. But Prohibition gave it the perfect conditions to grow. Gangsters took over the sale and distribution of alcohol, and since very many people wanted to drink, there were plenty of customers and plenty of profit. Gangsters ran gambling dens, fixed the betting at dog and horse races and ran brothels and clubs as well. Because they were making a great deal of money, they could often bribe the police, prohibition agents, judges, juries and local officials. Each gang controlled its own area and, inside that area, it was the law. Many businesses had to pay 'protection' money to the local gang, who would otherwise damage their business, or even destroy it.

> **Did you know?**
>
> The US government has two levels of government. Each state has its own local government. There is also a federal government that makes laws that affect the whole country. Congress (made up of the Senate and the House of Representatives) makes federal laws. If Congress wants to change the Constitution it has to have the agreement of three-quarters of all the states.

A major underlying cause of the corruption in cities like Chicago was Prohibition. The corruption created by this unenforceable law became part of city life. Police and officials saw bribes as part of their income and the reporters who publicly scorned gangsters privately drank their illegal alcohol.

Source A: *From a biography of the gangster Al Capone, written in 1994.*

alcohol sales	$60m
gambling	$25m
brothels, dance halls	$10m
other illegal activities	$10m

Source B: *Profit made by Al Capone, a Chicago gang leader, in 1927 (from a biography of Capone written in 1930).*

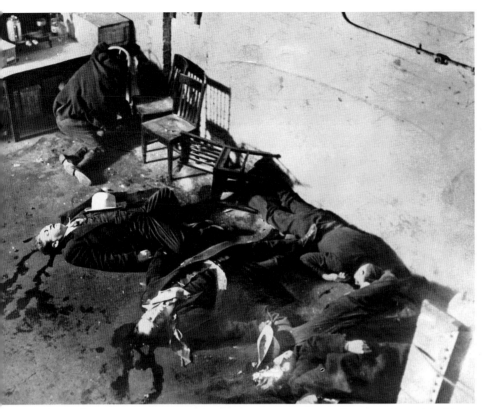

Source C: *The St Valentine's Day Massacre of 14 February 1929. Seven members of the Moran gang were trapped in a garage, lined up against the wall, and shot by Al Capone's gang.*

Source D: *A cartoon call 'The King still reigns', published in 1930.*

Gang war

The powerful rival gangs fought each other for control of parts of cities such as Chicago. The most notorious example was on 14 February 1929, the St Valentine's Day Massacre, when Al Capone's gang killed seven members of the rival Bugs Moran gang in Chicago. No one was ever arrested. This was one of the more spectacular killings, but it was not unusual – that year there were about 400 gang-related killings in Chicago.

Many people blamed Prohibition for the gang violence. Prohibition gave the gangs money and power, and reduced respect for the law, because it involved millions of ordinary Americans in breaking the law. But there were other factors. The war meant there were many ex-soldiers, who were used to killing. Cars made it possible to make a surprise attack and a quick get-away. The fact that gangs made so much money meant that they could bribe politicians and the police. The fact that they were so violent meant that very few eyewitnesses were prepared to testify against them.

 Top tip

When asked how one source supports another source, always consider **how** far one supports the other. Look for evidence of support, lack of support, and contradiction. Then make a judgement about how far support is given.

Activities

1 List four reasons for Prohibition.

2 Write a paragraph explaining how gangsters benefitted from Prohibition.

3 List four factors that led to the increase in gang violence in the 1920s.

4 Copy the following statements. For each, explain if it is an inference about organised crime from Source C. *It was dangerous. It was profitable. It involved mostly men. It involved rival groups. It controlled the cities.*

Why Prohibition failed

Learning objectives

In this chapter you will learn about:

- the problems of enforcing Prohibition
- how gangs exploited these problems
- How the public reacted to Prohibition.

Why Prohibition failed

Prohibition failed for three main reasons.

- There were not enough officers to enforce it.
- The law enforcement system was corrupted by organised crime.
- There were too many Americans who wanted to drink alcohol.

Enforcement problems

The US border with Canada (excluding the Canada-Alaska border) was 6,416 km. Its border with Mexico was 3,141 km. The only way to stop alcohol being smuggled into America was to have constant patrols along the borders. Worse still, smuggling from other countries was only a small part of the problem. Gangs made alcohol. Many people made their own alcohol. Prohibition enforcement officers were supposed to stop all this activity. They were also supposed to operate on a federal level, right across the USA. They often did not get co-operation from state police forces. In 1920 there were 1,512 enforcement agents, rising to 2,320 in 1925 and 2,836 in 1930.

Corruption

Prohibition enforcement officers were not well paid. On average, they earned slightly less than a skilled worker such as a carpenter or bricklayer. This was not much for the risks they took – gangs were likely to beat up or kill Prohibition officers who threatened their businesses. On the other hand, if they co-operated with the gangs they were given bribes. Some of them even worked for the gangs selling or delivering alcohol. Even if Prohibition officers were not corrupt, they could be obstructed by state police, judges and government officials who were.

Public opinion

In many ways, the biggest problem for the government was that most people disagreed with Prohibition. The effects were not what the lawmakers expected. People who would not normally break the law were happy to break this one. The problems with enforcement and corruption meant the chances of them getting caught were not high. Even if they were, juries often did not convict people prosecuted for making or selling alcohol, or for going to speakeasies. Ordinary people often had the sympathies of both judge and jury. Gangsters might get less sympathy, but could afford to try to bribe both judges and juries.

> The federal agent Izzy Einstein reported that in most cities it took only 30 minutes to find alcohol. Chicago was 21 minutes, Atlanta 17, Pittsburgh 11, and New Orleans 35 seconds. Izzy asked the taxi driver where he could get a drink. 'Right here,' said the driver, producing a bottle.

Source A: From The American Century, written by Harold Evans in 1998.

> In time, I learned that not everything in America was what it seemed to be. I discovered, for instance, that a spare tyre could be filled with something other than air, that some binoculars did not help you to see, and that the teddy bears that were suddenly popular with ladies very often had hollow metal stomachs.
>
> Prohibition has created a new, universally respected, well-loved, and very profitable occupation, that of the bootlegger who imports forbidden liquor. Everyone knows this, even the government.

Source B: Written by Felix von Luckner, a German who visited America with his wife in 1927.

Did you know?

Illegal drinking didn't just go on in bars run by gangsters. Many very respectable restaurants and private clubs also served bootleg alcohol. Poorer people bought moonshine, or made their own.

Source C: *Texas Guinan, a nightclub owner, singing with some of her customers in one of her speakeasies in the 1920s.*

Build Better Answers

How far does Source B support the evidence in Source A about popular feeling about Prohibition in the 1920s? Explain your answer. **(7 marks)**

Paper 2, Section A part b) questions will ask if one source supports the evidence in another source.

■ **A basic answer (level 1)** will compare the two sources for evidence of support or the lack of it, giving generalised examples from the sources. For example, ... *they both agree that Americans didn't obey the law about Prohibition.*

● **A good answer (level 2)** will consider support OR the lack of it, using detail from the sources. For example, *The sources don't support each other. Source A shows how people could buy alcohol very quickly in many different parts of America. Source B doesn't talk about different places, not does it talk about the speed with which you could get alcohol or getting it from taxi drivers.*

▲ **A better answer (level 3)** will consider both support and lack of support and make an overall judgement on the extent of the support using phrases such as very little support or strong support. For example, *Source B doesn't mention the different cities or that taxi drivers sold alcohol, as in Source A. But overall B does support A because they both show how easy it was to find alcohol and the fact that many people were not prepared to respect the law – they wanted to go on drinking.*

Activities

1 It is 1925. Write a letter from the person in charge of Prohibition enforcement to President Coolidge, explaining why Prohibition was failing.

2 Write your own definitions of 'bootleg' and 'moonshine' alcoholic drinks.

3 What inference about the reasons for the failure of Prohibition can you make from Source B?

4 'The main reason Prohibition failed was that too many ordinary people broke the law.' Draw up lists of ways in which the sources and the text support and do not support this statement.

Mass production

Mass production was one of the important factors behind the economic boom. Mass production meant goods could be made more quickly and more cheaply. The pioneer of mass production was Henry Ford, who applied the system to car manufacture just before the war.

Mass producing a Ford

This is how the Ford motor works applied the principles of mass production.

- They made just one kind of car, so the parts were a standard size and shape. This saved on money, storage and time. Standardisation also saved on labour, as workers only had to learn how to deal with one set of parts.
- They introduced division of labour. Instead of one or two workers building a whole car, the work was split up into a series of jobs, with one worker doing the same job over and over on lots of cars. They found splitting up the jobs into lots of steps made assembly faster.
- In 1914, they introduced a moving assembly line. Each worker stayed in one place and the job came to them on a moving line. Using an assembly line and breaking the jobs into smaller steps to suit the line meant that the time taken to produce a car dropped from 12 hours to 1 hour and 33 minutes.

Not just cars

Once Ford had shown how effective mass production was, many other businesses began to apply mass-production methods in their factories. The assembly-line system was especially suitable for newer industries that produced finished goods such as radios and fridges.

In April 1913, we experimented with an assembly line, just on the magneto. We try everything in a little way first – we'll rip out anything once we find a better way, but we must be certain the new way will be better before doing anything drastic.

One workman could make one magneto in 20 minutes. Dividing his job into 29 steps cut the assembly time to 13 minutes, 10 seconds. Then we raised the height of the line 8 inches. This cut the time to 7 minutes. Changing the speed of the line cut the time down to 5 minutes.

Source A: *From* My Life and Work, *Henry Ford's autobiography, first published in 1922.*

Did you know?

Ford began by experimenting with a number of different models of car. In 1909, he decided to manufacture just one design, the Model T, and to make it in just one colour – black. This was because black paint was the quickest to dry.

The Model T led to the weaving of the first highways, then freeways and the interstate. Beginning in the early 1920s, people who had never taken a holiday beyond the nearest lake or mountain could explore the whole United States. Most of all, the Model T gave to the farmer and rancher, miles from anywhere, a new pair of legs.

Source B: *From* America, *written by Alistair Cooke in 1976.*

The effects of mass production

Mass production made goods cheaper, because they could be produced faster and so for less cost. But it had far more widespread effects, too. Consider again the example of Ford cars. In 1908 a Ford car, produced with standard parts and some labour specialisation, cost $950. In 1926, an improved version of the car cost $350. This goes some way to explaining why there were 1m cars in the USA in 1915, but 28m in 1939.

Factories employed more people to make cars and car parts. Ford dealerships not only sold cars, they also provided mechanics to look after the cars and replace parts that wore out or were faulty. By 1912, there were 7,000 Ford dealerships in the USA and they spread rapidly. As the number of cars in the USA grew, so did the number of garages providing petrol and mechanics, all providing jobs. By 1929, over 4 million workers depended on the car industry. Industries that provided raw materials for parts (glass, steel, rubber and leather) also grew. By 1929, 75% of all leather, glass and rubber went to the car industry. The demand for petrol and oil grew, too.

More employment meant that more people had money to spend, which boosted industry. The growth in the number of cars led to more garages and surfaced roads (about 400,000 km were built in the 1920s). Road travel became quicker and easier. So people travelled more often, spreading their spending. Travelling salesmen took to the road too, selling everything from vacuum cleaners to underwear.

Activities

1 Explain the effects of:
   a Experimentation on the development of mass production by Ford.
   b Mass production on the cost of a Model T Ford.
   c The fall in the price of cars on sales of Ford cars.

2 Read *The effects of mass production* on this page. List the effects that Source C shows, explaining each one fully.

3 Draw a diagram to show the effect of mass production of cars on the US economy. The diagram on page 175 may help you.

Source C: *A garage in Atlanta, Georgia, photographed in 1936 as part of a government photographic survey of living conditions all over the USA.*

CHEROKEE PARTS STORE
GARAGE WORK
973
USED C

Boom!

Learning objectives

In this chapter you will learn about:
- the way new industries grew
- the effects of hire purchase
- the influence of advertising.

When Hoover took the oath as President in March 1929, he was proud and confident. 'We are a happy people – the statistics prove it. We have more cars, more bathtubs, oil furnaces, silk stockings and bank accounts than any other people on earth.'

Source A: *From* The Free and the Unfree. A New History of the United States, *written by Peter N Carroll and David W Nobel in 1988.*

At the end of the war, the new industries that had been growing slowly before the war suddenly exploded into life. It seemed as if everyone was buying radios, cars, fridges, washing machines and telephones. What set off this sudden outbreak?

Reasons to buy

There were several reasons for the increase in demand for these new goods. Mass production made them cheaper. Prices of radios, cars, fridges and other goods were falling all through the 1920s. But mass production was not the only factor. Wages were rising – the average wage rose 8% in the 1920s. Many of these goods ran on electricity, and after the war many more homes were connected to the electric grid. Advertising became big business in the 1920s, creating demand by persuading people they wanted and needed a fridge or a car.

Perhaps the biggest factor of all in the growth of these new industries was hire purchase. The fact was that many people could not afford to buy the new luxury goods outright. So shops and businesses set up payment-in-instalments schemes to get over that difficulty. Customers signed a hire-purchase agreement and put down a deposit on a radio or car. They then took the goods and paid off the rest of the cost in regular instalments. Before the war, some businesses had offered schemes like this. But they were seen as not quite respectable – a way of paying that poor people had to use because they could not buy even their necessities outright. After the war, more and more people made purchases this way. Many people took out mortgages on their homes, too. Being in debt was no longer shameful.

Year	Fridges made	Radios made
1921	5,000	No record
1923	18,000	190,000
1925	75,000	2,350,000
1927	390,000	1,980,000
1929	890,000	4,980,000

Value of goods produced in millions of dollars			
Year	Radios	Electrical goods	Toys and sporting goods
1921	12.2	63.2	124.1
1923	50.3	76.3	167.1
1925	168.2	106.3	164.2
1927	181.5	146.3	182.5
1929	366.0	176.7	214.6

Source B: *Some US government statistics that show the growth in production of consumer goods.*

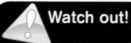 **Watch out!**

Section B part (b) asks you to consider how one source supports another 'about...'. Make sure you consider the support about that particular issue.

The boom cycle

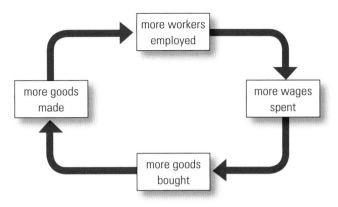

Source C: *An advertisement for a fridge from 1931. Unlike many adverts, it actually does mention hire purchase ('a few dollars down places one in your home today!'). This may well be because General Electric, the manufacturers, had their own hire-purchase schemes.*

Activities

1 Turn the *reasons to buy* section into a list of bullet point headings.

2 Re-draw the 'boom' diagram, adding: 'higher demand for goods', 'more profits' and 'more demand for goods' in the right places on the cycle.

3 Which of the following can you **not** infer from Source C? Explain your answer.

- In 1931 women had a wider range of food available to them in 1900.
- In 1931 fridges were a desirable item.
- In 1931 most women were expected to be housewives.

Build Better Answers

How far does Source B support the evidence in Source A about American prosperity in the 1920s? Explain your answer. (7 marks)

Paper 2, Section A part (b) questions will ask if one source supports the evidence in another source.

■ **A basic answer (level 1)** will compare the two sources for evidence of support OR the lack of it, giving generalised examples from the sources. For example, *They both suggest that Americans were well off.*

● **A good answer (level 2)** will consider support OR the lack of it, using detail from the sources. For example, *A says they have more things than any other people on earth and B supports the idea that people bought lots of consumer goods, millions of dollars worth of goods.*

▲ **An excellent answer (level 3)** will consider the overall support given making a judgement on the extent of the support using phrases such as *very little support* or *strong support*. For example, *Source B doesn't mention the items (cars, stockings etc) in Source A. But the millions of dollars spent and amount of goods made gives strong support to the idea in A that the country was prosperous.*

Buying shares

The confidence that came with the boom cycle and boosted it, led to a new development – ordinary people began to buy and sell shares.

What are shares?

Shares are just that, a 'share' in a company. If a person needs money to set up a company, or money to expand an existing company, the owner can raise that money by selling shares in the company. When the owner does this, he or she no longer owns all the company – the shareholders, the people who buy the shares, do. What they get in return for their shares is a yearly dividend. Each year, if it has made a profit, that profit is divided up between the shareholders. The amount they get is calculated according to the number of shares they have. Before the 1920s, only wealthy people or banks bought shares. They bought shares in companies they thought would be successful and would pay a good dividend, and they usually kept the shares for a long time. If shareholders needed money, they could sell their shares. Shares were not sold from person to person. For most companies they could only be bought and sold at a stock exchange – the most important was the New York Stock Exchange in Wall Street.

How the stock market worked

The **stock market** is the general name for buying and selling shares. Shares had no set value. They were worth whatever someone was prepared to pay for them. If you bought a share in a company for $10 one week, it could be worth $10 the next week, or $100 or $1. It all depended on the demand for the shares. The people who traded shares were called 'brokers'. If trading was 'slow', the prices of shares could stay the same for days, weeks or months. But, if there was a lot of buying and selling in the stock market, prices could go up and down several times a day.

In the 1920s, because new companies made such big profits, the prices of their shares went up and up. More and more people bought shares. People started to buy shares not for the dividend, but to sell them again at a profit.

In 1929, Samuel Crowther interviewed John J Raskob [from the finance section of General Motors] about how an ordinary person could get rich by investing in stocks. Crowther published Raskob's ideas in a *Ladies' Home Journal* article, 'Everybody Ought to be Rich'. In the interview, Raskob claimed that putting just $15 a month into shares would make investors $80,000 over the next 20 years. The prospect of building such a great fortune seemed possible in the atmosphere of the 1920s market. Shares excited investors; millions put their savings into the market hoping for a quick profit.

Source D: *From* Stocks for the Long Run, *written by Jeremy J Siegel in 2008.*

Year	$ millions spent on share trading
1926	450.8
1927	576.6
1928	919.7
1929	1,125.0

Source E: *From* A History of the Federal Reserve, *written by Allan Meltzer and Alan Greenspan in 2003.*

Company	3 March 1928	3 Sept 1929
Woolworths	$1.81	$2.51
Radio	$0.94	$5.05
AT & T (telephone company)	$0.77	$3.04
Westinghouse (electrical goods)	$0.92	$3.13
General Motors (cars)	$1.40	$1.82

Source F: *The price of a share in selected companies in 1928 and 1929.*

The stock market boom

As more and more people began buying shares, demand for shares, especially in new industries such as radios or electrical appliances, went up sharply. Because more people wanted to buy shares, the prices of shares rose and kept rising. From 1927, it seemed that everyone was buying shares and no one could lose.

Buying on the margin

People became so confident that the price of shares would keep going up that they began to borrow money to buy shares, confident that they would be able to sell them for more and repay the loan. Banks began to use their money to buy shares. They were gambling with people's savings. By autumn 1929, even the banks were beginning to forget that the price of stocks could go down as well as up.

Activities

1 Turn the 'What are shares?' paragraph into a flow diagram like the one on this page. Begin with someone wanting money to start a business.

2 Turn the 'How the stock market worked' paragraph into a similar flow diagram.

3 **a** If you had bought $30 worth of shares in radio and $30 worth of shares in AT & T on 3 March 1928, what would they be worth on 3 September 1929?

   b If you wanted to keep making money, what would you do with the profits?

4 Write a paragraph to explain how Source E supports Source F's pattern of rising share prices.

How people hoped to get rich by 'buying on the margin'.

Not all winners

Not everyone shared in the boom of the 1920s. Some older industries suffered after the war. Farmers had problems too – and about 40% of all workers were farmers and farm workers. Other people who suffered were black people and poor immigrants, many of whom could hardly afford food, let alone radios or cars.

The older industries

Older industries such as coalmining, shipbuilding and the railways could not benefit from new ideas such as the assembly line. During the war, the coal and shipbuilding industries were at full production. After the war, the use of coal dropped rapidly. More people used electricity – cheap, clean, and convenient – for heat, light and cooking. Businesses switched to electric power, too. The railways lost custom as people bought cars. They lost freight customers too, as many businesses chose to transport goods by truck on the network of surfaced roads that spread across the country. The war had increased the need for new ships, but demand had fallen now.

Problems for farmers

During the war, farmers bought more land (often by borrowing money on a mortgage), and they bought tractors and combine harvesters (again, with borrowed money) to grow more food. They were growing for the European market as well as the home market. After the war ended, European farm production took a couple of years to recover, but then Europe needed much less food from the USA. Demand fell for other reasons too:

- in 1920, Prohibition reduced demand for grapes and barley (used to make wine and beer)
- many clothes were made from new, synthetic, fabrics such as rayon: demand for cotton and wool fell.

Farmers' costs were high, and prices were falling. Mechanisation meant they needed fewer workers, but they were growing more crops than the country needed. Prices fell, and farmers started to go bankrupt.

Year	Wheat ($ per bushel)
1919	$2.16
1921	$1.01
1923	$0.92
1925	$1.44
1929	$1.04

Source A: *From US government records of wheat prices in the USA.*

1900 to 1920 was a time of general farm prosperity and rising prices. Farmers opened up poor lands and began to buy goods and machinery they could not afford before. But by the end of 1920, with the end of wartime demand, the price of crops such as wheat and corn fell into sharp decline. The most important cause of problems in agriculture was the loss of foreign markets. Farmers could not easily sell to countries where the United States was not buying goods because of its import tariff.

Source B: *From a Library of Congress on-line history of the USA.*

In 1919 Uncle Amos mortgaged his property to buy another farm, just as the farming boom of the World War was busting. A second farm meant hiring a man to run the machinery and buying extra horses. Low prices have made it impossible to pay the mortgage. Last fall [autumn of 1927] the bank foreclosed [took the mortgaged farm to pay his debts].

Source C: *From* Dust Bowl Diary, *Ann Marie Low's memories of growing up in North Dakota in the 1920s and 30s, based on her diary from the time.*

Source D: *A cartoon from a US newspaper, published in 1920.*

Examination question

How far does Source C support Source B's views about the reasons for the problems faced by farmers in the 1920s? Explain your answer.

(7 marks)

Low paid workers

The other people who suffered during the boom were low paid workers. These included farm labourers (many of whom were black) and workers in the worst-paid industries (e.g. mining), as well as those who could find no work. Workers in the South were often paid less than those in the North. Wages varied all over the country. The average wage for a farm worker in 1919 was $13.5 a week. In 1925, it was $11.3 and by 1930 it had dropped to $7.5. And while some farm workers will have earned more than this, others will have earned less. Meanwhile the average teacher's wage had risen from $15.5 in 1919 to $29.9 in 1930, and a skilled factory worker's wage had gone from $22.3 to $28.6.

Activities

1 **a** About what percentage of the people in the USA worked on farms?

   b Why does this make problems in farming so significant for the US economy?

2 List four reasons why farmers were having financial problems in the 1920s.

3 How far does Source B support Source C's view that farmers could not make a living in the 1920s? Explain your answer.

The Roaring Twenties

Learning objectives

In this chapter you will learn about:

- the key elements of 'the Roaring Twenties'.

The 1920s are often called 'the Roaring Twenties'. They were seen as a time of change – everything was faster and louder; people were richer and more glamorous. Not everyone shared the wealth of the boom years, but those who did not were, to an extent, the forgotten people of the 1920s. To most people at the time, and since, the image of the 1920s is of youth, wealth and confidence. Even the gangster culture of Prohibition seemed thrilling.

Key elements of the Roaring Twenties

- **Wealth**, fuelled by the manufacturing boom. People who made more money spent more money, which helped the economy to keep expanding.
- **Novelty** became fashionable. New kinds of music (such as jazz) swept America and new dances came with them. New consumer goods, such as radios, fridges and record players, were produced cheaply enough for many Americans to be able to buy them.
- **Mobility** increased as more and more people could afford cars. People could work further from home. New jobs, such as travelling salesmen, relied on the car. More people had the spare time to 'motor' for pleasure, and that created a whole web of jobs such as garages, petrol stations, motels and diners along the rapidly expanding road system.
- **Leisure**, because people had more free time and more money to spend during their free time. So the leisure industry expanded. For example, many more people watched, listened to the radio (and even played) sport.
- **Changing morals and values** caused confusion for many people. Many otherwise law-abiding people broke the law for the first time during Prohibition. Some people felt it was immoral for young women to break away from the conventional role of women – yet many of them knew young women who dressed and behaved unconventionally without being immoral.

Cities were the focus of the Roaring Twenties. The pace of small-town and rural life was far slower, and change came more slowly too, although people used new inventions such as mail-order catalogues to get a taste of the Roaring Twenties, no matter where they lived.

New technology – automobiles, airplanes and motion pictures – were transforming American life. Business was getting bigger. New products – toasters, vacuum cleaners and refrigerators – arrived in local shops. New cars rolled off the assembly line and then sped down city streets. Even the new music of the 1920s, jazz, was fast.

Source A: *From* America in the 1920s, *written by Edmund Lindop in 2010.*

Top tip

Remember that key factors in a situation are usually linked to each other. So, in the Roaring Twenties, the fact that there was more wealth **led to** people being able buy new consumer goods, such as fridges and washing machines. This **led to more** leisure time, which meant people could go to sporting events or the movies or even go motoring.

Activities

1 Write a sentence giving at least one example of how the increased wealth of many Americans affected each of the elements of the Roaring Twenties listed below:

novelty   motoring
mobility   leisure.

2 Novelty was an *effect* of wealth because people had more money, so they could pay for these new things. Novelty was also a *cause* of increased wealth because people had more money because they were paid to make and sell fridges, play jazz music etc.

Explain at least four more pairs of effects becoming causes like this.

Unit 4 The USA, 1917–29

Consumerism

> ### Learning objectives
>
> In this chapter you will learn about:
> - reasons behind the rise in consumerism
> - the power of advertising.

The 1920s boom grew rapidly as a wave of consumerism swept the country. Consumerism is the urge to spend money on goods and services. People bought more and more goods and spent more and more money on leisure. This was partly because they had more time and money. Working hours dropped after the war and most wages rose. At the same time, most prices fell. So people could buy more. New industries produced new goods for people to spend their money on.

The power of advertising

Advertising became big business. Adverts on billboards and in newspapers and magazines urged people to spend their money. They used pictures that showed a desirable lifestyle. The words they used tried to convince people that they needed the products in the advert. They also applied pressure by suggesting that by not buying these goods the consumer was in some way letting his family down. The idea of 'keeping up with the neighbours' had arrived.

Soon, advertising was everywhere: on billboards, in shop windows, painted on the sides of buildings. There were adverts on the radio, too. By 1925, 2,700,000 families had a radio, so it was a powerful tool for advertisers. Radio adverts had to be short – advertisers paid by the minute.

> ### Did you know?
>
> In 1922, the first radio advert was broadcast: by a radio company looking for advertisers. At first, radio adverts just described the product, then they used slogans. The first radio musical jingle was for Wheaties cereals, in 1926.

Activities

1. In pairs, turn the advert for a Victrola (Source A) into a jingle for radio. Keep it short, but use the same ideas.

2. Write a sentence to explain how you can make the inferences below from Source A.

    a. Advertisers tried to persuade people they really needed consumer goods.

    b. Consumer goods could be expensive.

    c. Record companies were making a lot of money.

Source A: *A magazine advertisement for the latest in record players, from 1920.*

181

That's entertainment!

> **Learning objectives**
>
> In this chapter you will learn about:
> - new forms of entertainment
> - reasons for the growth of the entertainment industry.

During the 1920s, people not only had more money to spend, they had more leisure time. They went out more – to theatres, sports stadiums and racetracks, recreation grounds and clubs – especially clubs playing the latest craze in music, jazz.

The Jazz Age

Jazz music swept from the South to the North in the 1920s, as black people moved from the South, especially to northern cities such as Detroit, Chicago and New York. Jazz music was seen as wild, and the dances that sprang up in these clubs, such as the Charleston, were wild, too. For many people it symbolised a new era, with more freedom. The record industry was soon selling jazz records: people could listen and dance at home, too.

The movies

The most important leisure activity of the 1920s was almost certainly going to the movies. Hollywood became a centre for making movies before the First World War. After the war, movie-making exploded. The first movies had no sound. The movie theatre hired a pianist or organist to play suitable music to go with the action on screen. Some places even hired orchestras. In 1922, cinemas made $4 million a week in ticket sales. Movies had a huge effect on people. The most famous stars were paid huge amounts. As early as 1916, Mary Pickford was paid $10,000 a week (the average national wage was $13 a week). People soon wanted homes, cars and clothes like the movie stars had.

The talkies

People wanted each new movie to be bigger and better than the last. Film directors hunted for the next star, the next 'big thing'. Then, in 1927, the 'talkies' arrived: speech to go with the images on screen. The talkies caused chaos in the movie industry because some famous film stars did not have good speaking voices. Their careers ended as audiences collapsed with laughter when they spoke.

The growing middle class, with larger paychecks and shorter working weeks, had the time and money to follow, even to play, sports. Radio broadcasts of football, boxing and horse racing, and newspaper sports columns boosted the popularity of spectator sports. Babe Ruth [baseball], Jack Dempsey [boxing] and Ruth Ederle [swimming] became national celebrities. Golf and tennis skyrocketed in popularity as men and women flooded to newly built golf courses and tennis courts.

Source A: *From* The 1920s, *written by Kathleen Morgan Drowne and Patrick Huber in 2004.*

People living in the inner cities mostly went to local boxing halls, pool halls or bowling alleys to play sport. Once public transport became more affordable they could go to outlying ballparks and racetracks and watch sport.

Source B: *Leisure activities in the 1920s, described in* City Games, *written by Steven A Reiss in 1991.*

Did you know?

When the movie star Rudolph Valentino died, aged 31, in 1926, over 100,000 people mobbed the undertakers in New York where his body was taken. When his brother took the body to California for burial by train, he said: *you could see men and women kneeling on both sides of the rails, waiting for it to pass through.*

An immoral age?

Not everyone was swept away with the glamour of jazz and the movies. Some people thought they encouraged immorality. They thought jazz music, and the dances that went with it, were too sexual. They worried about the lifestyles shown in the movies. Women in the movies smoked and drank. Movies showed crimes being committed. Couples kissed on screen. Critics of the movies argued that this meant that people, especially women, eager to copy film stars would want to start smoking, drinking and kissing (and more) before marriage.

The wild lives of some film stars, reported in movie magazines and the newspapers, gave critics of the movies more ammunition. They said it was time for the movies to have a set of rules that limited what could be shown on screen. In 1930, the Hays Code was published. It set down rules for movies to make sure that, 'no picture shall be produced that will lower the moral standards of those who see it.'

Source C: *Filming the 1933 movie* King Kong. *The movie cost about $650,000 and made over $4m profit after paying off its costs.*

New women

Effects of the war

Before the war, women in the USA were still struggling for suffrage (the right to vote). When the USA entered the war, the government asked women to do the work of men who had gone to war. Women went to work in their millions.

The war gave women the experience of independence, of earning wages and of showing what they were capable of doing. They had to work for lower wages than men, but even this was a victory. In 1918, even before the war was over, President Wilson urged the Senate to pass a federal law giving women equal voting rights, saying: 'We have made partners of the women in this war. Shall we allow them only a partnership of suffering and sacrifice and toil, and not a partnership of privilege and right?' The 19th Amendment to the United States Constitution, giving women equal suffrage, became law on 18 August 1920. After the war, women were expected to let the returning men have their jobs back. Most young women worked. But this was seen as only temporary, until they married.

	1910	1920	1930
White-collar workers			
Male	6,019	7,176	9,564
Female	1,943	3,353	4,756
Manual and service workers			
Male	13,469	16,172	18,956
Female	4,327	4,115	5,088
Farmworkers			
Male	10,359	10,221	9,414
Female	1,175	1,169	908
Total workers, male and female	**37,292**	**42,206**	**48,686**

Source B: *Men and women in the workforce, taken from US government statistics (in thousands).*

Examination question

'In the 1920s the position of women changed enormously.'
Use the sources and your own knowledge to explain whether you agree with this view.

(15 marks)

Source A: *This 'Votes for Women' stamp from 1913, despite its positive message, shows that less than half the US states allowed women the vote on an equal level with men. The map shows states where women have 'partial suffrage' – some voting rights, but not equal to men.*

Flappers

'Flappers' was the name given to some young women in the 1920s. They did not depend on men to support them. They helped change western attitudes to women.

Flappers wore silk stockings and short dresses made from modern fabrics. They did not wear the traditional layers of underclothes or corsets, so their bodies were far more evident. They cut their hair short, in a 'bob'. They wore make-up and many of them smoked and drank. Most of them worked, alongside men (if not for equal pay). They went to racecourses, boxing matches and clubs. In short, they did things that previously only men had done. They did not conform to the image of women as home-based wives, mothers and daughters.

Many flappers married eventually. When they did, they had to change their behaviour. However, many of them took advantage of all the new household gadgets to live as labour-saving a home life as possible, and some even continued to work.

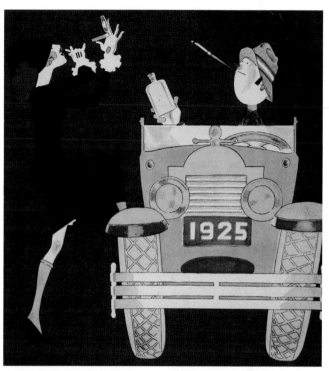

Source D: *One of the covers of a weekly magazine called* Judge *for the year 1925.*

> Women were now competing with men in the business world more than ever before. Whereas before prohibition the saloon bar had been a male space, women now drank with men in speakeasies. Women had taken to swearing, smoking and using contraception. They were not keeping inside the limits of their traditional role. They were becoming financially, and therefore in other ways, independent of their fathers and husbands in record numbers.

Source C: *From an article on 'flappers', written in 1969.*

Activity

Some of the statements below are correct, some are wrong. Copy the correct ones. Copy **a corrected version** of the wrong ones.

a American women got equal voting right to men in 1918.

b The number of women working rose sharply between 1910 and 1930.

c 'Flappers' was the name given to young, single, independent women who did not conform to the traditional image of women.

d Flappers who married changed their ways and behaved exactly as their mothers and grandmothers had.

Build Better Answers

'In the 1920s the position of women changed enormously'. Use the sources and your own knowledge to explain whether you agree with this view.
 (15 marks)

Paper 2, Section A part (c) questions expect an extended piece of writing, weighing up how far the sources and your own knowledge support a statement.

■ **A basic answer (level 1)** will make a generalised statement.

● **A good answer (level 2)** will give an answer supported by the sources and/or own knowledge. An answer for and against the view will gain higher marks.

▲ **A better answer (level 3)** will use detail from three or more of the sources for and against the statement. Adding own knowledge will gain higher marks in the level.

▲ **An excellent answer (top of level 4)** would use detail from three or more of the sources and their own knowledge to give an overall view on the level of support (for and against) the statement.

More open-minded?

Learning objectives

In this chapter you will learn about:

- the significance of radio
- the significance of motoring
- how intolerance restricted education.

The 1920s were a time when some people became more open-minded. Women had greater freedom. There were more ways to bring people together and let them find out about new ideas and other points of view.

- Millions of radios were sold in the 1920s – 10 million by 1929. They brought people in rural areas news and information as well as music and advertising. Radio producers claimed to bring the world to your living room and, while they did not exactly do that, they certainly brought a wider range of experiences.

- Motoring meant that people could move around their state, even travel to other states. On a smaller scale, rural families could drive to a large town more easily, rather than relying on the nearest small town for supplies and entertainment.

Intolerance

However, the 1920s was also a time of intolerance. The USA withdrew into isolationism after the First World War and many groups were intolerant of people whose race, politics or religion were different from their own.

There were groups that were very concerned about morality. They feared the movies and all the other elements of the Roaring Twenties would bring disaster as people abandoned their morals and social responsibility. These were mainly older people and members of church groups, especially fundamentalist church groups.

Some states tried to control 'immoral' behaviour. Ohio brought in laws about the length of dresses. Smoking was banned in North Dakota until 1925.

Fundamentalist church groups believed in accepting every word of the Bible as the actual truth. This meant they not only objected to the different morals of the 1920s. They also objected to any teaching that conflicted with the 'truth' of the Bible.

The new style of dancing was denounced in religious journals as "impure, polluting, corrupting and destroying spirituality." All church members were urged to instruct young people to raise their 'spiritual tone'. In Philadelphia a Dress Reform Committee was set up which, after consulting hundreds of clergymen, designed a 'moral gown' approved of by most of the churches in the city. It was loose with elbow length sleeves and reached down to the ankle.

Source A: *From a history of the 1920s written by Frederick Lewis Allen in 1931.*

Moralists complained that the American family was being weakened, that homes were becoming little more than places to stop to eat and sleep. In Atlanta, Georgia, a grand jury investigated the link between automobiles and moral degeneration. Elsewhere, people expressed concern over young people in cars on secluded country roads.

Source B: *From a 2005 web history of the 1920s.*

The 'Monkey Trial'

Many religious groups rejected the theory of **evolution**. A conservative politician, William Jennings Bryan, campaigned to ban any teaching of evolution in schools. Bryan and his supporters poked fun at the theory of evolution by suggesting it said we were related to monkeys. In 1925, the state of Tennessee passed a law that banned the teaching of anything that contradicted the Bible's Creation story.

John Scopes, a high-school biology teacher in Dayton, Tennessee, deliberately taught evolution so there would be a court case to test whether the law was allowable under the Constitution. The trial caused a sensation. On the first day about 1,000 people crammed into the courtroom: 300 of them had to stand. The case was broadcast live on radio in Chicago. The defence said the state law was against the Constitution and should be overruled. The judge did not accept this argument. The defence then tried to call witnesses to test the idea of Creation in the Bible and the idea of evolution. The judge heard some evidence, then decided that this was irrelevant. He finally told the jury that the decision was simple. Was teaching against the Creation story illegal? Yes. Had Scopes done this? Yes. So he had broken the law. The jury found Scopes guilty and fined him $100. Despite appeals against the case, the Tennessee law was not repealed until 1967.

Source C: *A cartoon about the Scopes trial, published in a New York newspaper at the time.*

Activities

1 Write a sentence each to explain how radio ownership might:
   a broaden the mind
   b encourage immorality.

2 Write a short opening speech for a debate on 'The motor car encourages immorality'. Choose either to support OR oppose the motion.

3 How far does Source B support Source A in its implication that concerns about immorality came from the churches in the USA?

4 Source C supported Scopes against the law banning teaching evolution. Copy this table. Add more rows to explain how we know this.

Feature	Explanation
Teacher wears black glasses	Blind people wore black glasses, suggests teacher is made to wear dark glasses so he can't see the truth.

Racism

By 1870, the USA had abolished slavery and given black people equal rights as American citizens. In reality, however, black people still faced racism, unequal treatment and violence. All over the USA, black people often did the most unpleasant jobs and were 'last hired, first fired'.

Racism in the South

In the South, '**Jim Crow**' laws enforced **segregation** – the policy of making black people use different, usually worse, facilities from whites. This covered everything from cafés to transport to toilets. States gave black schools less money, so it was hard to pay for books or building repairs. Black people had the right to vote, but white southerners often stopped them from registering to vote. Sometimes they told black people they would lose their jobs if they registered. Sometimes they threatened violence. The law in some states said voters had to be literate (able to read). So in those states, the (always white) person registering voters gave black people a hard test passage to read and white people a simple one. This 'legally' disqualified black people as illiterate.

Racism in the North

The North had no segregation laws, but black people often lived in separate neighbourhoods – usually in the worst parts of towns. So local schools and facilities were often all black anyway. But black people did have more opportunities to live a more equal life. They were more likely to get an education, and that education went on for longer. Many black people hoped that their contribution to the forces and war work during the war would help to change racism, especially in the South. It didn't, so many of them left. In the 1920s, black people moved north in their millions. In 1910, the black population of the Harlem area of New York was 10%. In 1920, it was 33% and by 1930 it was 70%.

[In 1896] Homer Plessy went to court to challenge a Louisiana railroad's forcing him to sit in a 'separate but equal' carriage, saying it was a violation of his rights under the constitution. Justice John Marshall Harlan said on his behalf: 'Our constitution is colour-blind'. The other justices did not agree; they ruled for the railroad. Separate but equal was legal. Jim Crow laws affected: public transport, shops, post offices, drinking fountains and libraries. Until the 1940s, the American Red Cross kept negro blood segregated in blood banks.

Source A: *From* Black History for Beginners, *written by Denise Dennis in 1984.*

The attitudes that many white people had towards black people in the South and in the North.

South

North

I, Too

I, too, sing America.

I am the darker brother.
They send me to eat in the kitchen
When company comes,
But I laugh,
And eat well,
And grow strong.

Tomorrow,
I'll sit at the table
When company comes.
Nobody'll dare
Say to me,
"Eat in the kitchen,"
Then.

Besides,
They'll see how beautiful I am
And be ashamed, –

I, too, am America

Source B: *From a poem written by Langston Hughes, a black poet, in 1926.*

Source C: *A segregated drinking fountain in the South in about 1930. The 'colored' label has been nailed to the nearest tree. Legally, segregated facilities had to be clearly marked.*

Activities

1   Turn Source B into a letter, giving the same information and feelings.

2   Write an short article for a magazine outlining the differences between racism in the South and racism in the North.

3   Plan out an answer for the exam question in the Build Better Answers box. Make a table listing the evidence from the sources the text for and against the statement. Write the final summing-up paragraph saying what you think.

Build Better Answers

'Americans in the 1920s saw segregation as perfectly acceptable.' Use the sources and your own knowledge to explain whether you agree with this view.

(15 marks)

■   **A basic answer (level 1)** will make a generalised statement.

●   **A good answer (level 2)** will give an answer supported by the sources and/or own knowledge. An answer for and against the view will gain higher marks.

▲   **A better answer (level 3)** will use detail from three or more of the sources for and against the statement. Adding own knowledge will gain higher marks in the level.

▲   **An excellent answer (level 4)** will use detail from three or more of the sources and their own knowledge to give an overall view on the level of support (for and against) the statement.

Racist violence

White racism was not just a matter of enforcing separation on black people. It was not even a matter of routinely treating them as inferior. There were racist groups who were quite happy to beat up, terrorise, or even murder black people for any reason or, sometimes, for no reason at all.

Lynch law

A **lynching** is when a mob kills somebody, because the people in the mob believe the person they lynch has committed a crime. In the USA in the early twentieth century it was usually (but not always), a white mob killing a black man. Sometimes the mob hauled their target from jail, sometimes the person had not even been arrested. Lynch mobs almost always beat or tortured their targets, then hanged their bodies from a tree. Many people at the time thought lynching only went on in the South. This was not true. But it was easier to get away with there.

About 75 people battered down the door in the jail to reach the yard. They stripped Thomas Shipp, dragged him out to the jail yard and hung him from a window until he was dead – the 10th person lynched in Indiana this year. They beat Abe Smith unconscious with a sledgehammer, let women trample & scratch him, carried him a block away and hung him to a maple tree in the yard of the courthouse – the 11th person lynched in the state this year. Then they hung Shipp's body by Smith's.

Source D: *A* Time *magazine article, 18 August 1930, about lynchings in Indiana.*

Along the way most of his clothes were torn off. When the men dragging Smith stopped briefly, several women rushed forward to stomp on his head and chest and to scream insults.

Source E: *From an eyewitness account of the lynching of Shipp and Smith.*

Source F: *In 1930, Tom Shipp and Abe Smith were arrested on suspicion of murder in Indiana (not a southern state). Before they could be tried, they were taken from jail, beaten, then hanged by a mob of about 1,000 people.*

The Ku Klux Klan

The first Ku Klux Klan was a set up by a group of soldiers from the South in 1865, after they lost the Civil War. Its aim was to stop blacks gaining any real freedom. It was suppressed in the 1870s. In 1915, William Simmons re-formed the Ku Klux Klan. It was still a terrorist organisation, but it expanded its targets a little. The Klan wanted America to be a WASP nation (white Anglo-Saxon Protestants). They saw black people, Jewish people, immigrants from non-Anglo Saxon countries, Catholics and people who belonged to left-wing political groups (for example Communists) as 'un-American'. They believed these people should be driven out of the country. The Klan became very powerful, especially in the South. They wore white robes and hoods, to keep their identity secret. In fact, almost everyone knew who was a local Klan member. In some states the police, the law courts and local government were all full of Klan members. It was hard for anyone they persecuted to bring charges against them.

Activities

1 Write one or two sentences each to explain what Source D tells you about:
   a the feelings of the lynch mob
   b how the reporter felt about the lynching.
2 What three inferences can you make about the Ku Klux Klan from their song-book (Source G)?
3 List the problems faced by a governor of a Southern state in 1925 who was not a member of the Ku Klux Klan and wanted to stamp it out.

⚠ Watch out!

Many people make the mistake of calling the 'Ku Klux Klan' the 'Klu Klux Klan'. This is because the last two words both start with 'Kl-'. But the first word does not have an 'l' in it.

Build Better Answers

How far does Source E support the evidence of Source D about what happened to Shipp and Smith?
(7 marks)

■ **A basic answer (level 1)** will compare the two sources for evidence of support OR the lack of it, giving a generalised answer. For example, *No, because Source E does not mention Shipp at all.*

▲ **A good answer (level 2)** will quote examples of support, OR lack of support. For example, *Source D says women trampled him, and Source E says women stomped on his head.*

▲ **An excellent answer (level 3)** will explain the ways in which the E both does and does not support Source D, and make a conclusion about how far this is support using phrases such as *very little support* or *strong support.*

Source G: *One of many songbooks produced for the Ku Klux Klan. 'Uncle Sam', the symbol of America, is carrying a US flag and leading a group of Klansmen.*

Integration or separation?

Learning objectives

In this chapter you will learn about:
- principles of integration: e.g. W. E. B. Du Bois
- principles of separation: e.g. Marcus Garvey.

Black Americans reacted differently to racism. Some decided to work for greater **integration**. As American citizens, they should have the same rights and opportunities as white Americans. They didn't. So they campaigned for these rights. In 1905, the Niagara Movement was set up, to speak up for the rights of black people. It was followed, in 1909, by the National Association for the Advancement of Colored People (NAACP) and other, more local, groups. **Separatist** black Americans thought integration was impossible. It was better for black people to live in separate communities.

W. E. B. Du Bois 1868–1963

W. E. B. Du Bois helped to set up the Niagara Movement and the NAACP. He also set up and edited a monthly magazine for the NAACP – *Crisis*. He was born in the North and took degrees at Nashville and Harvard before settling to teach at Atlanta University. In 1909 he left the university to work for the NAACP as Director of Publicity and Research. He worked for integration and the rights of black Americans. He travelled widely, speaking on integration and studying the way other countries ran their societies. In 1961 he became a communist and moved to Ghana, Africa, where he spent the last years of his life.

We claim for ourselves every single right that belongs to a freeborn American, political, civil and social; and until we get these rights we will never cease to protest and assail the ears of America. The battle we wage is not for ourselves alone but for all true Americans. It is a fight for ideals, lest this, our common fatherland, false to its founding, become in truth the land of the thief and the home of the slave.

Source B: *The aims of the Niagara Movement, set up in 1905.*

Did you know?

In 1923, Du Bois went to Liberia as a US 'special ambassador' for the inauguration of Liberia's president. After this, he tried to persuade companies and the US government to give Liberia aid and develop its industry. In the early 1920s Marcus Garvey became interested in Liberia. He said he hoped to move the UNIA there to make it a base to defend black interests worldwide. Many Liberians thought he wanted to build a black empire in Africa, from Liberia, with himself as emperor.

Source A: *A photograph of Du Bois (standing at the back) photographed in the* Crisis *office, in about 1910.*

Marcus Garvey 1887–1940

Marcus Garvey was born in Jamaica, studied in England, then returned to Jamaica in 1914 to set up the Universal Negro Improvement Association (UNIA). He moved to the USA in 1916. The UNIA wanted an end to racism, just like the NAACP. But Garvey was a **separatist**. He said whites ran all aspects of life in the USA and other countries and black people would always feel second-rate trying to live in an integrated way. He said he believed in Europe for the Europeans, Asia for the Asians and Africa for the Africans – all Africans who had been scattered by slavery. He set up an African Orthodox Church (a Christian Church with black images of God and the holy family). Some people laughed at his ideas, but he had a huge following, especially among ordinary people. He used donations to help black people set up their own businesses in black areas of US cities.

Garvey began a Back to Africa campaign, with Liberia (a country set up in 1817 as a new country for black colonists from the USA) as the country to settle in. In 1919 he set up the Black Star Line to take black people to Liberia. He funded it with $10,000 collected from his followers. The ships did make several trips to Liberia and back. However, they were in bad condition and the company shut down in 1922. In 1923 Garvey was arrested for fraud and he was deported to Jamaica in 1927.

Garvey and Du Bois

At first, Du Bois was supportive of Garvey's ideas. He said that, while he believed in integration, he also believed that people should be allowed to choose separation. In 1921, he wrote in *Crisis* that Garvey was an inspiring leader, with some good ideas, but that he should be careful how he put them into practice. When Garvey was accused of fraud, he withdrew his support.

Source C: *Marcus Garvey, photographed in Harlem, New York, in August 1922 when he was at the height of his popularity.*

Activities

1 Write, in your own words, definitions of 'integration' and 'separation'.

2 Use Source B to write two slogans for the Niagara campaign: one to show their aims and another to show why they see their fight as a fight for all Americans.

3 **a** Does Source C support the fear of some Liberians mentioned in the Did you know box? Explain your answer.

   b Does this mean that Garvey really was empire-building?

In the Paper 2 final examination in Section A you will have to answer one question on the historical investigation you have studied. You will be given four sources and asked to answer three questions. Question (a) asks you to make inferences from a source, (b) asks you to cross reference between two sources, and (c) asks you to write an essay. You will be asked to make a judgement about a view using the sources and own knowledge.

You have about 45 minutes to answer the three sub-questions on the in depth study, so the examiners are not expecting you to write huge amounts. The number of marks helps you to judge how much to write. For Question (a) allow 5 minutes, Question (b) 10 minutes and Question (c) 30 minutes.

Build Better Answers

Let's look at an en example of a set of sources and questions for Section A.

This question is about the changing position of women in the USA in the 1920s.

Study Sources A, B, C and D and then answer all the questions that follow.

Source A: *A photograph showing flappers dancing the Charleston at a New York club in 1926.*

Source B: *An article with the title 'Flapper Jane' from a US magazine, 1925.*

> Jane's a flapper. Let us take a look at the young person as she strolls across the lawn of her parents suburban home, smoking a cigarette in public. She has just put the car away after driving sixty miles in two hours. She is, for one thing, a pretty girl. Beauty is the fashion in 1925. She is frankly, heavily made up with poisonously scarlet lips and richly ringed eyes. As for her clothes, Jane isn't much this summer. Her dress is brief. It is cut low. The skirt comes just below the knees. The bra has been abandoned since 1924.

Source C: *An English journalist writing about flappers in the USA in 1921.*

> Think of the modern young American girls of this great country, heavily made up and wearing brief skirts. Do they ever think? Do they ever ask whence they have come? It would seem not. Their aim appears to be to look good in order attract men and to secure money. What can a man with a mind find to hold him in one of these lovely, brainless, cigarette-smoking badly-behaved creatures whom he meets continually?

Source D: *From a history of the USA, published in 2009.*

> The position of women in the USA in the 1920s changed for several reasons. Women were given the vote in 1920 and there were increasing numbers of women in employment. The popularity of the cinema, radio and dance halls provided further opportunities. Advertising was aimed specially at women whilst labour-saving devices released women from some of the time previously spent on domestic chores. However, the main reason for change was the influence of the flappers.

Study Source A.

What can you learn from Source A about women in the USA during the 1920s?   **(3 marks)**

Study Sources B and C.

How far does Source C support the evidence of Source B about the flappers? Explain your answer.   **(7 marks)**

Study Sources A, B, C and D, and use your own knowledge.

'The main reason for progress for women in the USA in the 1920s was the influence of the flappers'.

Use the sources, and your own knowledge, to explain whether you agree with this view.   **(15 marks)**

(Total for question: 25 marks)

Build Better Answers

Question (a)

Examiner tip: Part (a) questions will ask you what you can learn about a particular topic from the source provided. This is worth 3 marks, so spend about 5 minutes on this question.

Let's look at an example.

What can you learn from Source A about women in the USA in the 1920s?　　　　**(3 marks)**

- The question is asking you to infer something from the source. An inference means working something out from a source that the source doesn't actually tell you. For example, we often make inferences (get messages) from body language. If a student yawns during a lesson the teacher may well get the message, or make the inference, that the student is bored.

- Be careful not just to write down what you can see from the source. In other words, the contents. For example, 'The student is yawning' is a description, not an inference.

- You need to support the inferences with information from the source. Begin each answer with the phrase 'This source suggests…'

Women are in a club. This suggests that women had greater social freedom in the 1920s.

All the women are dancing the Charleston while men watch them. This suggests that women danced openly in public.

Woman wearing a short dress. This suggests that women's fashions had become much more daring in the 1920s.

The women are smiling and waving at the camera. This suggests that women are happy to have their picture taken, and proud of what they are doing.

Build Better Answers

What can you learn from Source A about women in the USA in the 1920s? **(3 marks)**

Student answer

Source A shows me a group of women who are dancing in a New York club. The women are wearing short skirts. Two of the women have pulled their skirts up. The women are posing for the camera. Some of them are smiling and waving at the camera. They are wearing high heels and have short hair styles. The women only seem interested in having a good time.

Examiner comments

This answer mainly describes what can be seen in the source and more or less repeats the information given above the source. It does, however, make one inference in the last sentence when suggested that the women only seem interested in having a good time. This would be awarded two marks.

Let's rewrite the answer, making inferences from the source.

Source A suggests that women's fashions had become more daring. This is because the women are shown wearing high heel shoes and short dresses. The source also suggests that women now had the freedom to dance in public. This is because the photograph shows them dancing in a night club.

In this answer there are two inferences from the source which are underlined and each of the inferences is supported with evidence from the source. Moreover, the candidate has used the word 'suggest' to encourage an inference rather than simply describing what is in the source. The answer would get full marks. Remember that you only need one supported inference to achieve full (three) marks. It is not the only possible answer as there are several other supported inferences that could be made from the source. However, marks are often lost at the end of an examination by spending too much time on the first question in a section. Make sure you spend no more than five minutes on this question as it is only worth three marks. As you can see, you do not have to write much for this question to achieve full marks.

Build Better Answers

Question (b)

Examiner tip: Part (b) questions will ask you to **compare** two sources by looking for support and disagreement between the two sources as well as making a judgement about the extent of support. This is worth 7 marks, so spend about 10 minutes answering the question.

Let's look at an example.

Study Sources B and C.

Source B: *An article with the title 'Flapper Jane' from a US magazine, 1925.*

> Jane's a flapper who is responsible for the advancement of women in the USA. Let us take a look at the young person as she strolls across the lawn of her parents' suburban home, smoking a cigarette in public. She has just put the car away after driving sixty miles in two hours. She is, for one thing, a pretty girl. Beauty is the fashion in 1925. She is frankly, heavily made up with scarlet lips and richly ringed eyes. As for her clothes, Jane's dress is brief. It is cut low. The skirt comes just below the knees.

Source C: *An English journalist writing about flappers in the USA in 1921.*

> Think of the modern young American girls of this great country, heavily made up and wearing brief skirts. Do they ever think? Do they ever ask whence they have come? It would seem not. Their aim appears to be to look good in order attract men and to secure money. What can a man with a mind find to hold him in one of these lovely, brainless, cigarette-smoking, badly-behaved creatures whom he meets continually? They do little for the image of women in the USA.

How far does Source C support the evidence of Source B about the flappers? Explain your answer.　　**(7 marks)**

To answer this question you need to be clear which areas of the sources say the same things; which, if any, contradict; and which just don't overlap. A good way to plan the answer to the question is to:

- Highlight any areas of support in what the sources say. These are shown in red above. Explain these similarities.
- In a different colour, highlight any areas of challenge in what the source say. These are shown in green above. Explain these differences.

Are there any differences in the overall attitude or tone of each of the sources, in what they are suggesting? For example, the overall tone or attitude of Source B approves of flappers while Source C is very critical of their influence.

Here is a grid to help you to plan your answer:

	Source B	Source C
Support		
Challenge		

Now make a judgement on the extent of support between the two sources. Try to use judgement phrases such as *strongly support, some support, very little support*. Remember to explain this judgement. Here is another grid to help you make this judgement.

Strong support	Some support	Little support	No support

Build Better Answers

Student answer

Source B says that flappers wear short skirts and a lot of make-up. It also says that they smoke and drive cars. Source C tells us that they smoke and wear short dresses and that they are only interested in attracting men. It says they are not very intelligent.

Examiner comments

This student summarises the contents of the two sources but makes no real attempt to compare or contrast them. This would be awarded a mark in Level 1.

Let's look at a better answer.

Source C does support the evidence of Source B about the appearance of the flappers. Source B says that Jane the flapper is wearing a brief skirt while Source C tells us that flappers wore short skirts. Both sources mention that flappers wore heavy make-up and smoked.

This student has directly cross-referenced the two sources and given evidence of support. However, there is no mention of differences between the two sources. In addition, the student does not make a judgement about the extent of support between the two sources. This would be awarded a mark in Level 2.

Now an answer that is better still.

Source C does support the evidence of Source B about the appearance of the flappers. Source B suggests that Jane the flapper is wearing a brief skirt while Source C tells us that flappers wore short skirts. Both sources mention that flappers wore heavy make-up and smoked.
However, Source C also challenges the views of Source B about the role of flappers. While Source B suggests that flappers have done much to improve the position of women, Source C is very different, believing that they have done little to advance the role of women and are brainless. Overall, there are strong differences in attitude and tone between the two sources, with Source B supportive of the flappers and Source C much more critical.

This student has directly cross-referenced the two sources, giving evidence of support and challenge. In addition, there is a final judgement on the extent of support between the two sources. This would be awarded a mark in Level 3.

Build Better Answers

Question (c)

Examiner tip: Part (c) questions will ask you to discuss a view using the sources and your own knowledge. Remember to keep focused on the view and consider support and lack of support. You will need to make a quick plan before writing your answer. It is worth 15 marks so spend about 30 minutes on this question.

Let's look at an example.

Study Sources A, B, C and D, and use your own knowledge.

'The main reason for progress for women in the USA in the 1920s was the influence of the flappers'.

Use the sources, and your own knowledge, to explain whether you agree with this view.   (15 marks)

A good way to answer this type of question is to:

• Decide which sources can be used to support the view.

• Decide which sources can be used to challenge the view. Some sources can be used to give both sides.

• Use the sources to stimulate your own knowledge. Remember that if you develop information from the source then it becomes own knowledge. For example, Source D will often provide several opportunities to develop your own knowledge.

Source D: *From a history of the USA, published in 2009.*

> The position of women in the USA in the 1920s changed for several reasons. Women were given the vote in 1920 and there were increasing numbers of women in employment. The popularity of the cinema, radio and dance halls provided further opportunities. Advertising was aimed specially at women whilst labour-saving devices released women from some of the time previously spent on domestic chores. However, the main reason for change was the influence of the flappers.

You should be able to explain more about some of the factors highlighted in blue in this source.

Here is a grid to help you plan your answer.

	Support the view	Challenge the view
Source A		
Source B		
Source C		
Source D		
Own knowledge		

• Ensure you write a balanced answer in which you use one or more of the sources and your own knowledge to support the view and one or more of the sources and your own knowledge to challenge the view.

• Write a conclusion in which you make a final judgement on the view given in the question.

Student answer

Source A shows a group of flappers in a club. They are wearing short skirts and dancing. Source B tells us more about the flappers. It says that they drive cars, smoke, use a lot of make-up and wear short skirts. Source C also says that they wear short skirts and lots of make-up and smoke, but says they are brainless. The flappers did change the position of women because they made them more confident. Source D gives other reasons for changes. It mentions advertising and labour-saving devices.

Examiner comments

This student summarises the contents of the first three sources and makes no attempt to focus on the question. There is more attempt to focus on change with Source F and a hint of own knowledge about making women more confident. This would be awarded a mark in Level 1.

Let's look at a better answer.

Sources A and B suggest that it was the flappers who encouraged change in the position of women. Source A shows a group of flappers dancing in a club and wearing short skirts. Their **favourite dance was**, as mentioned in the source, the Charleston. **They also listened to controversial new music known as jazz.** This would have shocked many Americans.
The writer of Source B believes they have done much to further the position of women. This was because they encouraged greater freedom for women. The source mentions how they drive cars, smoke in public, are heavily made up and wear very short skirts. **They went to cinemas and speakeasies without a chaperone.**

This is better because the student focused on the question and has organised and used some of the sources to support the view. The answer has also used information in the sources to stimulate own knowledge (in bold). However, the student has only given one side of the question and does not come to a conclusion. This would be awarded a mark in Level 2.

What takes an answer to Level 3?

Sources A and B support the view that the flappers did most to encourage progress in the position of women in the USA in the 1920s. They show how flappers challenged the traditional role of women (dancing in clubs, wearing short skirts, driving cars). Flappers **also listened to controversial new music known as jazz and went to cinemas and speakeasies. This would have shocked many Americans. Joan Crawford, a popular film star, was a flapper who did much to encourage a freer lifestyle for women.** However, Source C doesn't suggest flappers furthered the position of women. Quite the opposite. It says they were brainless and were only interested in attracting men. Moreover, Source D suggests there were more important reasons for progress – labour-saving devices, for example. **These reduced the amount of time women spent on housework, giving them more leisure time to socialise and drive cars. Many people, especially in rural areas, saw flappers as too extreme while others agreed with the views of Source C that they were simply pleasure-seeking females. Neither view furthered the position of women.**
Overall, although A and B support the view that flappers were the most important reason, Source D suggests good arguments for other more important reasons.

This is an even better answer. The student has focused on the question and has organised and used all the sources to support and challenge the view. Moreover, there is much more own knowledge to back up both sides of the view. The student has written an answer of four paragraphs and a conclusion on the view given in the question. This would be awarded a high mark in Level 3.

In 1919, at the end of the First World War, the leaders of the victorious powers met near Paris to create a peace treaty. They wanted a treaty to ensure that there would never again be a world war on that scale.

Part of their treaty was the League of Nations – an international organisation which was intended to help keep the peace. It set out to solve international disputes and improve people's lives, to remove the causes of war. Although it had several successes, it did not prevent the Second World War.

Undeterred, the leaders of the victorious powers in the Second World War tried again in 1945. They created the United Nations, with exactly the same aims as the League.

In this section you will study:

- the creation and aims of the League and UN
- the similarities and differences in the organisation of the League and UN
- changes brought about by the work of the League and UN
- successes of the League and UN
- weaknesses in the peacekeeping of the League and UN.

As you go through the course, you will be able to compare the key features of the League and UN and their work and study the changes which took place as they worked to make the world a safer place.

The exam

This page shows you exactly what your Paper 2, Section B exam paper will look like. In Section B you answer the one breadth study in change that you studied.

There are three questions, parts (a), (b), and (c). **You must answer all three.**

B3: The changing role of international organisations: The League and the UN, 1919–2000

Source: From a modern history textbook, published in 2001.

The League failed for several reasons. The sanctions the League imposed were often ineffective. It did not have its own military forces to use against an aggressor. In any case, countries were reluctant to act against an aggressor unless their own interests were at stake. However, the most important reason was the absence of key nations, especially the USA.

(a) What does this Source tell us about the reasons for the failure of the League of Nations?

(3)

(b) Explain the key features of the peace-keeping role of the United Nations in **either** the Korean War (1950–53) **or** the Congo (1960–64).

(7)

(c) How far did agencies of the League of Nations and the United Nations improve the lives of people in the years 1920–2000?

You may use the following information to help you with your answer.

- The International Labour Organisation
- The World Health Organisation

(15)

(Total for Question B3 = 25 marks)

Notice (a) asks what the source tells us. Don't add things from your own knowledge – the marks are only for explaining what the source says.

Pay special attention to part (b). You have to choose **one** of the two alternatives: in this case, to write either about the Korean War or about the Congo.

Notice the marks for each question. Part (a) is worth 3 marks, but part (b) is worth 7 and (c) 15. You need to spend more than half the time on part (c).

In part (c) you get two bits of information, called 'scaffolding', to help you structure your answer. You may use the scaffolding information and/or any other information of your own, including (where appropriate) case studies you have worked on. With 15 marks this question needs you to write at length, supporting your answer with detailed information.

The pattern of questions will be the same.
a) source comprehension
b) writing about the key features of an event
c) making a judgement in an essay.

The birth of the League of Nations

The League of Nations was an international organisation of states from all over the world. It was based in Geneva, Switzerland, and its main aims were to keep peace and improve people's lives. It started with 42 members in 1920 and grew to 58 members by 1934. It was dissolved in 1946.

The background of the League

The idea of nations co-operating to avoid war was not new. In 1815, after the Napoleonic Wars, the leading powers started the Congress System. They met to solve disputes which might lead to war. But it was limited to Europe and met only occasionally.

The idea of nations co-operating to improve lives was not new either. For example, the International Red Cross had been started in 1864. However, this was limited to helping the wounded during wars.

So the idea of a permanent group of states from all around the world, meeting to discuss a range of issues, was a change. It was driven by two things.

- Internationalism: people tried to make things better by international co-operation. In 1874, the Universal Postal Union started, for example.
- But even more important was the First World War. Over 8 million combatants died; and over 20 million were wounded. There was widespread destruction. People wanted to prevent this ever happening again.

As a result, by 1918, a number of politicians were proposing a league of co-operating states. One of these was Jan Smuts, prime minister of South Africa, who published *The League of Nations – a Practical Suggestion* in 1918. Another was British prime minister Lloyd George. But the most important was Woodrow Wilson.

Activities

1. Make a timeline to show the events from 1918 to 1920 which led to the start of the League of Nations.

2. International co-operation had taken place before the League of Nations. In what ways was the League of Nations a change from earlier international co-operation?

3. a Make a list of ways in which Woodrow Wilson can take the credit for the start of the League of Nations.

   b Make a list of other factors which explain the start of the League of Nations.

   c How far do you think Wilson was the 'father of the League'?

Watch out!

Woodrow Wilson was the driving force behind the founding of the League. But he was not the only reason it was founded.

Make sure you balance his role with other factors, like the growth of internationalism and the death toll in the First World War.

...a great attempt must be made to establish by some international organization an alternative to war as a means of settling international disputes.

Source A: *An extract from a speech about British war aims by David Lloyd George, British prime minister, 5 January 1918.*

Setting up the League

On 8 January 1914, while the First World War was still going on, US president Wilson set out his peace plans. He said peace should be based on Fourteen Points. The Fourteenth Point said:

'A general association of nations must be formed under specific covenants for the purpose of affording mutual guarantees of political independence and territorial integrity to great and small states alike.'

This was Wilson's plan for a League of Nations.

In January 1919, when the war was over, world leaders met at the Paris Conference. Wilson wanted to make his Fourteen Points the guide to peace. But other leaders, like Lloyd George, Clemenceau and Orlando, had their own views. Many people in Britain wanted Germany punished. France wanted Germany weakened. Wilson gave way to many of these demands. But, in doing so, he did get agreement on his main demand: the founding of the League of Nations.

As a result, a special commission was set up, with Wilson as its chairman, to work out a proposal for a League of Nations. Some countries, like France, wanted it to have a very narrow role, only concerned with settling disputes between nations. Others, like Wilson, wanted it to have a more wide-ranging role. Wilson's vision of the League won the day.

So, when the peace treaties with Germany and its allies were eventually agreed, every one of them had, as Part 1 of the treaty, an agreement setting out the aims and rules of a new body: the League of Nations. This agreement was called the Covenant of the League of Nations.

Woodrow Wilson became the 28th president of the United States in 1912. He was a professor of politics and law and a committed Christian, and both these outlooks shaped his politics.

In 1917, German U-boat attacks on US ships led Wilson to join the Allies and declare war against Germany. But he was determined that some good should come from the war. So, in the peace settlements, although Wilson had to compromise on many of his Fourteen Points, he refused to compromise the on League of Nations.

Woodrow Wilson is seen as the father of the League and, for this work, he was awarded the Nobel Peace Prize in 1919.

However, the US Congress did not want the USA to be drawn into international disputes. They voted against joining the League. Soon after, Wilson suffered a stroke which ended his political career.

Source B: *The key leaders at the Paris Peace Conference in 1919, from left to right: Lloyd George, prime minister of Britain; Vittorio Orlando, prime minister of Italy; Georges Clemenceau, prime minister of France; and Woodrow Wilson.*

The Covenant of the League

The Covenant of the League stated its aims and its rules. It consisted of 26 articles.

Article 1 dealt with membership. It said that all the 44 states who signed the Covenant in June 1919 were members of the League. Any other state could join if two-thirds of the existing members voted for it.

Articles 2–7 set up the main bodies of the League – for example the Council and Assembly (see pages 212–13). Although the major powers dominated the Council, both it and the Assembly needed unanimous support for any decision. This shared power but delayed decision-making.

Articles 8 and 9 committed members to reduce military armaments and limit arms production.

Articles 10 –17 dealt with disputes which could lead to war.

- All member states had to promise not to take any aggressive action against other member states.
- Instead, they had to agree to take any disputes to the League and try to solve these with discussion.
- If discussion failed, they had to go to **arbitration**.
- Any state that refused to accept a League decision could have **economic sanctions** imposed – such as stopping trade to deny them essential supplies.
- If this was not sufficient, member states agreed to take military action against the offending member.

Articles 18–21 banned any secret treaties or treaties which endangered peace.

Article 22 set out rules for governing colonies taken away from the defeated powers.

Articles 23–25 promised work on labour conditions and drug trafficking and links with other international bodies, like the Red Cross.

Article 26 said the Covenant could be changed if the Council and a majority of the Assembly agreed.

The Covenant was written as Part 1 of the peace treaty with every defeated nation.

Activities

1 a How did the Covenant say that members of the League should deal with disputes which threatened peace?

   b In what other ways did the Covenant try to ensure peace?

2 Wilson was determined that the League should not just have a narrow role, concerned only with keeping peace. How did the Covenant try to ensure that this would happen?

3 In pairs or groups, set up a debate.

   One side should argue that *The Covenant contained measures which would make the world a safer place.*

   The other group should argue that *The Covenant was flawed; it would never make the world safer.*

Key Features

Section B part (b) questions always ask you to *Describe the key features of … (something).*

Firstly, what is a key feature?

It's an important aspect or part of something.

The key features of the Covenant of the League of Nations could be…

- Article 1 – which said who could join.
- Articles 2-7 – which described the way the League was organised.
- Articles 10-17 – which said how the League would try to stop wars.
- Articles 23-25 – which said how the League would help people's lives around the world.

Secondly, what makes a good answer?

The best answers will:

- give **at least two** key features
- give details of each one
- explain each one
- explain links between the features.

Weaknesses built into the Covenant	
The Covenant set out to use a system of collective security. This means that it said that the security of all nations should be protected by all the members agreeing on one policy and applying it collectively – together.	But it was optimistic to think that all members could agree on one policy. Sometimes individual members ignored the League's policy. In 1935, rather than upset an ally, Britain and France ignored the League's policy towards Italy.
The Covenant also said that members would act against any act of aggression towards a member state.	But members didn't always think this was the best policy. Sometimes they thought it best to appease – calm – the aggressor, by turning a blind eye.
The Covenant also said that, after discussion, arbitration and the use of economic sanctions, its members would use military action to enforce its decisions.	But the Covenant was woolly about this. It did not say how it would use military force. It gave the League no army and, by disarmament, it made its members less able to enforce its decisions.
Finally, the Covenant was phrased as if it was interested in the security of all nations and the quality of life of all the people of the world.	But the Covenant expressed the aims of the Allies, not the defeated powers, who saw its creation as the League of Victors, not the League of Nations.

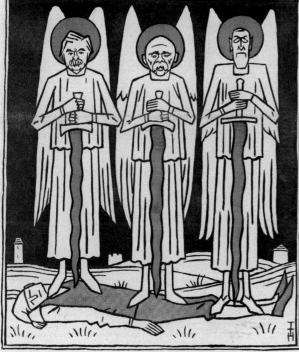

Three of the great powers were not members. To succeed, the League needed the support of all the great powers. The United States did not join. Because Germany was a defeated nation, it did not join until 1926. Russia was in the middle of a civil war and was not allowed to join. The League also had no power to enforce its decisions; it had no police force or army of its own. Finally, the League could only use force in a dispute if all the members agreed.

Source C: *From a modern history textbook, published in 1984.*

Source D: *The cover of this German magazine, from 1919, shows Lloyd George, Clemenceau and Wilson. They look like angels, but they are trampling on a symbolic German peasant to set up their League of Nations. The expressions on their faces are not angelic. Many Germans were hostile towards the League from the outset.*

The birth of the United Nations

> **Learning objectives**
>
> In this chapter you will learn about:
> - the start of the United Nations
> - US president Roosevelt's part in starting it
> - the Charter of the United Nations.

The United Nations is an international organisation of states from all over the world. It is based in New York, USA, and its main aims are to keep peace and improve people's lives. It started with 51 members in 1945. By 2000, it had 189 members.

The background of the UN

In August 1941, there was a secret meeting, on board HMS *Prince of Wales*, between Franklin D. Roosevelt, president of the United States, and Winston Churchill, prime minister of the UK. They met to discuss how to organise the peace at the end of the Second World War. In a document that echoed Woodrow Wilson's Fourteen Points, they decided the world needed:

- democracy in all countries
- free trade and prosperity shared by all nations
- arms reduction
- 'a wider, permanent system of security'.

These ideas were written into the Atlantic Charter. This was signed in January 1942 by the Allies, the 26 nations fighting the Axis powers (of Germany, Italy and Japan). The Allied countries called this treaty *'A Declaration by the United Nations'*.

The 'Big Four' in the Allies – the USA, UK, Soviet Union and China – made more detailed plans.

- In 1943, they issued the Moscow Declaration. It said that a 'general international organisation' would be set up to maintain peace.
- In 1944, the Big Four met at Dumbarton Oaks, in Washington USA. Here, they set out a basic framework for the United Nations organisation.
- In 1945, at the Yalta Conference, the USA, UK and Soviet Union added details, including who could be members, and decided voting rights.

Activities

1 Read the Key Features box on page 150.

   a Use that as a guide to create your own list of the key features of the Charter of the United Nations.

   b Compare your answer with other people.

2 Think about who set up the United Nations.

   If playing no part is 0% and being totally responsible is 100%, how much do you think the following groups contributed to setting up the United Nations?

   a the United States

   b all the Allies combined

   c other international organisations

   d the Axis powers.

   Compare your answer with other people. Come to your own final decision and write a justification for it.

> **Franklin Delano Roosevelt** was the person who coined the phrase 'the United Nations'.
>
> The relationships among the main Allies – the USA, UK, Soviet Union and China – were not easy. Roosevelt managed to keep them all agreed on the United Nations. Unlike Wilson, he also managed to ensure that the US Congress supported it too.
>
> When Allied leaders met at Yalta, Roosevelt was already ill. On 12 April 1945, 13 days before the San Francisco Conference was due to begin, Roosevelt suffered a brain haemorrhage and died. Consequently, though in some ways the father of the United Nations, he never lived to see it start.

Setting up the United Nations

All these preparations meant that, as the Second World War came to an end in Europe, the victors were ready to set up the United Nations Organisation. So, between April and June 1945, the United Nations Conference on International Organisation was held in San Francisco, USA. It was attended by 50 nations, all of whom had joined the Allies by March 1945. Many other international bodies, representing groups such as trade unions, health experts and economists, also attended and were able to submit papers to the Conference.

During debates some changes were made to the Dumbarton proposals. For example, the smaller states inserted provisions on human rights and racism. Eventually, all 50 nations agreed and signed the draft United Nations Charter, which set out its aims and rules.

Finally, on 24 October 1945, the Charter of the United Nations was ratified in Washington by the majority of its members. This officially brought the United Nations into existence, and 24 October is still celebrated annually as United Nations Day.

Did you know?

When Roosevelt first used the term 'The United Nations', he meant the Allies.

So, when the Allies set up their new peace-keeping organisation, they called it 'the United Nations Organisation' – or UNO.

As time went by, the last word was dropped.

We now talk about the organisation as just *the United Nations* – and in normal usage, it is often just called *the UN*.

Fifty nations met in the San Francisco Opera House and signed the UN Charter. They agreed to keep the peace, encourage co-operation between nations and defend human rights. Wilson's League had failed because some of the largest nations had not joined and because it had no armed forces at its disposal.

Source A: *from a modern textbook, published in 1968.*

Examination question

What does Source C on page 154 tell us about the aims of the United Nations? **(3 marks)**

Source B: *Roosevelt and Churchill, planning for the end of the war, aboard HMS* Prince of Wales *in August 1941.*

The Charter of the United Nations

The Charter of the United Nations set out its aims and rules. It starts with a preamble (introduction) and then has 111 articles, in 19 chapters.

The Preamble sets out the aims of the UN as:

- maintaining of peace
- upholding human rights
- supporting international law
- promoting social progress.

Chapter 1 sets out the key aim of the UN: to preserve international peace and security.

Chapter 2 defines the rules for membership.

Chapters 3–15 describe the organisation of the UN, all its institutions and their roles. A key change here is that the major powers were given a veto over decisions in its Council and majorities are sufficient for decisions in the Assembly. This limited the influence of small powers.

Chapters 16–17 put the UN into international law.

Chapters 18–19 explains how the Charter can be amended.

All states who sign the Charter are bound by it. The Charter states that obligations to the United Nations overrule any other treaty obligations.

WE THE PEOPLES OF THE UNITED NATIONS DETERMINED: to save succeeding generations from the scourge of war, which twice in our lifetime has brought untold sorrow to mankind, and to reaffirm faith in fundamental human rights, in the dignity and worth of the human person, in the equal rights of men and women and of nations large and small, and to establish conditions under which justice and respect for the obligations arising from treaties and other sources of international law can be maintained, and to promote social progress and better standards of life in larger freedom.

Source C: *The opening words of the Preamble of the UN Charter.*

Activities

1 Practise your source comprehension skills.

 a Write out the phrases in Source C which tell us the aims of the United Nations. Keep them short.

 b Compare your answer with other people and discuss any differences.

 c Now write out your final decision.

2 In preparation for the examination question in this chapter, make a list of headings which describe the ways in which the Charter was:

 a the same as the Covenant of the League

 b different from the Covenant of the League.

Source D: *An American poster supporting US membership of the UN. It shows similarities with 1919, when the war dead were also a cause of the League. But it also represents widespread US support for the UN, a difference from 1919.*

The Covenant and Charter were the idea and the work of the victors in World War.

The USA was the driving force and the 4 major powers proposed all the main features.

Both put their faith in **collective security** – the countries working together to preserve peace

Similarities

Both reflect the end of World Wars, not normal times. So, for example, Germany was snubbed by both.

THE CHARTER AND THE COVENANT

Differences

The Charter was not part of peace treaties, so it was seen less as part of the punishment of defeated powers.

The Charter says members must provide armed forces for the UN to use to ensure peace. All this was left very vague in the Covenant.

The Covenant gave smaller powers more influence. The Charter gives the major powers more control.

Build Better Answers

In what ways was the Charter of the United Nations a change from the Covenant of the League of Nations? You may use the following information to help you with your answer and any other information of your own. (15 marks)

- **The aims of the United Nations**
- **The Big Four – USA, UK, USSR, China**

Paper 2, Section B part (c) questions of the exam will ask you to analyse change.

The best answers will:

1 Discuss at least two – and preferably more – examples which show change or lack of change.

2 Explain how far each example shows change or lack of change and show how the examples are linked.

3 Use information to support the view explained.

4 Make a judgement on the extent of change or lack of change.

The organisation of the League of Nations

> **Learning objectives**
>
> In this chapter you will learn about:
> - the key features of the organisation of the League
> - the strengths and weaknesses of the organisation.

Membership to 1926

All nations of the world were invited to join the League of Nations, with two important exceptions.

- Countries that had fought against the Allies were not invited. So countries like Germany, Austria, Hungary, Bulgaria and Turkey could not join.
- Russia was in the midst of a civil war and was not invited. By the end of 1920, it was controlled by a communist government of which many European states did not approve, so was still not invited.

In addition, the USA did not join. Despite Wilson's efforts, its Congress decided it wanted isolation from world affairs.

So, in 1920, the League had 42 members – the Allies and 13 neutrals. A majority came from outside Europe, but the European members were the most powerful. By 1923, Austria, Hungary and Bulgaria had all been invited to join and membership stood at 54. Furthermore, in a move which shows the early success of the League and the desire for peace across Europe, Germany joined in 1926.

The League of Nations.

" I bring you our brothers from Germany and Russia."
" No, thank you. See what they bring : they are flame projectors, not extinguishers."

Source A: *This cartoon throws light upon the debate about membership of the League. What different opinions about membership does it reveal?*

Activities

1 List four ways in which the membership of the League weakened its ability to be an international peacemaking organisation. Sources A and B may help you.

2 Draw your own diagram to show the organisation of the League of Nations. Use the text in this chapter to annotate your diagram with the key points about each part of the organisation.

3 With the exam question on page 159 in mind, use what you know so far and give each body of the League a mark out of 10 for success. Write a sentence or two to justify your mark.

> The peace-makers thought mainly in terms of Europe and it was sometimes said that the League of Nations was just something of a European club.

Source B: *From a modern history textbook, written in 1984.*

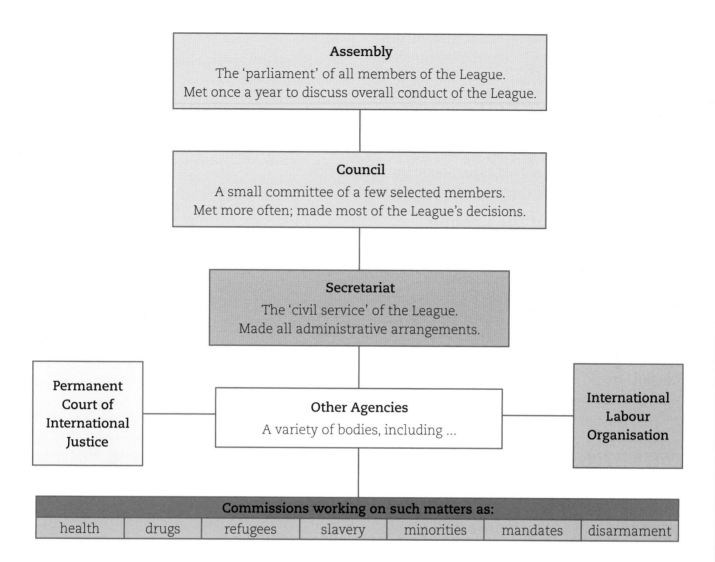

The Assembly

One key feature of the organisation of the League was the Assembly. This was like the parliament of the League. It met once a year, normally in September, but extra meetings could be called by a majority of the members. Every member sent three representatives, although each member state had just one vote. The Assembly reviewed all the League's activities. It could also elect new members, by a two-thirds majority, and controlled the League's budget. Some decisions had to be unanimous. In theory, this gave every member a veto, which could have made decisions impossible. In fact, it slowed the League down and watered down its actions; but compromises were usually made. In this sense, the Assembly was a good example of international co-operation.

The Council

Another key feature of the League was the Council. This was a smaller, more manageable body. It met four to five times a year and if there was a crisis. Again, decisions had to be unanimous, making actions less decisive. At first there were four permanent members: Britain, France, Italy and Japan. This became five when Germany became a member in 1926. There were also temporary members, elected by the Assembly. There were four temporary members in 1920: Belgium, Spain, Greece and Brazil. This increased to six in 1922 and nine in 1926. Permanent places in Council assured that major powers had their say. However, the growing number of temporary members and non-European members meant that the League was, increasingly, genuinely international.

The Secretariat

The Secretariat was a key feature of the structure of the League of Nations. It consisted of experts, officials and clerical workers who administered the League. They prepared briefing papers and agendas for meetings, made records of debates and put the decisions of the League into practice.

An Englishman, Sir Eric Drummond, was the first Secretary-General of the League. He led the Secretariat and presided over Assembly meetings.

Other agencies of the League

Resolving disputes which upset peace was one aim of the League. But it had others. Article 23 of the Covenant said the League would also address social issues. So another key feature of its structure was a variety of other agencies (known as Commissions) to fulfil these roles.

The Permanent Court of Justice

The Permanent Court of International Justice sat in the Hague in Holland. It had 15 judges, elected by the Assembly from various nations. The Assembly or the Council dealt with political disputes between nations; the Court heard legal disputes – for example, over borders or fishing rights. It had no power to enforce its rulings, which was a weakness. But it only accepted cases if both parties agreed to accept the outcome. By 1939, it heard 70 major cases and made 400 international agreements. It was successful enough to be continued by the United Nations after 1945.

International Labour Organisation

This was set up to improve working conditions around the world. It met annually and dealt with issues like pay, hours and trade union rights. Each member sent two delegates from its government, one from employers and one from its workers.

Again, the ILO had no power to enforce its will on members. But its first director, a Frenchman, Albert Thomas, used the status of the League to prod members to follow ILO advice. For example, a minimum working age of 15 and trade union rights for all were adopted by many member states. The danger to workers of lead in paint was widely publicised. Membership of the ILO was open, so even the USA joined and, after 1945, the ILO became a part of the United Nations.

Did you know?

The Secretariat suffered from poor funding. To run a world-wide organisation, in 1920, it had only 158 staff. In contrast, in 2009, the United Nations Secretariat had 40,000 workers around the world.

Health

Article 23 of the Covenant said the League would address the 'prevention and control of disease'. So the Health Organisation was set up to help members tackle diseases like malaria, typhus and leprosy and to use radiation to treat cancer. It had to work with other international agencies, as it could only work directly with League members.

Drugs

Article 23 also gave the League 'supervision of traffic in opium and other dangerous drugs'. Useful work was done. For example, the Permanent Central Board was set up in 1925 to oversee trade in drugs like opium – which is useful in medicine, but can also be turned into dangerous drugs like heroin. As a result of its work, the production and sale of these drugs fell between 1920 and 1935.

Refugees

The First World War had left many homeless; some had fled fighting, some were prisoners of war. So the Commission for Refugees was set up, led by Fridtjof Nansen. The Commission improved living conditions in **refugee** camps. It also helped prisoners of war and other refugees return home or re-settle elsewhere. For example, in 1925, Nansen helped 40,000 Armenian refugees fleeing from Turkey to resettle in Lebanon and Syria. Nansen died in 1930, but his agency went on. It was awarded the Nobel Peace Prize in 1938.

Slavery

The League tried to end slavery. For example, it insisted on the abolition of slavery in Ethiopia when it joined in 1926. A Slavery Commission was formed in 1924. In 1926, this set up a treaty, called the Slavery Convention. Countries which signed promised to work to end slavery. Britain freed 200,000 slaves in its colony of Sierra Leone.

Mandates

In the peace treaties at the end of the First World War, the defeated powers lost all their colonies. In addition, Turkey lost large areas of its empire. Article 22 of the Covenant said that member states should be 'mandated' to govern these territories, on behalf of the League. Britain, France, Belgium, New Zealand, Australia and Japan were the main mandatory powers.

The Covenant said that the mandate territories should be given independence as soon as possible. In the event, the mandatory powers were slow to do this. Only Iraq gained its independence before 1939; some had to wait until the 1990s.

Disarmament

The League's success in reducing armaments was disappointing. Article 14 of the Covenant called upon member nations to **disarm**; but nothing much happened. The League set up a military commission to advise members on disarmament, but this also had little success. It was replaced by a Temporary Mixed Commission, with military and civilian members; this also made no progress.

The League then began to hold a series of World Disarmament Conferences. The first, in 1926, could not even agree what armaments were so that they could count them. When the Conference met in 1932 it was actually debating an increase in German arms when Hitler came to power there. Not satisfied with its progress, Germany withdrew and, to the embarrassment of the League, rearmed anyway. The Conference ended, without agreement, in 1934.

There was some progress. In 1921, several League members, including the USA, Japan, Britain and France, agreed to limit their navies. The Locarno Treaties (1925) and Kellogg–Briand Pact (1928) reduced tensions. But these were not the work of the League. The world's press were very critical of the League's failure over disarmament, but hardly reported the successes of its other agencies.

UNDER THE SPREADING ARMAMENT TREE
THE DISARMAMENT CONFERENCE SITS

(Yesterday Was Chestnut Sunday)

Source C: *This cartoon, from 1934, shows the Disarmament Conference meeting under a massive 'tree' of bombs and planes, while its worthy aims on paper are no more than rubbish in a bin.*

The organisation of the United Nations

> ### Learning objectives
>
> In this chapter you will learn about:
> - the key features of the organisation of the UN
> - the strengths and weaknesses of the organisation
> - similarities and differences to the League of Nations.

Membership of the United Nations

There were 51 founding members of the UN in 1945. But any nation could apply to join. Membership grew to 144 by 1975 – much bigger than the League. This was one change. It is linked to other changes.

- The new smaller states often worked together. In 1964, they set up the Group of 77 to strengthen their voice by voting as a block.
- Most of the new members were smaller and poorer. This increased the UN focus on economic and social projects.

The General Assembly

Like the Assembly of the League, the General Assembly is the main discussion forum for the United Nations. Like the League, it needs a two-thirds majority to elect new members. But, unlike the League, it meets from September to December. Each member has one vote. A simple majority vote is enough for some decisions, whereas the League required all votes to be unanimous.

The Security Council

The Security Council is the UN body which deals with international disputes. Unlike the League's Council, it is in permanent session, so can discuss any crisis quickly. The major powers dominate its membership and decisions.

- The Security Council has 15 members. The USA, UK, France, Russia and China have five places permanently. The other 10 members (it was only 6 before 1966) are elected by the General Assembly for terms of two years.
- A majority is enough to pass a resolution. But each permanent member has a veto. This was a serious problem in the Cold War (from about 1945–90) when the USA and USSR headed two opposing alliances. Co-operation stopped. By 1950, for example, the USSR had used its veto over 100 times to block decisions.

During a threat to peace, the Security Council will try to arrange arbitration. If fighting occurs, it can use economic sanctions – as it did against Rhodesia in 1964. So far, this is just like the League. But the UN can also use military force. The UN has no army of its own, but the Security Council can deploy troops from member states.

Activities

1. Draw your own diagram to show the organisation of the United Nations. Use the text in this chapter to annotate your diagram with the key points about each part of the organisation.

2. Make a grid to analyse the degree of change between the organisation of the League and United Nations. Your grid should have two columns, headed *No change* and *Change*; the grid should have rows for the Assemblies, the Councils, etc.

3. Now decide whether each change was an improvement. Write a sentence to justify each decision.

Source A: *A UN peacekeeper, deployed by the Security Council, rescuing a child from danger in the Congo in the 1960s.*

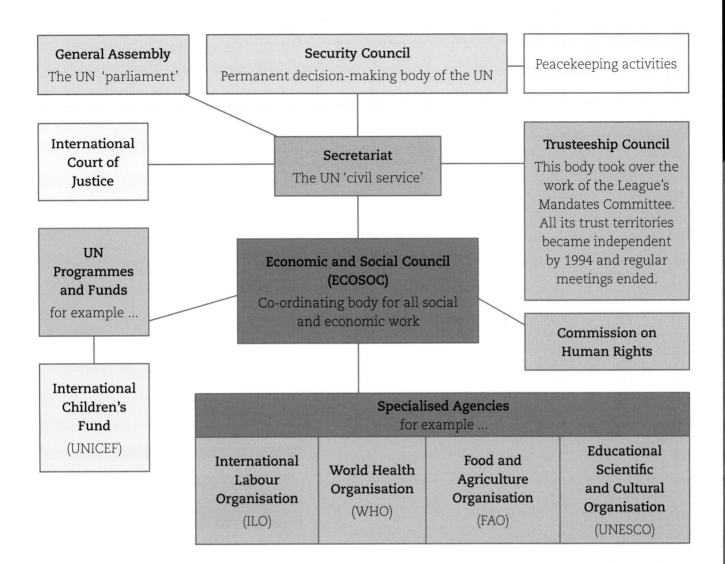

Peacekeeping forces

Unlike the League, the UN can use troops to help keep the peace. Peacekeeping troops were first used in 1948 to keep a ceasefire between Israel and Arab nations. But they have had mixed success.

- States have ignored the UN and used force. For example, the USSR sent troops into Hungary in 1956.
- UN troops have been deployed but failed to prevent serious loss of life. For example, in Bosnia in 1995.
- The UN has also managed to intervene successfully. For example, in Korea in 1950.

In its first 60 years, UN sent peacekeepers on 60 missions.

In 2005, the UN had 70,000 troops on 17 separate missions.

Disarmament is also a Security Council task. Like the League, it has had little success. Arms holdings have increased hugely since 1945. Any recent cuts have come from independent negotiations between individual states.

Top tip

In your examination, there will always be a question asking you to explain the key features of something – like the question on page 159.

If you need to practise questions on key features, take the question on page 159 and substitute *United Nations* for the *League of Nations*.

If you answered the question on page 159, you can analyse that answer, find the things which you could have done better and then practise those in your answer on the United Nations.

The Secretariat

The UN's Secretariat has the same role as the League's (see page 213 for details). However, there are several changes. One is location. The UN General Assembly, Security Council and Secretariat are all based in New York. Another change is scale. The UN Secretariat had 40,000 staff by 2009. It controlled an annual UN budget of $2 billion – excluding peacekeeping costs, which, in 2007-9, for example, added a further $6.8 billion.

The International Court of Justice

The Permanent Court of International Justice of the League of Nations had been a success, and it was included in the structure of the United Nations under a shortened title. It kept its seat at the Hague in Holland; it kept its 15 judges. Its role remained unchanged: hearing legal disputes between nations and giving legal advice to the UN. Like its predecessor, it has done useful work, though it remains limited by being unable to enforce its rulings.

The Economic and Social Council

ECOSOC is the body which co-ordinates all the UN's economic and social work. Its creation, as one of the UN's six main bodies in 1945, reflects the greater emphasis in the UN on humanitarian work than in the League. This is perhaps a change of tactics rather than a change of direction. It is still meant to achieve peace. For example, the third UN Secretary-General, U Thant, said:

I became increasingly convinced that the division of the world into rich and poor…is much more explosive than division of the world based on differing ideologies.

Commission on Human Rights

This was a new body, created in 1946 by ECOSOC. It is the UN's main body for trying to protect human rights around the world. It has emphasised rights such as freedom of speech, freedom from arrest without trial, women's rights, etc. It has had two distinct phases since 1946.

At first, it just defined human rights and recommended good practice. This was widely regarded as ineffective. So, from 1967, it set out to investigate and publicly condemn violations of human rights. This brought much greater public debate, but little real change. The Commission was often embarrassed by the poor human rights records of its own members, who spent more time criticising other members than making improvements of their own. In 2006, it was replaced by the Human Rights Council.

Similarities and Differences

In some ways, the organisation and work of the UN was the same as that of the League.

- Some UN agencies just carried working (for example, the ICJ and ILO).

Sometimes the UN kept a feature of the League, but changed part of it, e.g. voting.

- The Assembly, like the League, uses vetos and needs a two-third majority to elect new members.
- But the UN mostly uses majority votes; the League wanted everyone to agree.

Some things are different.

- The UN's has more members, with no major powers missing.
- The Security Council meets all the time; major powers dominate it.
- The UN has peacekeeping troops and can use military force.
- There is much more humanitarian work (e.g. by UNICEF).

Build Better Answers

In what ways did the organisation of the United Nations improve on the organisation of the League?   (15 marks)

You may use the following information to help with your answer and any other information of your own.

- funding
- voting arrangements

■ **A basic answer (level 1)** will often just repeat the scaffolding points.

● **A better answer (level 2)** will describe things with good detail, but not talk about improvement.

▲ **An excellent answer (level 4)** will not only describe the factors in detail, but also show both improvements and failures, explain the links between the factors, and make a judgement on the extent of the improvement or lack of improvement.

Specialized agencies

The specialized agencies are like the Commissions of the League (see page 213). They do the work of the UN, but are separate organisations, with their own membership. The main ones are set out below. They have had mixed success.

The World Health Organisation

Since 1948, WHO has continued the work of the League's Health Organisation. It has helped to develop new vaccines, for example, against influenza. It has also led campaigns against diseases like malaria and AIDs. In 1980, it said smallpox had been eradicated. WHO has also helped in crises. In 1947 it supplied drugs to Egypt in a cholera epidemic. The death rate fell from 85% to 50%, and WHO's intervention stopped the disease spreading to Africa and the Middle East. In 1960 in the Congo, when medical care collapsed during civil war, WHO sent 150 doctors.

The International Labour Organisation

The ILO was set up in 1946, taking over the League's work in Geneva unchanged. Its success continued and, in 1969, the ILO was awarded the Nobel Peace Prize. For example, in 1992, it set up the International Programme on the Elimination of Child Labour (IPEC) to campaign to end child labour in 88 countries. In 2008 it spent over $60 million on this work.

The Food and Agriculture Organisation

The FAO was set up in 1943 and became part of the UN in 1945. It is based in Rome. Its work has included:

- in 1994, a campaign against crop diseases and pests. This boosted the rice harvest in Asia and eliminated rinderpest, a cattle disease in parts of Asia and Africa
- in 1996, the World Food Summit: 112 states signed the Rome Declaration to halve numbers in hunger by 2015.

By 2000, the FAO had an annual budget of $345 million. It has not always been well spent. The FAO has been critised for allowing bureaucracy to swallow too great a proportion of its funds.

UNESCO

The UN Educational, Scientific and Cultural Organisation is based in Paris. It was set up in 1946 to gain peace through education and culture. Its aims say 'Since wars begin in the minds of men, it is there that peace must be built.' It has:

- in 1948, recommended that all members should adopt free and compulsory primary education for all children
- since 1972, established almost 900 World Heritage Sites, to protect unique cultural features around the world.

Source B: *A child in need at a UNICEF camp in Biafra, 1968.*

But UNESCO has not always been well run. Both the UK and USA left UNESCO for a time, claiming waste of funds. Both returned (the UK in 1997, the USA in 2003) after reforms.

UNICEF

The UN International Children's Fund was set up in 1946 as a temporary measure to help children suffering the effects of the Second World War. In 1953 it was made permanent, with the aim of tackling issues – like poverty, illness or lack of education – that affect children. Achievements include:

- in 1979 launching the Year of the Child to highlight children's problems
- by 1980 vaccinating 280 million children against tuberculosis and 32 million against malaria.

For a body that relies entirely upon voluntary contributions from governments and private donors, UNICEF has been a great success. In 1965 it was awarded the Nobel Peace Prize. In 2006 its annual income was $2.7 billion.

Successes of the League of Nations

Activities

1 As you read this chapter, draw a timeline showing the dates of the successes of the League of Nations. What does your finished timeline tell you?

2 Two vital stages of the League's work in Aaland, Silesia and Bulgaria were a) investigation b) action. Make a small table showing details of these stages for each of the three episodes.

3 **a** List the League's actions on drugs and refugees.

   b Identify the most successful one. Justify your answer to someone else.

Aaland Islands (1920)

The Aaland Islands are in the Baltic Sea, midway between Sweden and Finland. For some time, they had been governed as part of Finland. However, they had once been ruled by Sweden, most of the 25,000 people there spoke Swedish and many of them wanted to become part of Sweden.

During the territorial changes after the First World War, both Sweden and Finland claimed the Aaland islands. The Swedish Navy and Finnish troops were both sent there. War loomed. So, in 1920, the League was asked to arbitrate.

The League appointed legal experts from France, Holland and Switzerland to investigate. A report was written in weeks. In June 1921, the Council of the League ruled that the islands should remain Finnish. For Swedish security, they said that no weapons should ever be kept there. Sweden, reluctantly but honourably, agreed to accept the settlement; it has lasted to this day.

Each occasion in which the question of sanctions arises will have its own special circumstances, requiring individual treatment. One general point is worth making. When there is real danger to world peace, the use of economic weapons, in preference to any other, is one of the essential bases of the Covenant.

Source A: *Written by the League of Nations Secretary-General in December 1925 in response to pressure to lay down rules about when to apply sanctions.*

Upper Silesia (1921)

Upper Silesia was part of Germany, a valuable industrial area. The population was partly German and partly Polish. At the end of the First World War, Poland claimed it. In 1919, the Treaty of Versailles said that there should be a plebiscite (public vote) among the people who lived there to decide whether it should be part of Germany or Poland.

In the meantime, Allied troops were stationed there to keep the peace because local feelings were divided and very strongly held. In 1919 and again in 1920, local Poles attacked German residents. Many were driven from their houses; a few were killed.

In March 1921, the Silesian plebiscite was held. 700,000 voted for German rule; 500,000 for Polish.

Germany claimed victory; Poland claimed a split vote. Rioting started again. The Allies had to send six new troop battalions. Open warfare threatened.

The League was asked to settle the dispute. Its first step was to send in a commission with members from Belgium, Brazil, China and Spain. Their enquiry lasted six weeks. Next, they announced a decision. Upper Silesia should be divided between Germany and Poland. Finally, they called the two sides to Geneva to work out the details. It took five tense meetings. Eventually Germany was given two-thirds of the land; but Poland's part had half the population and most of the mineral reserves and industry. Neither side was happy, but they accepted the outcome and it lasted until the Second World War.

The Greek-Bulgarian war (1925)

Greece and Bulgaria had been long-time rivals in the Balkans. In 1925, there was a series of incidents on the border between the two countries. In one, shots were fired by border guards on both sides and a Greek soldier was killed. The Greek public were angry. Three days later, Greek troops invaded Bulgaria. War had broken out.

Successful interventions by the League of Nations in the 1920s.

The Bulgarians looked to Europe's leading powers for help. They were advised to appeal to the League of Nations.

The League's first response was to order both sides to stop fighting. The Bulgars therefore offered only token resistance. They evacuated over 10,000 people from the border area and withdrew their troops. Eventually the Greeks complied too and pulled out their troops.

Next, the League sent in a team of investigators to make a recommendation. The outcome was that Greece was held to blame. It was told to pay £45,000 to Bulgaria in compensation.

Greece grumbled that the League was not consistent; it had acted very differently two years before over Corfu (see page 228). However, the League's ruling was accepted and the danger to peace was ended.

> For once, this showed that force did not bring rewards. But it did seem to Greece that the League of Nations had one law for the large states and another for the small fry. Nevertheless, after Bulgaria there was a new hopefulness for peace and goodwill among nations.

Source B: *From a modern history textbook, published in 1984.*

Build Better Answers

What does Source A tell us about the use of economic sanctions by the League of Nations?
(3 marks)

Paper 2, Section B part (a) questions will ask you to show that you understand the content of a source.

To get full marks, your answer must contain **three** things which the source tells us about the use of economic sanctions by the League. For example, that they did not think a single rule on economic sanctions would work (1) **but** that they felt economic sanctions should always come before war (2). They were under significant pressure to issue a single rule (3) otherwise they would not have issued the statement.

Drugs

By 1900, addictive drugs like opium and cocaine were an international problem. From 1850 to 1900:

- output of opium in China reached 39,000 tons
- use of opium in the USA quadrupled.

When the League of Nations set up its Opium Advisory Committee in 1920, it found that the trade in opium and coca leaves (which produced cocaine) was ten times bigger than medical needs.

The Committee held international conferences in 1924 and 1925 which produced two treaties.

- In the first, seven major nations agreed that only their governments, not private individuals, could trade in opium.
- In the second, 56 nations agreed to use export and import certificates for dangerous drugs to control trade. A Permanent Central Board (PCB) was set up to control the certificates. It is a system which is still in use today.

This had some impact. For example, from 1920–1933, exports of coca leaves from the two biggest producers, Java and Peru, fell by 88%.

However, the volume of trade was still too high. The Committee held another conference in 1931. It led to a treaty signed by 67 states. They said that:

- each state would estimate, in advance, its medical and scientific need for dangerous drugs and limit their imports to this
- a Drug Supervisory Board would monitor trade by each nation and challenge discrepancies.

By 1935, the PCB reported that legal manufacture and trade in dangerous drugs had fallen to a level equal to medical and scientific need.

However, this still left illegal manufacture and trade. A conference in 1936 led to a new treaty. Thirteen states set strict guidelines to punish those who illegally made or traded in drugs.

Some treaties were signed by very few states.

The League had only about 50 members. This made it difficult to involve non-League states like the USA. And some states had reasons not to collaborate. They were making too much money from the drug trade.

But much progress had been made. It was the foundation for the work of the United Nations.

Top tip

Paper 2, Section B question (c) in your examination is a 15-mark question about change. It has a big impact on your grade. An example is on the opposite page.

Here's some inside information. For the top marks, examiners expect you to make a judgement. You will be expected to consider how things have changed and how they have stayed the same. You will almost always need to compare the League and the UN unless the question asks about just one. Ask yourself:

- how have things changed
- how have they stayed the same
- have they changed more than they have stayed the same
- (and if comparing the League and the UN) have I considered both organisations each time and given them roughly equal amounts of space?

Source C: *This cartoon, called* The Opium Devastation of the First Conference, *shows the scale of the League's problems. A flood of opium from the mountains of China creates a sea of drugs, drowning adults and children. Observers from around the world look on. One puts out a rather useless helping hand.*

Displaced people

After the First World War, there were millions of people displaced from their homes. The League took on the responsibility of helping them.

Many were prisoners of war, stuck in camps across Europe. In 1920, the League asked a Norwegian, Fridtjof Nansen, to help. He set up an organisation that helped 425,000 prisoners return home from 26 separate countries.

Refugees

Other people were refugees who had left their homes to flee fighting. At first, the League assumed this was a temporary problem. But in fact it got worse. In 1921, millions of Russians fled the civil war there. The League appointed Nansen as High Commissioner of a new Commission for Refugees. It helped in two ways.

- Firstly, where refugees were struggling to survive, it arranged shelter, food and medical help.
- Secondly, it helped refugees return home or settle elsewhere. A key to this was the 'Nansen passport', created in 1922. These were identity papers issued by the League to homeless refugees. 450,000 were issued. Nansen persuaded 52 states to recognise them. The passports allowed refugees to cross borders and settle in any state that would accept them.

The work of Nansen and the League's Commission for Refugees was therefore extremely important in the 1920s. Sadly, it was different in the 1930s.

Nansen died in 1930. The League abolished the post of High Commissioner. Instead, from 1931, it funded Nansen's staff to finish his work. They felt refugee problems would diminish. So the funding was for eight years only and reduced year by year.

The Nansen Office did vital work. By the time it closed, in December 1938, it had given legal or financial help to almost a million refugees. But in the late 1930s a flood of refugees fled repression in Germany, Italy, Spain and Russia. The problem of refugees was getting worse, not better. In 1939 a new Commission for Refugees was created, based in London. But its activities were soon engulfed by the Second World War.

Key Features

The key features of League successes that worked in the Aaland Islands, Upper Silesia and Bulgaria were:

- a quick League response
- the use of arbitration
- willingness to accept the League's judgement.

Other key features were:

- the use of committees, commissions or agencies (drugs, displaced people and refugees)
- the use of binding treaties (drugs)
- the influence of individuals (refugees).

Build Better Answers

In what ways did the work of the League improve the problems of drugs and refugees? **(15 marks)**

You may use the following information to help you with your answer and any other information of your own.
- The Opium Advisory Committee
- The Permanent Central Board

Paper 2, Section B part (c) questions will ask you to analyse change.

■ **A basic answer (level 1)** will make simple generalisations. For example, *they cut drug trading and got people home.*

● **A good answer (level 2)** will use the two information points and/or their own knowledge to give relevant detail. For example, *... the Opium Committee got nations to sign treaties that limited drug trading. The Commission for Refugees got displaced people home.*

▲ **An excellent answer (level 4)** will not only describe the factors in detail, but also show both improvements and failures, explain the links between the factors, and make a judgement on the extent of the improvement or lack of improvement.

Successes of the United Nations

Learning objectives

In this chapter you will learn about:

- threats to peace solved by the UN
- key features of UN success.

Korea (1950–53)

On 25 June 1950, communist North Korea invaded South Korea. Its army, boosted by weapons from Russia, crossed the 38th parallel, the border created at the end of the Second World War.

The Security Council of the UN met at once. For some time, the Council had been weakened by arguments between the USSR and USA. The USSR used its veto 79 times from 1945 to 1955. However, at this time, the USSR was boycotting the UN. The Council therefore passed Resolution 82, condemning North Korean aggression and ordering them back across the 38th parallel. They refused. Two days later, the Council passed a further resolution, authorising the use of military force.

Led by US General Douglas MacArthur, it had 600,000 troops. About 90% of these were American, although troops from 15 other countries also took part, including Britain.

In September 1950, MacArthur made a bold amphibious landing behind North Korean lines. Under attack on two sides, the North Koreans retreated north, having suffered heavy losses.

The US was keen to press on and reunite Korea. A UN vote agreed and MacArthur crossed the 38th parallel into North Korea. But this took the UN troops close to the border with China. In October, there were clashes betwen South Korea and Chinese troops. Unwilling to have democratic, capitalist South Korea on his doorstep, the Chinese leader (Mao Zedong) sent troops to support the North Koreans in November.

Rather than escalate the war by attacking China itself, the UN force withdrew behind the 38th parallel. By 1951, a stalemate had developed.

Fighting dragged on for two years before a ceasefire was agreed in July 1953. Losses had been heavy on both sides. However, the UN had

- shown it could act quickly and assemble a strong military force
- repelled an aggressor and saved a state that had been attacked.

Source A: *UN troops crossing back into South Korea in 1951.*

The Suez Crisis (1956)

From 1954, Egypt's new leader, Gamal Abdel Nasser, had been causing increasing international tension. He had, for example, supported rebels in nearby Algeria against France. He had also supported terrorist attacks by Egyptians on the neighbouring country of Israel. Then, on 26 July 1956, he nationalised the Suez Canal.

The Suez Canal runs through Egypt. By taking over the company that managed the Canal, Nasser was breaking a treaty obligation. He was also taking the property of the shareholders – mostly British and French. Most seriously, he was threatening trade; Western Europe's oil supplies came through the Canal. In October 1956 Britain, France and Israel secretly agreed that Israel would attack Egypt. The attacks began on 29 October; Israel sent troops into Egypt's Sinai Peninsula. On 30 October, Britain and France demanded that Egypt and Israel should withdraw all troops from the area around the Suez Canal. For Egypt, this meant removing its troops from an area of its own country. Nasser refused. In response, on the next day, British and French troops bombed Egyptian air fields and destroyed the Egyptian air force.

The UN Security Council was stopped from acting by British and French vetoes. But, on 2 November, the General Assembly passed Resolution 997. This called for a ceasefire and the withdrawal of all troops. It was passed by 64 votes to 5.

On 5 November, following the secret plan, British and French forces invaded Egypt. They captured key ports and the Canal Zone. The invasion was a military success. But political support in Britain was waning. Stung by the strength of the UN vote, people demanded 'Law not War'. Prime Minister Anthony Eden's own party wavered; two ministers resigned in protest. In addition, the USA threatened to withdraw help with Britain's war debts. The USSR made dark warnings of rocket attacks. On 6 November the Anglo-French forces agreed to the UN demand for a ceasefire.

To help preserve this peace, a UN force of 6,000 peacekeepers arrived in Egypt on 15 November. It stayed until 1967. During this time there were many clashes and the operation cost the UN 89 lives as well as $200 million. But the UN had:

- quickly used political and military pressure
- repelled aggression and preserved peace.

Top tip

Your examiners will expect you to give key features that are clearly explained, and detail provided of needed in the explanation. To get to the top level, you will need to look for links between the explanations and point them out. Ask yourself have I:

- given more than one key feature
- given detail about the feature
- looked for links between the features and clearly discussed them?

Activities

1   The stages of UN action towards threats of war are:
    - discussion, warning, attempts at arbitration
    - economic sanctions
    - military sanctions.

    Make a table with these 3 stages as columns, and each of the crises in this unit as rows. List in each column the UN's actions during the 5 episodes described in this chapter.

2   This chapter describes 5 successes of the UN. List them in order of how successful the UN was, starting with the most successful.

3   **a** Explain the key features of the successes of the League of Nations 9 (see pages 220–23).

    b Explain the key features of the successes of the United Nations (see pages 224–27).

    c Make a table with two columns headed 'Successes of the League and the UN, with two columns, 'Similarities' and 'Differences'. Study your answers to parts **a** and **b** and complete the table.

The Congo (1960–64)

In June 1960, the Congo, which had been a Belgian colony, was given its independence. After elections, Patrice Lumumba took office as prime minister. But unity didn't last long.

In July, two areas, Kasai and Katanga, broke away, demanding their own freedom. The army mutinied and civil war broke out. The Belgian government feared for the lives of the 100,000 Belgians still in the Congo. They sent in paratroops to protect them, which increased tension. On 12 July, Lumumba asked the UN for help. The UN acted quickly. On 14 July Security Council Resolution 143 ordered Belgian troops out and sent its own peacekeeping force. This was in the Congo within two days. At its peak, it totalled 20,000 men. The force was ordered to:

- protect Congo's government against rebels
- restore political stability.

The UN's problems became worse when Prime Minister Lumumba was removed in a military coup, led by his own army leader, Colonel Mobutu. However, UN troops stayed and the UN took further measures. First, the UN Secretary-General went to the Congo in person. He met the warring parties and acted as an arbitrator. In early 1961, his diplomacy was partially successful. Fighting in Kasai ended. But the dispute Katanga went on.

So, during 1962, the UN launched a military offensive called Operation Grand Slam. This defeated the rebels in Katanga. In January 1963, Katanga was reunited with the rest of the Congo.

The UN force was withdrawn in June 1964. The Congo was not stable; political confusion continued for some time. But the UN action did have a number of successes. For example, it had:

- acted quickly, using arbitration and troops
- prevented outside troops intervening
- given humanitarian aid
- prevented the Congo from breaking up
- achieved a settlement to the civil war.

The Gulf War (1991)

On 2 August 1990, Iraq invaded its much smaller neighbour, Kuwait. The UN acted at once. The Security Council condemned the action and demanded withdrawal. On 6 August, it passed Resolution 661, imposing economic sanctions. A period of diplomacy followed. But Saddam refused to budge. Finally, in November 1990, Resolution 678 authorised military action if Iraq failed to withdraw by 15 January 1991.

The United States arranged a coalition of 34 nations and an armed force of 500,000 troops. On 16 January, Coalition planes began 'Desert Storm', an aerial assault that destroyed the Iraqi air force on the ground. Then Coalition planes dropped 88,000 tons of bombs on Iraqi troops.

Source B: *The wreckage of Iraqi vehicles after Coalition aircraft attacked fleeing Iraqi troops on the 'Highway of Death'.*

Then, on 23 February, the Coalition launched its land attack, called Desert Sabre. By this time the Iraqi army was so weak that hundreds of thousands of troops surrendered. The Coalition lost only 350 men. Kuwait was freed.

A ceasefire was called on 27 February. Saddam Hussein, the Iraqi leader, was allowed to continue in power, but UN weapons inspectors would be allowed into Iraq to make sure he didn't pose a threat to peace again.

The UN had:

- used diplomatic, economic and military means
- raised a powerful military force
- repelled an aggressor
- done all this by consensus among major powers, avoiding any wider conflict.

Mozambique (1990–94)

Civil war had broken out in Mozambique in 1977. In 1990, the UN was asked to arbitrate. Talks began in Rome. It took 12 separate rounds of meetings over two years to reach agreement. The UN is credited with keeping the talks alive. Eventually, arbitration worked and, in October 1992, the two parties signed the General Peace Agreement.

Under the Agreement, the UN was asked to:

- monitor the peace and disarm all illegal troops
- arrange elections for a new government
- provide humanitarian assistance as needed.

The UN mission arrived early in 1993. It had about 6,600 troops, 1,100 civilian police and 900 election observers from 41 different nations.

UN troops demobilized 76,000 soldiers and seized 155,000 weapons. This allowed humanitarian work to begin. By 1994, 2.5 million displaced people were resettled in their homes. And, during the UN mission, the death rate of children was cut by half.

In 1994 elections were held and a new government formed. When the UN mission ended in December 1994, it had suffered 26 deaths and cost $500 million. But it had helped achieve peace.

Some conclusions

We can now draw some conclusions about the key factors in the successes of the League and the UN.

- Speed of response seems to have been a key factor. The League suggested solutions to disputes in the Aaland Islands and Upper Silesia in weeks. But the UN Security Council sits in permanent session. It can act even more quickly.
- Arbitration has been a key factor too, for example, when the League or the UN has offered solutions to international disputes or drug or refugee issues. But it has only worked if the nations concerned have been willing to accept the outcome.
- Military force has been a key factor in solving international problems for the UN (not the League, which had no army), but only relatively small states.

Key Features

The key features of UN's successes were:

- a quick UN response (Korea, Egypt, the Congo, the Gulf War)
- the use of arbitration (the Congo, Mozambique)
- willingness to accept the League's decision.
- the use of troops (Korea, Egypt, the Congo, the Gulf War, Mozambique)
- humanitarian work in areas of intervention (the Congo, Mozambique).

Examination question

Explain the key features of the action of the United Nations in either the Congo (1960–64) or Mozambique (1990–94). **(7 marks)**

Failures and weaknesses of the League of Nations

> **Learning objectives**
>
> In this chapter you will learn about:
> - times when the League failed to solve threats to peace
> - the key features of its weakness against aggression.

Corfu (1923)

The peace treaties at the end of the First World War had not made a clear ruling on the new border between Greece and Albania. This caused tension between them. Fighting on the border between unofficial armed gangs became common.

So the Conference of Ambassadors arranged for the border to be properly mapped. In August 1923, the Italian leader of this mapping group, General Tellini, and four of his staff were ambushed and murdered. They were in Greek territory at the time.

The public in Italy were outraged; their new prime minister, Benito Mussolini, was keen to benefit from the crisis. He demanded 50 million lire compensation from Greece and the execution of the killers. But the Greek authorities could not identify the culprits. So Mussolini sent ships from the Italian navy to bombard the Greek island of Corfu, near the coast of Albania. Several local inhabitants were killed. Italian troops then occupied the island; Mussolini said they wouldn't leave until the compensation was paid.

This was an act of aggression by one League member against another. Greece appealed to the League of Nations for help. The League condemned Mussolini's actions. But no nations were keen to evict the Italians by force. The League did not act. The occupation dragged on. Meanwhile, Mussolini referred the matter to the Conference of Ambassadors. The Conference said that Greece should apologise and pay the fine. Without practical support from other nations, the Greeks agreed and the Italians left the island.

The League had shown itself to be weak against a determined aggressor. Mussolini clearly thought so, because a year later he caused another confrontation. The Treaty of Versailles had given the port of Fiume, near the Italian border, to Yugoslavia. But, in 1924, not worried about the League, Mussolini demanded that Yugoslavia should give Fiume to Italy. Yugoslavia gave in – understandable, considering the bombardment of Corfu.

> **The Conference of Ambassadors**
>
> The Conference of Ambassadors was set up in 1920 to make sure the treaties were put into practice. It had representatives from Britain, France, Italy and Japan. If disputes arose out of details of the peace treaties, these were sometimes referred to the Conference of Ambassadors, which advised the League of Nations.

Activities

1 As you read this chapter, make a table to record the key events of the three episodes described. Your table should have three columns, headed:
   - aggression
   - the League's response
   - reasons why the League failed

   and a row for each crisis.

2 Look at the key features of the weakness of the League on p.175.
   a Can you find any links between the key features?
   b Give each key feature a mark out of 10 for *importance*. Debate your reasons for these marks with someone else. Record the most important along with the reasons.

Manchuria (1931–33)

Manchuria was a province of China. But Japan owned industries there; it also had army and navy bases there. On 18 September 1931, near Mukden, the capital of Manchuria, a section of railway owned by the Japanese was blown up.

It's not clear who caused the explosion. Some suspect local Japanese army officers. But Japan blamed China. Then, when the Japanese army went to the explosion site, they said that they were fired upon. As a result, Japan invaded Manchuria, claiming it had to protect Japanese interests.

Japan and China were both founding members of the League. Both had signed the Covenant. So China appealed to the League for help. The League:

- appealed to both parties to separate their armies
- set up a commission, under the Englishman Lord Lytton, to investigate. The Commission set sail from Europe to Japan, a journey which took several weeks.

In the meantime, Japan ignored the League and carried on with its invasion. By February 1932, it had captured the whole of Manchuria and re-named it Manchukuo.

Eventually, in October 1932, the Commission reported. Four months later, in February 1933, the League accepted their report – 17 months after the invasion began. It:

- condemned Japan as the aggressor
- demanded that Japan should free Manchuria.

Japan ignored the order and left the League of Nations.

The League took no further action. No economic sanctions were applied. Countries were unwilling to damage their trade and, anyway, Japan's main trading partner was the USA, a non-member. No military force was used. The League had no army and members were unwilling to consider a far-off and costly war.

In 1933 Japan invaded another province of China, and in 1935 another two. In 1937 it declared all-out war on China.

China appealed to the League under Article 11 of the Covenant, which, in the event or threat of war, empowered the League to take 'any action that may be deemed wise and effectual to safeguard the peace of nations'.

Source A: *An American cartoon from 1931. Japan blasts holes in a number of treaties, including the League's Covenant and the Kellogg–Briand Pact.*

Source B: *From a modern history textbook, published in 1966.*

The Kellogg–Briand Pact

The Kellogg–Briand Pact was an international treaty signed by 65 nations. It said that war should not be used as 'an instrument of national policy' except for self-defence.

- It was signed by Japan and the USA.

When Japan attacked Manchuria, China said this broke the Pact and appealed to the USA for help. As a result, the US allowed its ambassador in Geneva to sit in on Assembly meetings about Manchuria. But it never offered any practical help.

Abyssinia

Abyssinia (now called Ethiopia) was a free country in East Africa. In December 1934, there was a clash on Abyssinia's border with Somaliland, an Italian colony. Italian troops claimed that the fort at the oasis of Walwal belonged to Italy. Thirty Italian soldiers were killed in the fight. Italy's leader, Mussolini, demanded financial compensation and ownership of the oasis.

Italy and Abyssinia were both League members. The Abyssinian emperor, Haile Selassie, appealed to the League for help. The League started discussions. It sent a commission to investigate. Eventually, this declared neither side to blame and advised Abyssinia to sort out a solution with Italy. Meanwhile, Mussolini sent troops to the Abyssinian borders. The League made warning noises. In September 1935, Hoare, the British Foreign Secretary, addressed the League. He stressed 'the interest of the British in collective security' and said it would 'fulfil obligations in the Covenant'.

Ignoring all this, 250,000 Italian troops invaded Abyssinia on 3 October. On 7 October, the League's Council denounced Italy as an aggressor and demanded withdrawal. On 9 October, the Assembly imposed economic sanctions. No arms, iron or rubber could be sold to Italy. There were problems with these measures.

- Coal, steel and oil were not part of the sanctions. They were vital for war. But it was thought that Italy could get them from non-members, like the USA, Germany or Japan.
- Austria, Switzerland and Hungary were members, but refused to apply the sanctions.

Britain and France, the major powers in the League, had just made a treaty with Italy, called the Stresa Front, to oppose German expansion. So, rather than offend Italy, they worked *outside* the League. They secretly proposed the Hoare-Laval Pact, offering two-thirds of Abyssinia to Italy. Ignoring all this, Italy completed the conquest of Abyssinia by May 1936. On 15 July 1936, the League called off sanctions and accepted the situation.

THE SWEETS OF AGGRESSION.

HAILE SELASSIE. "HAVE I GOT THIS RIGHT?—HE'S TAKEN NEARLY HALF OF W. HAD AND NOW YOU GENTLEMEN WANT TO DISCUSS WHETHER HE SHOULD ANY MORE!"

Source C: *A British cartoon from 1935. Mussolini, hands in pockets, seems unconcerned about the British and French policemen outside the League of Nations police station. Its original caption was:* The Sweets of Aggression. *Haile Selassie [left] is saying: 'Have I got this right? He's taken nearly half of what I had and now you gentlemen want to discuss whether he should take any more!'*

I assert that the problem submitted to the Assembly today is much wider than…Italian aggression. It is collective security. It is the very existence of the League.

Source D: *Haile Selassie appealing to the League of Nations. Quoted in the* New York Times, *1 July 1936.*

Weaknesses

These three episodes show four key features of the weaknesses of the League in dealing with aggression.

1 Organisation of the League

One key feature was League's organisation. Council resolutions had to be unanimous. Some decisions of the Assembly (about 50 members) also had to be unanimous. This had two effects.

a It could make the League slow to act; decisions often took months and debates were overtaken by events (as in Corfu, Manchuria and Abyssinia).

b It showed a contradiction in the voting system.

- Believing in collective security means that members should act as a group.
- Needing unanimous votes for decisions meant each member had a veto over the group.

2 Missing members

Another key feature of the League's weakness was missing members. The USA and, at various times, key states like the USSR, Germany, Italy and Japan were outside the League. This had effects.

- When the League used diplomacy, it lacked the authority of representing all major powers.
- When it used economic sanctions, some key trading nations continued to trade normally (as in the Abyssinia crisis).
- If it considered military force, it depended too much on just two members: Britain and France.

> The League had no military power of its own. It depended on its members' contributions; and its members were not willing to use sanctions, economic or military. Moral authority was insufficient.
>
> Several Big Powers failed to support the League: the United States crucially never joined; Germany was a member for only seven years from 1926 and the USSR for only five years from 1934; Japan and Italy both withdrew in the 30s. The League then depended mainly on Britain and France, who were understandably hesitant to act forcefully.

Source E: Cyberschoolbus, *a website run by the United Nations.*

3 Military weakness

Another key feature was that the League had no army and the Covenant gave no clear way to use members' troops (although it said the League could raise troops from member nations). This cut options in Corfu, Manchuria and Abyssinia. Members opposed military force to solve problems at this time because:

- the First World War was fresh in people's minds, most did not want another war
- worldwide economic depression after 1929 meant no nation wanted the expense of war.

So the League often fell back on moral authority – just saying that nations should uphold the law.

This sometimes worked. But some aggressors knew it made the League weak (see Source F).

4 National self-interest

Another feature was national self-interest. In one sense, the League did not fail. *Nations* failed. The League was set up by nations that were against aggression and wanted collective action to prevent it. But they did not keep their promises.

- Some member nations ignored the Covenant to commit aggression, such as Italy and Japan.
- Other member nations ignored the Covenant and refused to take effective action, as Britain and France did over Abyssinia.

> The League is very well when sparrows shout, but no good at all when eagles fall out.

Source F: *Supposedly said by Mussolini.*

Failures and weaknesses of the United Nations

Learning objectives

In this chapter you will learn about:

- times when the UN failed against aggression
- key features of the UNs weaknesses
- weakness of the League and UN.

Activity

1 As you read this chapter, make a table to record the key events of the five episodes described. Your table should have three columns, headed

- details of aggression
- UN's response
- reasons why the UN failed

and a row for each episode.

Hungary (1956)

In October 1956 there were violent protests on the streets of Hungary. Hungarians wanted a new government, not one controlled by the USSR. By 30 October, the rioters were in control of the capital. A new government was formed under Imre Nagy. This was too much for the USSR. On 4 November, 200,000 Soviet troops invaded Hungary.

The USSR and Hungary were both members of the UN; the invasion was a breach of UN Charter. So the General Assembly met on 4 November. It passed Resolution 1004, which:

- condemned the Soviet invasion and demanded the withdrawal of Soviet troops
- called for humanitarian aid to be allowed in.

The USSR ignored this. On 7 November, it occupied Budapest and installed its own leader of Hungary.

About 20,000 Hungarians died; 200,000 fled to nearby countries. Nagy, the deposed Hungarian leader, was arrested and executed on 16 June 1958.

This was a terrible humiliation for the UN.

- Its weakness against a major power was clear.
- Key members gave it no real support. Britain and France were busy with Suez. The USA was in the middle of a presidential election.
- Anyway, the USSR was a nuclear power. If it refused to listen, what could the UN do?

> "We have designed an organisation that can control the mice, but the tigers are still on the loose."

Source A: *Mexican delegate to the United Nations, in 1945.*

Source B: *A British cartoon from 1956. It shows the UN taking a different line over Suez and Hungary. UN Secretary-General Dag Hammarskjold makes the leaders of France, the USA and Britain write out lines, saying "I must not bully". In the background, Khrushchev, the Soviet leader, is busy beating up Hungary.*

Palestine (1947–49)

In February 1947, Britain's mandate to govern Palestine was nearing its end. It asked the UN to decide Palestine's future. Palestine's population were mostly Muslim Arabs. They wanted control of Palestine. But the number of Jews living there had recently boomed, as they fled persecution in Europe. The UN's response was as follows.

- First, it set up a committee of enquiry. It could not agree; in August, it put forward *two* plans.
- In November, the General Assembly chose a plan. In time, Palestine would be split into an Arab state and a Jewish state. Arab Palestinians were not happy. Violence broke out.
- So, in April 1948, the UN called for peace.
- It also sent a Truce Commission, diplomats to negotiate a peace. No soldiers were sent.

The UN plan fell apart almost immediately. On 14 May 1948, on the very same day the British troops left Palestine, two things happened.

- First, the Jews said they would not wait for the UN plan to unfold. They set up the Jewish state of Israel in the area the UN plan had set aside.
- Secondly, Arab states, like Egypt, Jordan, Syria and Saudi Arabia, declared war on Israel.

Fighting lasted until 1949. Remarkably, the new Jewish state survived. But the UN was damaged.

- It had been divided about its plan for Palestine.
- It had not sent troops to enforce its plan.
- 520–800,000 Arabs fled Israel as refugees.
- Armed force decided who won; the UN didn't.

Lebanon (1975–87)

Lebanon is a country on Israel's northern border. During the 1948 war in Palestine, 100,000 Palestinian Arabs had fled from Israel to Lebanon. They settled, in huge refugee camps, in southern Lebanon along the Israeli border. Many supported a militant group called the Palestinian Liberation Front (PLO), which wanted to destroy Israel. In March 1978, a PLO commando attack into Israel left many Israeli civilians dead or wounded.

Israel retaliated: Israeli troops attacked PLO bases inside Lebanon – in effect, invading another state's land.

In Resolution 425, the Security Council urged Israel to withdraw and sent a peacekeeping force of 4,000 men, called UNIFIL, to prevent further fighting.

However, PLO raids continued. As a result, in June 1982, Israel invaded Lebanon again. The UN was ignored. Israeli troops swept past UNIFIL. This time, Israeli troops advanced as far as Beirut itself.

It was the United States, not the United Nations, that brokered a peace. In 1985, pressure from US President Reagan achieved a settlement.

- The armed PLO groups left the Lebanon.
- Israel withdrew most of its troops, but insisted upon keeping a small armed presence there.

UNIFIL remained in Lebanon, helping to keep peace there. However, the UN:

- had been unable to prevent Israeli aggression
- relied upon the USA to negotiate peace
- despite continued requests by the UN, it was 2000 before the Israelis left Lebanese soil.

Somalia (1991–95)

Somalia is a very poor country in East Africa. In 1991 civil war broke out. Two million refugees became homeless and 4.5 million faced starvation. The UN's response was fourfold.

1 In 1991 a special envoy was sent to mediate between warring factions.

2 In January 1992 the Security Council announced a ban on trading arms to Somalia.

3 In April 1992 3500 troops, called UNOSOM I, were sent to keep the warring factions apart.

4 The UN sent humanitarian aid.

The UN was using all its powers. But it didn't work.

- Ceasefires were agreed, but didn't last.
- UNOSOM I was too small to prevent fighting.
- Weapons were smuggled in.
- Humanitarian aid was hampered by fighting.

In 1992 the USA offered to lead a stronger military force in Somalia. The UN agreed. A US-led United Task Force of 37,000 men arrived in December. This worked for a while; fighting died down. So, in March 1993, the UN decided it could withdraw the United Task Force. Instead, it sent its own force, UNOSOM II. But this had only 22,000 men.

Fighting broke out again, with disastrous effect. In a long battle with rebels in the capital, Mogadishu, 24 UNOSOM soldiers died in June and 18 US troops fighting with UNOSOM were killed in October. The battle was portrayed in the film *Black Hawk Down*.

In August 1994, the Secretary-General announced 'members are not prepared to continue costly commitments...when there are no signs of... reconciliation.' UNOSOM II cost $1.6 billion. By 1995 the USA and UN had withdrawn all troops. Civil war went on. The UN had failed in Somalia.

- Diplomacy failed.
- The embargo on arms sales failed.
- Military efforts to stop fighting failed.
- The UN's only real success was humanitarian help – and this was limited by military failure.

Bosnia (1991–95)

In 1991 civil war broke out in Yugoslavia. It broke up into six republics. Of these, Bosnia was divided ethnically (between Serbs, Croats and Bosnians) and religiously (between Muslims and Christians). Civil war broke out in 1992. The situation was very complex; fighting broke out between different groups over ethnic or religious issues. Many groups carried out 'ethnic cleansing' – driving out or killing minority groups.

The UN had been trying to stop fighting in Bosnia. In May 1992, it passed two resolutions, one urging a ceasefire, the other imposing trade sanctions on Serbia to hinder its aggression.

But fighting continued. Ceasefires were broken. UN diplomacy and trade sanctions failed to stop the fighting. And there were other UN failures.

- In October 1992 the UN banned military flights in Bosnia. Bombing reduced but did not stop.
- In July 1993 the UN debated border patrols to seize weapons. But its peacekeeping budget was overspent. No patrols started.
- In 1993, the UN set up 'safe areas' for civilians. But these were constantly shelled by the Serbs.

Worse came in 1995. A UN safe area at Srebrenica was defended by 600 UN troops who did not resist when Serbian troops entered the town. The UN troops bussed the women out but 8,000 Bosnian men were taken away by Serbs and shot.

In 1995, diplomatic pressure by the Contact Group – a number of states, led by the USA – forced peace on the Serbs and Croats. The UN could only look on.

Source C: *Bosnia 1995. Women and children leaving Srebrenica. Unknown to them, their sons, brothers, husbands and fathers had just been shot.*

Weaknesses

These five episodes show four key features of the weaknesses of the UN.

1 Military weakness

Like the League, the lack of an army has been a key feature of the UN's weakness. The cost of a military force also limits what it can do. It was not strong enough, militarily, to enforce its policies in Palestine, Lebanon, Somalia or Bosnia. It certainly lacked the power to oppose the USSR in Hungary.

2 National self-interest

Like the League, the biggest weakness of the UN is the national self-interest of its members. For example, the USSR was a member of the UN during the crisis in Hungary and Israel was a member during the crisis in Lebanon. Both ignored the UN to followed their own interests.

3 The Cold War

The Cold War was a key feature of the UN's weakness. With the USSR and USA at each other's throats, it was impossible for the UN to get collaboration. You can see its impact by noting the Soviet vetoes 1945–55, the UN's impotence over Hungary and the lack of progress with disarmament.

4 The USA

Another key feature of its weakness has been the UN's military and financial dependence upon the USA. When the USA acted with the UN, it was strong, as in Korea. When the USA withdrew support, as in Somalia, the UN it was weaker. Worse still, the USA sometimes ignored the UN and pursued its own solutions to problems (as in Bosnia and Lebanon).

Some conclusions

We can now compare the key features in the weaknesses of the League and the UN. Two key factors are common to both the League and the UN. They stayed the same and are examples of continuity.

- The League and the UN have both been limited by military weakness. The League had no army and it's Covenant gave it no clear way to raise troops from member states. The UN has no army but has a system for using troops from member states. But it is limited by what they can provide and by cost.

- The League and the UN have been weakened by member states choosing to follow their own interests rather than co-operating with other nations (Britain and France over Abyssinia in 1935 and the USSR over Hungary in 1956).

There are other weaknesses which are specific to the League or the UN. These are examples of difference or change. For example:

- the League was weakened by organisation and missing members (see page 231)
- the UN has been weakened by dependence upon the USA and the Cold War (see this page).

see page 231

Examination question

How far did the role of the USA change in its dealings with the United Nations 1945–2000?

You may use the following information, or other case studies, to help you with your answer.

- setting up the UN (1941–45)
- Lebanon (1975–87). **(15 marks)**

A study in change

This unit is not like the others in this course. You study one theme – international co-operation to avoid war and improve people's lives – over about 80 years. These two pages help you to summarise what you have learned so far about the change which took place during that time.

Key Words

Change is the most inclusive word – it means anything that is different.

Improvement is a special sort of change – when things get better. Not all change is an improvement.

Continuity is when things don't change, they stay the same.

Similarity and **difference** is a way of looking at something in history, to see the *change* and the *continuity*, by looking at what is the same and what is different.

Organisation of the League and UN – similarities and differences

Make two tables:

1 Organisation of the League and UN – *Similarities*
2 Organisation of the League and UN – *Differences*

Use the same rows on each table:
General Assemblies; Council/Security Council; Secretariats; Leadership; Forces; Agencies and commissions; Membership in 1920/1945; Human Rights Commission.

Read through pages 148–155, and your own work on the creation and aims of the League and the UN. Fill in as much as you can in the two tables.

Organisation of the League and UN: Similiarities		
	League	**UN**
General Assemblies		
Council/Security Council		
Secretariats		
Leadership		
Forces		
Agencies and conmmissions		
Membership in 1920/ 1945		
Human Rights Commission		

Key features of League and UN peacekeeping successes

Make a table like the one below.

Use the information on pages 164–71 to give specific details to support each key feature. We have done the first row for you.

Under your table list:

- the key features of success which are the *same* for the League and UN
- the key features of success which are *different* for the League and UN.

Key Features of successes of the League and UN in peacekeeping		
key feature which helped to solve a crisis	**League of Nations**	**United Nations**
speed of response	e.g. in Aaland Islands (1920) recommendation in weeks e.g. in Upper Silesia (1921) recommendation in 6 weeks	e.g. in Korea resolutions within days e.g. in Egypt Resolution 997 within 4 days
arbitration or diplomacy		
member states accepting League/UN recommendation		
influence of key people		
use of military force		
humanitarian success		

Key features of League and UN peacekeeping weaknesses

Make a table like the one below.

Use the information on pages 172–79 to give support each key feature. We have done the first row for you.

Under your table list:

- the key features of peacekeeping weaknesses which are the *same* for the League and UN
- the key features of peacekeeping weaknesses which are *different* for the League and UN.

Key Features of weaknesses of the League and UN in peacekeeping		
key feature which made it harder to solve a crisis	detailed support League of Nations	detailed support United Nations
military weakness	e.g. unable to prevent Japan taking over Manchuria (1931–33) e.g. unable to prevent Italy taking over Abyssinia (1935)	e.g. UN unable to force USSR out of Hungary (1956) e.g. unable to protect Bosnians at Srebrenica (1995)
national self-interest		
organisation (e.g. voting rules)		
missing members		
dependence on USA		
the Cold War		

Change in the work of the League and UN agencies

First we need a table to summarise the work of the committees, commissions and agencies of the League and the UN. Then we can use this information to identify how much *change* occurred.

We have started the table for you by summarising what work the League and UN agencies did to improve health. We have also identified what *changed* and what *did not change* about this work.

Make your own copy of the table.

Then, your task is to use pages 156–163 to add details of the work of the League and UN agencies in each of the following areas:

- working conditions
- legal disputes
- suffering (e.g. hunger, refugees, child suffering)
- social injustices (e.g. slavery, lack of education, human rights abuse)
- dangers to society (e.g. drugs, armaments, loss of heritage).

Changes in the Work of League and UN Agencies			
	work of the League of Nations	work of the United Nations	change and continuity
health	Aimed to prevent and control the spread of disease (Article 23). Set up agency. Attacked diseases like malaria, typhus, leprosy. Missing key members, so had to work with other international organisations.	Set up WHO (1948) to continue the work of the League. new vaccines (e.g. influenza). Fought disease like malaria, AIDS and smallpox. Helped in crises – Egypt cholera 1947, Congo 1960 UNICEF cut TB/malaria in children.	**Continuity** • continued an organisation to improve world health • Fought diseases (e.g. malaria) **Change** • new vaccines (e.g. influenza) • dealt with new diseases (e.g. AIDS) • helped in crises (e.g Egypt/Congo) • UNICEF targets help on children
working conditions			
legal disputes			
suffering			
social injustices			
dangers to society			

In the Paper 2 final examination in Section B you will have to answer questions on the one breadth study in change you have studied. You will be given one source (from a modern textbook or written at the time covered by the question) and asked to answer three questions. Question (a) will ask you to extract three points from the source, (b) asks you to explain the key features of an event, and (c) will ask you to write an essay on change with the assistance of two points known as scaffolding. You can use this information or your own knowledge to answer the question.

You have about 45 minutes to answer the three sub-questions, so the examiners are not expecting you to write huge amounts. The number of marks helps you to judge how much to write. For Question (a) allow 5 minutes, Question (b) 10 minutes and Question (c) 30 minutes. Let's look at a set of questions for Section B.

Build Better Answers

Source: *From a modern history textbook, published in 2001.*

> During the 1920s the League of Nations became involved in a series of disputes in Europe. It was successful in the dispute between Sweden and Finland over the Aaland Islands in 1921, deciding these should go to Finland, a decision accepted by both countries. There was further success in the Greece-Bulgaria dispute of 1925, when the Greeks were forced to back down. However, the League was not successful in dealing with Italian aggression during the Corfu Incident of 1923. Mussolini forced the Greeks to back down.

(a) What does the source tell us about the peacekeeping role of the League Nations in the 1920s? **(3 marks)**

(b) Explain the key features of the peace-keeping role of the United Nations in either the Korean War (1950–53) or the Suez Crisis (1956). **(7 marks)**

(c) In what ways did the work of international organisation agencies change the lives of people during the twentieth century? **(15 marks)**

You may use the following information to help you with your answer and any other information of your own.

- The Slavery Commission of the 1920s
- The World Health Organisation (WHO)

Build Better Answers

Question (a)

Examiner's tip: Part (a) questions will ask you to get three points from the source. This is a comprehension question, worth three marks, so spend about 5 minutes on this question.

Let's look at an example.

(a) What does the source tell us about the peacekeeping role of the League Nations in the 1920s?　　　　**(3 marks)**

- Ensure you understand the focus of the question. Highlight or underline key words or phrases in the question.
- As you read the source, highlight at least three points in the source.

In this question you should highlight 'the peacekeeping role'.

> During the 1920s the League of Nations became involved in a series of disputes in Europe. It was successful in the dispute between Sweden and Finland over the Aaland Islands in 1921, deciding these should go to Finland, a decision accepted by both countries. There was further success in the Greece-Bulgaria dispute of 1925, when the Greeks were forced to back down. However, the League was not successful in dealing with Italian aggression during the Corfu Incident of 1923. Mussolini forced the Greeks to back down.

- Describe these points. You could signpost your answer by telling the examiner each time you get a point from the source.
- You do not need to include your own knowledge, in other words knowledge from outside the source. Own knowledge will not be credited and will waste valuable time.

Student answer	Examiner comments
The source tells me that the League was not successful in the Corfu Incident of 1923. Following a dispute in which five Italian surveyors were killed by Greek soldiers, Mussolini occupied the Greek island of Corfu. The League did little to stop Italian aggression because Britain and France did not want to take action against Mussolini. The Greeks eventually apologised.	This answer picks out one point from the source, about the failure of the League in the Corfu Incident of 1923. The rest of the answer is own knowledge (underlined) and cannot be credited. Moreover, the student has used up valuable time on this unnecessary information. It would be awarded 1 mark.

Let's rewrite the answer and focus on three points from the source.

The source gives me three examples of the peacekeeping role of the League of Nations in the 1920s. The first is the success of the League in Aaland Islands with Sweden and Finland. The second example is the success of the League in the Greek-Bulgaria dispute, forcing the Greeks to back down. Finally, the source mentions the failure of the League with Italy over the Corfu Incident of 1923.	The student has described three points from the source of the peacekeeping role. In addition, the answer has signposted each point to help the examiner. There is no additional unnecessary own knowledge which would not be credited. This answer would be awarded three marks.

Build Better Answers

Question (b)

Examiner tip: Part (b) questions will give you a choice of two topics. You have to choose one of these and explain its **key features**. This question is worth 7 marks, so spend about ten minutes writing your answer.

Let's look at an example.

- Highlight or underline key words or phrases in the question. This should ensure that you focus on the question.

(b) Explain the key features of the peace-keeping role of the United Nations. **(7 marks)**

Choose **either** | the Korean War (1950–53) | **or** | the Suez Crisis (1956).

- In this example the examiner wants to know about peace-keeping, and you have a choice to make – whether to write about peace-keeping during the Korean War or the Suez Crisis.

- Ensure you make the right choice. It might help to list the main things you know about each one. Normally, you will choose the conflict you can write most about.

- Stick to your choice. Some students write a paragraph about one conflict, cross it out and write about the second conflict. This wastes valuable time.

- Key features include any part of the given conflict – including causes, events and results – as long as they are relevant to the question. Here are some examples of key features of the two conflicts mentioned in the question.

Korean War	The Suez Crisis
• The first actions of the UN when they condemned the invasion of South Korea by North Korea	• Reactions of the UN to the actions of Britain, France and Israel
• The Security Council resolution	• General Assembly resolution
• The UN force in Korea	• Despatch of UN forces to Suez
• Effects of UN intervention on Korea	• Effects on UN actions on the Suez Crisis
• Effects of UN intervention on the role of the UN	• Effects of UN intervention on the role of the UN

- You need to explain at least two key features. Try to write a paragraph on each. Ensure that these are significant features of the given event.

Make a link or links between the key features. In other words how one key feature led to or was connected to the next key feature. Link words or phrases often help to achieve this. Here are some examples: *this led to, as a result, moreover, furthermore, as a consequence, in addition.*

Here is a grid to help you plan your answer to this question.

First reason	Give the feature.
	Fully explain it.
Link	Make a link with the second feature.
Second reason	Give the feature.
	Fully explain it.
Conclusion	Sum up the two features stressing the links between them.

Build Better Answers

Student answer

The United Nations condemned the invasion of South Korea by North Korea. The Security Council condemned North Korea. The United Nations sent an army which supported South Korea.

Examiner comments

This student writes two simple statements about United Nations involvement in the Korean War. Each statement is a key feature but has not been explained. This answer is too brief and would be awarded a mark in Level 1.

Let's look at an answer where the student has used some of his or her own knowledge.

In June 1950, communist North Korea invaded South Korea. The Security Council of the United Nations immediately passed a resolution condemning the invasion and called upon member nations to send help to the South. The Soviet Union, a member of the Security Council, would have vetoed this decision but their representative was absent because they were boycotting the Security Council.

This student has developed one of the key features of the United Nations role in the Korean War by describing the Security Council resolution condemning the invation and how this was passed. However, there needs to be at least one more key feature and links shown between the two. This answer would be awarded a mark in Level 2.

Let's re-write the answer to include the sources and own knowledge and two linked factors focused on features.

The first key feature of the United Nations peacekeeping role in the Korean War, was the reaction of the Security Council. In June 1950, communist North Vietnam invaded South Vietnam. The Security Council of the United Nations immediately condemned the invasion and called upon member nations to send help to the South. The Soviet Union, a member of the Security Council, would have vetoed this decision but their representative was absent because they were boycotting the Security Council.
As a result of the Security Council Resolution, troops from sixteen countries were sent on behalf of the United Nations, to South Korea to preserve the frontier between the two Koreas along the 38th parallel. The majority of the troops and the Commander-in-Chief, General MacArthur, were American. Their arrival was able to prevent the whole of South Korea from being overrun by the communists. In September 1950, the United Nations forces had counter attacked at Inchon and were driving the North's army back out of South Korea.

This student has described two features of the United Nations peacekeeping role in Korea, including the United Nations resolution and the early actions of the United Nations forces. Notice how the student has signposted the first feature. In addition the answer has made a link between the first and second key feature. This would be awarded a mark in Level 3.

Exam Zone

Question (c)

Examiner tip: Part (c) is asking you to write an essay about change over a period of time. This means you must show change, either by comparing the situation before and after the development or you must show how it developed during the period. The question will give you two points known as scaffolding to help you with your essay. You can use this information or your own knowledge to answer the question. Remember, this a the highest-scoring question on the paper (worth 15 marks) and it requires a substantial and detailed response. It is about change, and you must either show change by comparing the situation before and after the development, or you must show how it developed during the period. You should allow 30 minutes for this question.

Let's look at an example.

(c) In what ways did the work of international organisation agencies change the lives of people during the twentieth century? **(10 marks)**

You may use the following information to help you with your answer and any other information of your own.

> • The Slavery Commission of the 1920s
> • International Children's Fund (UNICEF)

- Focus on the question. It is about change, so ensure you write about changes. Do not just tell the story.

- You can make use of the scaffolding points or develop points of your own (for example you may wish to mention The Commission for Refugees of the 1920s and The United Nations Human Rights Commission as well as the organizations mentioned in the two points). However, you must make sure your answer covers the work of both organisations: the League and the United Nations, and the full time span – the 1920s to 2000.

- Write a paragraph on each of the agencies. At the beginning of each paragraph give the change and then fully explain it. Using the word 'because' helps you to give a developed explanation.

- For the higher marks you also have to make links between each agency. This means explaining how one change led to the next. Link words or phrases will help to achieve this. Here are some examples: *this led to, as a result, moreover, furthermore, as a consequence, in addition.*

- Write a conclusion showing how the agencies you have written about acted together to bring about change.

Here is a grid to help you plan your answer to this question.

First point	Give the change and then explain it. Make a link to the next change.
Second point	Give the change and then explain it. Make a link to the next change.
Third point	Give the change and then explain it. Make a link to the next change.
Fourth point	Give the change and then explain it. Make a link to the next change.
Conclusion	Explain how the factors you have written about acted together to bring about change.

Student answer

The Slavery Commission got rid of a lot of slavery in Africa. The Refugees Commission helped prisoners of war. WHO improved the health of many people.

Examiner comments

The student makes generalised comments about three points. This would be awarded a low Level 1 mark.

Let's look at an answer where the student has used some of his or her own knowledge.

The Slavery Commission was set up to abolish slavery and forcing women into prostitution. It freed 200,000 slaves in Sierra Leone and stopped forced labour in various African states. It did not completely stop slavery.
The World Health Organisation helped develop new vaccines, such as for influenza, and it led campaigns to eradicate diseases, like smallpox, which it declared eradicated in 1980.
The Human Rights Commission has tried to define the rights all people should have, including freedom from arrest without trial.

This student has described the work of three agencies with good supporting knowledge. However, there is no real focus on the idea of change and no attempt to link the work of some of the agencies. Moreover, the answer is not detailed enough for a 15 mark question. This would be awarded a mark in Level 2.

Let's re-write the answer to include the sources and own knowledge and two linked factors focused on change.

All four agencies did much to improve the lives of people in the 20th century. The Slavery Commission made important changes in Africa. Although slavery had been illegal for many years, it was still widely practiced in Africa in the early 20th century. The Slavery Commission, although it did not remove slavery, did much to reduce its effects. It freed 200,000 slaves in Sierra Leone and made ending slavery a precondition for Ethiopia's membership of the League and greatly reduced the numbers of women forced into prostitution. While the Slavery Commission did much to change the lives of people in Africa, a second League of Nations commission, did much to improve the lives of some people in Europe.
The Commission for Refugees did much to change lives. There were just under 500,000 prisoners of war at the end of the First World War. The Commission, run by a Norwegian, Fridtjof Nansen, ensured that 425,000 of them returned home from 26 countries within two years. He also set up the Nansen Passport, was used to identify stateless people. He got 53 states to accept them, and 450,000 passports were issued. In the 1930s the Commission did much to help refugees, especially those that were fleeing from Nazi policies. The changes to the lives of people brought about by League organisations was continued by various United Nations agencies in the second half of the twentieth century.
The World Health Organisation did much to change and improve the lives of people especially in Africa and Asia (example). While WHO changed people's health, the Human Rights Commission has done much to improve the treatment of people by their governments (example).
Overall, all four organisations did much to improve the lives of people in the 20th century. The Slavery, Refugee and Human Rights Commissions worked to protect freedom and political rights. WHO has brought changes to the health of many people more especially by reducing the effect of infectious diseases...

This is an excellent answer. The student has fully explained the changes brought about by four agencies. The answer consistently focuses on the idea of change (in   ) and make links between one factor and the next (in blue). Furthermore, there is evidence of carefully selected, precise knowledge (in red). In addition, there is a conclusion which links the changes brought about by the four agencies and makes a judgement on the extent of improvement. This would be awarded a mark in Level 4.

Term	Definition
alliance	A formal agreement between countries.
Anschluss	The formal union of Germany and Austria.
appeasement	A policy of keeping peace by negotiation and making concessions.
arbitration	When groups/countries that cannot agree in a dispute and so go to a third person to help them settle the dispute.
armistice	A truce or agreement to stop fighting.
arms race	When countries compete to have the most effective armed forces.
atomic bomb	A highly destructive nuclear weapon.
blockade	An attempt to prevent resources reaching their destination.
boycott	To refuse to take part in something.
capitalism	A way of running the economy (or a country) where individuals own businesses, fund them and take the profits from them.
censorship	Action by the government to prevent the publication of any material of which they disapprove.
CIA	Central Intelligence Agency – an American organisation designed to monitor foreign governments.
collective security	Nations acting together to prevent war.
communism	A way of running the economy where the state owns all businesses, funds them, takes the profits from them and supports all the people who are part of the economy (or country).
constitution	The rules for running a country or organisation.
containment	Stopping something from spreading.
demobilise	To stop a country being geared up for war.
depression	Used here to refer to economic depression. This is a downturn in trade where less is bought and sold, profits fall, more business fail and more people lose their jobs.
dictator	A person who rules a country using harsh or extreme methods.
direct action	Used here to mean organised public protests.
disarmament	Cutting down the numbers of troops and weapons a country has.
doctrine	A statement of ideas.
economic sanctions	Trade restrictions placed on a country to pressure it to behave in a certain way.
evolution	Changing and adapting to circumstances. The theory of evolutions states that new living things evolve from earlier types, they do not just happen.
fallout shelters	structures designed to protect people during a nuclear attack.
HUAC	the House Committee on Un-American Activities, also called the House Un-American Activities Committee, used after the war to investigate communism in the USA.

immigration	Coming to a country to live there.
impeach	To prosecute someone who has a government job for crimes they have committed while they were doing that job.
inflation	Rising prices, not accompanied by rising wages.
integration	Not separating groups of people or things.
isolationism	The policy of not becoming involved in the affairs of other countries.
Jim Crow laws	Laws segregating blacks and whites in the USA named after a black character played by a racist white performer in the 1820s.
judicial	To do with enforcing laws and punishing crime.
laissez-faire	The policy of not interfering in people's lives: not telling them how to run their businesses or providing welfare and other social care.
lynch	To execute someone without trial (with no legal right to do so), usually by hanging.
militant	Believing in violent action to resolve a problem.
NATO	The North Atlantic Treaty Organisation – a military alliance of the USA and European democracies.
picketing	Demonstrating outside a place that does something you consider wrong (e.g. discriminating against black people) and asking others not to use it.
propaganda	Information (true or false) given to people to make them think/behave in a certain way.
racism	Prejudice against people of a different race.
rationing	Government restriction of how much food or other goods people can buy.
rearmament	Increasing armed forces and weapons to restore a country's military strength.
refugee	Someone who is forced to leave the country they live in because of persecution or disaster.
reparations	Payments made to make up for damage caused, used here to mean the payments the Treaty of Versailles said Germany had to pay to the Allies at the end of the First World War.
sabotage	Damage done to machinery, equipment or buildings to cause disruption.
segregation	Separating things or people, used here to mean making different groups of people live separately and used different facilities.
sit-in	To sit down in a public place to demonstrate against something and to refuse to move.
stock market	Where shares are bought and sold.
summit	Used here to mean a meeting between important government representatives to reach an agreement on an issue.
totalitarian state	A country where the government controls all aspects of life.
unconstitutional	Against the constitution (rules for running a country).

abortion (USA 1960s and1970s) 144
atomic bomb 70, 82, 94, 95

Bay of Pigs (see Cold War)
Berlin Crisis (see Cold War)
Berlin Wall (see Cold War)
Birmingham civil rights protest 126
Black Panthers (see civil rights groups, Black Panthers)
Black Power 132
Brown v. Board of Education (see Brown v. Topeka) 120
Brown v. Topeka (175) 120
Capone, Al 168, 169
Castro, Fidel 96, 97
Churchill, Winston (British Prime Minster 1940–45) 68, 69, 70, 72, 74, 209
civil rights protest groups (USA)
    Black Panthers 132
    National Association for the Advancement of Coloured People (NAACP) 116, 118, 120, 122
    Congress of Racial Equality (CORE) 116
    Student Nonviolent Co-ordinating Committee (SNCC) 124
civil rights protest methods (USA)
    boycotts 118–9, 122
    freedom rides 122, 125
    non-violent 122, 123
    mass marches 122, 127, 128, 129
    militant 131
    pickets 122
    sit-ins 122, 124
civil rights legislation 116, 118, 120, 121, 125, 127, 128–9
civil rights voter registration 117, 123, 129
Cold War
    arms race 82, 94, 101
    Bay of Pigs 96
    beginnings 72–5, 110
    Berlin Crisis 80–3, 111
    Berlin Wall 92–3
    Cuban Missile Crisis 98–101
    Détente 100
    division of Germany 81, 90–1
    Eastern Europe's role in 68, 69, 70, 71, 78, 79, 82, 87, 88
    Hungary (1956) 86–9
    ideologies 68, 69, 74
    'peaceful co-existence' 86
    propaganda 72, 74, 75, 81, 91, 96
    post-war Germany 69, 70, 80, 81
    U2 incident 91
Comecon 79
Cominform 78–9, 86
Cuban Missile Crisis (see Cold War)

Dawes Plan 18

Death squads 36, 37
Ebert, Friedrich 7, 8, 9, 16
economic problems
    USA, 1920s (see USA)
    Germany, after First World War (see German economy)
Eisenhower, Dwight D (US president 1953–61) 89, 90, 91
Enabling Act 32

Final Solution 51–3
First World War 204
    effect on USA 160, 161, 162, 163, 164, 184, 186
    post-war Germany 6–7
    reactions to 204
Fourteen Points (Woodrow Wilson) 162, 204, 205
Freikorps 16, 17
Friedan, Betty 140, 142

gangsterism (USA 1920s) 168, 169, 170
German Constitution, 1918 8–9
German economy
    problems 6, 12–13, 18, 22, 26–7, 29
    recovery 25, 49
German Home Front (see Second World War)
German political parties to 1933
    Centre Party (ZP) 9, 15
    Communist Party (KPD) 15, 29
    Democratic Party (DDP) 9, 15
    German Workers' Party (DAP) 20
    National Party (DNVP) 15
    Nazi Party (NSDAP) 15, 21, 22, 23, 25, 28, 29, 30, 31
    People's Party (DVP) 9, 15
    Social Democratic Party (SPD) 7, 9, 15, 25, 29
German Revolution, 1918, 6–7
Germany, East (German Democratic Republic, GDR) 81, 83, 90, 91, 92, 93
Germany, West (Federal Republic of Germany, FDR) 81, 83, 90, 91, 92, 93
Gestapo 36, 37, 51
ghettos 50
Goebbels, Joseph 25
Goering, Hermann 21, 23

HUAC (see red Scare, HUAC)
Hindenburg, Paul von 25, 30, 31, 35
    views on Hitler 31
hippies 136
Hiss case (see red Scare, Hiss case)
Hitler, Adolf (see also Nazis entries for policies once Führer)
    appeal of 25, 28, 29
    anti-Semitism 20, 25
    death 59

elected Führer 35
    First World War 20, 21
    imprisonment 23, 24
    Mein Kampf 23
    Munich Putsch 17, 22–3, 24
    opposition to 55, 56–7
    role in growth of Nazi Party 21, 24, 25
    Treaty of Versailles 20
Hollywood Ten (see Red Scare, Hollywood Ten)
Hungarian Uprising 86–9
Hungary (1956) (see UN, Hungary (1956)
hyperinflation (Germany 1920s) 13, 18, 22

immigration, US restrictions of 164, 165
inflation (Germany 1920s) 12, 13, 25
integration 192–3
isolationism 74, 163, 164, 186

'Jim Crow' laws 116, 117, 188, 189

Kapp Putsch 17
Kellogg-Briand Pact 19
Kennedy, John F (US president 1961–63) 91, 92, 93, 96, 98, 99, 100, 122, 126, 127, 128, 134, 136
Khrushchev, Nikita 86, 90, 91, 92, 96, 97, 98, 99, 100
King, Martin Luther 118, 119, 122–3, 126, 127, 131, 134–5
Korean War (1950–53) 84–5, 111, 217, 227, 235
Ku Klux Klan 126, 127, 191

League of Nations 19, 162, 163
    Aaland Islands (1920) 220, 227
    Abyssinia (1934–36) 230, 231
    agencies 213, 214, 222
    Assembly 213, 223, 230, 231
    commissions 213, 214, 215, 223, 228
    Corfu (1923) 228, 231
    Council 210, 213, 220, 223, 230
    Covenant 206–7, 211, 214, 215, 235
    Disarmament Commission 213, 215
    drugs 214, 222
    Greek-Bulgarian War (1925) 221
    Health Organisation 213, 214
    ILO (International Labour Organisation) 213, 214, 223
    International Court of Justice 213, 223
    Manchuria (1931–33) 228, 231
    Mandates Commission 213, 215
    membership 212, 213, 222, 231
    Permanent Court of Justice 214
    Refugee Commission 213, 214, 223
    Secretariat 213, 214
    Secretary-General 214, 220
    set up 205
    Upper Silesia (1921) 220, 227
    US attitudes to 162, 163

Little Rock (1957) 121
Locarno, treaties of 19
Ludendorff, Erich von 21, 22, 23
McCarthy, Senator (see Red Scare, McCarthy)
Malcolm X 130–1, 134
Marshall Plan 74, 75, 78, 79, 80, 85
mass production (USA 1920s) 160, 172–173
'Monkey' trial 187
Montgomery Bus Boycott (1955) 118–119, 122
Munich Putsch, 1923 22–3

NATO (Northern Atlantic Treaty Organisation) 82, 101
Nation of Islam (NOI) 130, 131
Nazi Party to 1933 (see German political parties)
Nazi Party after 1933
Nazi policies
    censorship 40, 41
    churches 38–9, 57
    concentration camps 37, 50, 51
    death camps 52–3
    government 24, 33
    gypsies 37, 53
    Jews 20, 25, 29, 37, 42–3, 49, 50–3
    propaganda 21, 25, 40, 41, 50
    race (see racism, Nazi Germany)
    rearmament 49
    Treaty of Versailles 25, 28
    unemployment 29, 48, 49
    unions 33, 48
    women 46–7, 49, 54, 55
    young people 44–5, 56
Night of the Long Knives 34–5, 36
Nixon, Richard (US president 1965–74) 146, 147, 148, 149, 150, 151

Organised crime (USA 1920s) 168, 169, 170, 171

Potsdam Conference 68, 70
Prohibition 168–171, 178
protectionist policies, USA 163
protest groups (USA)
    anti-Vietnam (see Vietnam) 136, 137, 138, 139
    National Organisation for Women (NOW) 140
    Students for a Democratic Society (SDS) 138
    women's liberation 140, 141, 142

racism
    Nazi Germany 36, 42, 43, 44, 47
    USA 1920s 165, 186, 188, 189, 190
    USA 1950s & 1960s (general introduction) 116, 117
Red Scare 166–7
    HUAC 112, 113
    Hiss case 112
    Hollywood Ten 112
    McCarthy, Senator J 114–5
    reasons 110–1, 167
    Rosenberg case 113
reparations 10, 11, 69, 70, 162
Reichstag 25, 27, 30, 31, 32, 33, 35

Fire 32
Nazi election campaigns 21, 23, 25, 31, 33
set up 8
Rentenmark 13, 18
Roaring Twenties
    advertising 175, 181, 186
    cars 172, 174, 175, 180, 185, 186
    flappers 185
    hire purchase 174, 175, 180
    jazz 180, 182, 186
    morals 180, 183, 186
    movies 182, 183
    radio 174, 180, 181, 186
    women 184, 185
Röhm, Ernst 21, 24, 34, 35
Roosevelt, Eleanor 140
Roosevelt, Franklin D (US president 1933–45) 68, 69, 208, 209
Rosenberg case (See red scare, Rosenberg case)
Ruhr, French occupation of 10, 12, 18, 22
Russian Revolution 7, 15

SA (Sturmabteilung, storm troopers)
    role in Nazi Party 21, 22, 24, 25, 28, 32, 33, 34, 49
    set up 21
SS (Schutzstaffel)
    role in Nazi Party 24, 25, 33, 34, 36, 37, 49, 51
    set up 24
Sacco and Vanzetti case 165
satellite states (of USSR) 76–9
Schafly, Phyllis 145
Second World War 51, 54, 55, 58–9, 68, 69, 74, 80, 82, 90, 136, 208
segregation 188, 189
separation 192–3
Spartacists 15, 16–7
Stalin, Joseph (leader USSR from about 1929 to 1953) 68, 69, 70, 86
Stresemann, Gustav 13, 17, 18–9, 22, 25
Sturmabteilung (see SA)

Tehran Conference 68
Treaty of Versailles (see Versailles, Treaty of)
Truman, Harry S (US president 1945–53) 70, 84
    Doctrine 72, 74, 111

UN (see United Nations)
U2 incident (see Cold War)
USA agriculture (1920s) 161, 178
    economic problems (1920s) 161, 163, 178, 179
    economic production (1920s) 160, 161, 172, 173, 174
    trade (1920s) 74, 160, 161
    race riots (1960s) 133
    stock market (1920s)
    boom 173, 176–7
    Wall Street Crash (1929) 26, 30
United Nations (UN)
    agencies 217, 219
    Bosnia (1995) 217, 234, 235

Congo (1960–64) 226, 227
Charter 210–11
ECOSOC (Economic and Social Council) 217, 218
FAO (food and Agriculture Organisation) 217, 219, 223
General Assembly 210, 216, 217, 223, 232
Gulf War (1991) 226, 227
Human Rights Commission 217, 218
Hungary (1956) 217, 232, 235
ILO (International Labour Organisation) 213, 217, 219
International Court of Justice 217, 218
Korean War (see Korean War)
Lebanon (1975–87) 233, 235
membership 209, 216
Mozambique (1990–94) 227
Palestine (1947–48) 233
peacekeeping forces (see also individual country entries in this section) 217, 227
Secretariat 214, 217, 218
Secretary-General 218, 226, 232, 234
Security Council 216, 217, 224, 225, 226, 227
setting up 69, 209
Somalia (1991–95) 233, 234, 235
Suez Crisis (1956) 225, 227
UNESCO (Educational Scientific and Cultural Organisation) 217, 219, 223
UNICEF (International Children's Fund) 217, 219, 223
WHO (World Health Organisation) 217, 219

Versailles, Treaty of, 1919
    German reactions to 11, 15, 19, 20, 25, 28
    terms of 10
    US reactions to 162
Vietnam War
    US involvement in 137
    protests against 136, 137, 138, 139

Wall Street Crash (see USA)
Warsaw Pact 82, 87, 89
Watergate scandal 146–51
Weimar Republic 8, 9, 11, 12–19, 35
    constitution 8, 9
    chancellor 8, 9
    end of 32, 33
    National Assembly 8, 9
    opposition to 14–17
    president 8, 9
    successes 18, 19
    weaknesses 9, 11, 12, 15, 17, 26, 27, 29
Wilson Woodrow, (US president 1913–21) 11, 104, 162, 163, 205
women's liberation movements (see protest movements, women's liberation)

Yalta Conference 69, 208
Young Plan 19

Published by Pearson Education Limited, a company incorporated in England and Wales, having its registered office at Edinburgh Gate, Harlow, Essex, CM20 2JE. Registered company number: 872828.

www.pearsonglobalschools.com

Edexcel is a registered trademark of Edexcel Limited

Text © Pearson Education Ltd 2010 and 2012

First published 2010

16 15 14 13 12

IMP 10 9 8 7 6 5 4 3 2 1

ISBN 978 0 435141 90 5

Produced by Paul & Jane Shuter Ltd for Pearson Education
Edited by Lauren Bourque & Ag MacKeith
Photo research by Thelma Gilbert
Designed by Richard Ponsford and Creative Monkey
Layout by AMR Design Ltd (www.amrdesign.com), new material for the 2nd edition typeset by TechType
Original illustrations © Pearson Education Ltd 2010
Illustrated by AMR Design, David Woodroffe, Peter Bull Studio and Design Tribe
Cover design by Creative Monkey
Cover photo © National Archives and Records Administration
Printed in the UK by Scotprint

Acknowledgements

The authors and publisher would like to thank the following individuals and organisations for permission to reproduce photographs:

l = left, r = right, c = centre, t = top, b = bottom

akg-images Ltd: 4c, 9bl, 12tr, 12br, 14tr, 16br, 23tr, 27b; **Alamy Images:** 41br, 106c, 207bl, 215bl, 222br, 234b; **Bridgeman Art Library Ltd:** 15tr, 38tr, 46tr, 179bl; **British Cartoon Archive, University of Kent www.cartoons.ac.uk:** 35tr, 39b, 75cl, 83bl; © **Bildarchiv Preussischer Kulturbesitz, Berlin:** 32cr; **Conelrad.com:** 111tr; **Corbis:** 44br, 46br, 48br, 69br, 85b, 88br, 118br, 121tl, 123t, 131tr, 137tl, 139br, 145bl, 169tl, 184bl, 191bl, 192bl, 194b, 196b, 226br; **Getty Images:** 6bl, 19tr, 24br, 43b, 59br, 81b, 86tr, 88l, 88r, 99tr, 113br, 115t, 129b, 164bl, 190b, 193tr, 209bl; **Library of Congress:** LC-USZ62-122632 142br, LC-USZ62-125549 130bl, LC-USZ62-84483 108c, 117b, LC-USZ62-99711 135tl, LC-USZC4-6624 132br; **Mary Evans Picture Library:** 175bl; **Press Association Images:** 124bl; **Rex Features:** 93t, 96bl; **RIA Novosti Photo Library:** 95t; **TopFoto:** 21br, 28br, 31br, 36cr, 51bl, 53bl, 54b, 57b, 92br, 100cr, 126bl, 141tl, 147br, 151tl, 158c, 161tr, 162bl, 166bl, 169tr, 171l, 173b, 181br, 183b, 185tr, 187tr, 189tr, 202c, 205bl, 210br, 212bl, 216br, 219tr, 224b, 229bl, 230tr, 232br